# ROLL RED ROLL

## RAPE, POWER, AND FOOTBALL IN THE AMERICAN HEARTLAND

### NANCY SCHWARTZMAN

WITH NORA ZELEVANSKY

hachette
BOOKS

NEW YORK

Hachette Books
Hachette Book Group
1290 Avenue of the Americas
New York, NY 10104
HachetteBooks.com
Twitter.com/HachetteBooks
Instagram.com/HachetteBooks

First Edition: July 2022

Published by Hachette Books, an imprint of Perseus Books, LLC, a subsidiary of Hachette Book Group, Inc. The Hachette Books name and logo is a trademark of the Hachette Book Group.

The Hachette Speakers Bureau provides a wide range of authors for speaking events. To find out more, go to www.hachettespeakersbureau.com or call (866) 376-6591.

The publisher is not responsible for websites (or their content) that are not owned by the publisher.

Library of Congress Control Number: 2022936476

ISBNs: 978-0-306-92436-1 (hardcover), 978-0-306-92438-5 (ebook)

Printed in the United States of America

LSC-C

Printing 1, 2022

*For my beloved father, Dr. Robert J. Schwartzman,*
*a die-hard football fan, who held this story*
*with me, every step of the way.*

1939–2021

# CONTENTS

# AUTHOR'S NOTE

IN DECEMBER 2012, when I first learned of the Big Red football case in Steubenville, Ohio, I almost wrote it off as just another awful story. As a human rights activist and documentarian focused on gender-based violence, I'd seen countless rape cases played out in the press, the focus primarily on the victim's role and complicity, rarely on the perpetrators—their behavior, the need for consequences. The Steubenville story seemed like all the others. After all, the Department of Justice estimates that one in six women are the victims of attempted or completed rape annually, and we know that those numbers are higher in actuality, as rape is a vastly underreported crime. The risk for young women ages eighteen to twenty-four is three times higher than the average population. In reality, the average rapist has to commit twelve assaults before going to prison. Steubenville's story is practically the norm in the United States.

But as I learned more about what happened, adrenaline began to rise in my chest: this case, which involved the sexual assault of a teenage girl by high school football players in a downtrodden former steel town, offered a window into rape culture unlike anything I'd seen before. The rape was live-tweeted by the local teenage boys, who anticipated, observed, and recounted it without concern for privacy, accountability, or the girl's well-being. As a result of their tweets and texts, in the aftermath they couldn't deny what they'd done. This was a glimpse at the perpetrators' mindset, illuminating the different roles people play in an assault like this one—and why. It demonstrated how easily a seemingly average set of circumstances can spiral into something horrific when there's a culture of enablement, entitlement, and denial.

I set out to make a documentary film about the crime and ensuing case. I would ultimately arrive on the ground in Steubenville a year to the day after Jane Doe's assault, prepared to discover for myself what kind of environment birthed the incident. I spent the next three years filming, traveling in and out of the town, learning its rhythms, talking to locals, and recording their often-divided perspectives. Over that time, I learned that a powerful economic force of boosters funneled big money into Steubenville High School's "Big Red" football program. I learned that the depressed community's sense of self, fragile after years of economic instability, hinged on the success of that team. And I learned about a legacy of systemic sexual abuse that had hung over Steubenville for generations. That's one of the reasons why Jane Doe herself does not feature prominently in the work I've done around this case. What needs investigating and interrogation isn't about the victim. It's about the perpetrators, the bystanders, the culture that created them and then, inadvertently or not, allowed them to thrive. For a long time, nothing had changed. And I came to realize that the culture of this place didn't just reflect the residents of this Ohio town; it was the legacy of our shared history. This was a microcosm. This was our heartland. This was our America.

This is our future if we don't make a change.

I went to a high school with alcohol-fueled weekend parties not unlike those of Steubenville High School. A varsity tennis player, I came from a sports-loving family and understood intense relationships with coaches, what it meant to your family for you to succeed on the field or court. When the entire town of Steubenville, or any community, comes together to celebrate in the stands on Friday nights, it can be a beautiful thing, but not when celebrating the boys takes precedence over protecting the girls.

When digging into the trove of social media and text messages traded between those involved, I felt like I knew these teens, especially the ringleaders. They reflected some of the same attitudes of my peers growing up, and even some of my own. If I had stayed in my hometown, a tight-knit and somewhat conservative community outside of Philadelphia, my worldview might not have shifted. I took a different path—left home, moved to New York City, and traveled the world. Motivated by my own experiences and those of friends and even strangers, I chose activism, using storytelling and technology to create safer communities for women and girls. Before shooting my film, I created Circle of 6, an award-winning mobile app designed to reduce sexual violence among America's youth. Recognized by organizations from the Obama White House to the United Nations, it's been used by more than 350,000 people in thirty-six countries. The Steubenville story, at the intersection of rape culture, technology, and athletics, is an amalgamation of everything that makes me who I am.

Understandably, I was fascinated by the undercurrents of this disturbing situation. Rape culture wasn't unfamiliar to me—I could recognize that I was born and bred inside of it like everyone else—but the social media platforms were new. I wanted to understand what empowered boys to talk about rape so casually and broadcast it so publicly. What was specific to this place, and many others today, that enabled unabashed rape culture like this to fester? It was all out there. Prosecutors sifted through more than 360,000 text messages and hundreds of tweets to uncover the truth. And, as I read the texts and social media posts myself, the lack of empathy and remorse chilled me, as it did many others across the country who followed this story.

While technology is mainly neutral, the way we use it is variable. Seeing it overlap in the gender space, I was amazed at the power of social media: to incriminate, to empower, and to shine a light in the darkness.

What surprised me most was that despite the overwhelming evidence created by the teenage boys themselves, despite the ensuing rallies, the trial, and later the grand jury investigation of school officials and others charged with ignoring and/or covering up potential evidence, the town of Steubenville was divided. Instead of working to understand the root causes of this terrible rupture, many residents felt victimized by unwanted media attention and emphasized how overblown the reaction was to the rape. They stressed Jane Doe's complicity and split hairs about what constituted "rape." If we want to understand what defines "rape culture," then here it was, laid bare. I couldn't look away.

The Steubenville rape case, and the experience of the town, underscored the need for all of us to take responsibility as friends, parents, family members, classmates, teachers, school administrators, coaches, and community members. As adults and role models, when we don't stand in defense of a specific victim, we're making our own children and their peers vulnerable too. This case's national attention lit a fire under many Americans, who felt disturbed and angry and now understood, on a more visceral level, the need to actively create change. Steubenville helped spur what is, hopefully, the beginning of a transformation in cultural discourse and behavior via movements like #MeToo and the expansion of protections like Good Samaritan laws.

Today my film, *Roll Red Roll,* has screened at more than fifty festivals and 200 institutions and streamed in 190 countries. I've learned that telling and retelling these stories can change lives, and there is so much more to explore in hindsight ten years later: What impact did Steubenville have on the national discourse? What, if anything, has evolved? What can we be doing differently if we want to effect change? Jane Doe has since graduated from college, gotten married, and, by all appearances, done her best to move on with her life. But the story of this case remains incredibly important, as it's a mirror. If the retelling can help one young woman come forward or one young man intervene, then this book has done its job.

Rape is preventable. Steubenville is just like your community, filled with dimensional people whose views are formed from their own experiences and education in school, at home, and out in their world. The bystanders and even rapists are not all simply "monsters." They don't look different; they hide in plain sight. They are us—our sons, our fathers, our pastors, our coaches, our friends. In order to eradicate the problem, we as individuals and communities have to take responsibility and teach accountability to our children so that they understand right from wrong and learn to speak up, even if it's an unpopular choice or no one else is doing it. We have a chance to learn from our mistakes, call in a diversity of voices, and protect future generations. But first we have to be willing to take a hard look at the unconscious, entrenched behaviors that allow this type of culture to flourish.

*Roll Red Roll* is that opportunity.

# "SHE'S SO DEAD"

**M**ICHAEL "NODI" NODIANOS was having the night of his life.

Surrounded by half-empty plastic soda bottles and the pent-up energy of the athletes who ignored him during school hours, he couldn't miss. He was killing it. Lonely nights spent reading blogs and watching TV news with his family were finally a useful social advantage. He knew stuff. Not much. But stuff.

It was late on a muggy August night. His face was slick and flushed pink, eyes glazed from alcohol and sudden attention. He was landing almost every joke—and the crowd was too wasted to notice the duds. He was the headliner of the high school house party, a smaller pre-season gathering between bangers.

"She is so dead!" He cracked, pressing his fingers to the bridge of his nose. "She's deader than a doornail."

"How dead is she, Nodi?"

"She's deader than JFK! She's deader than Joe Pesci in *Goodfellas*."

His audience egged him on: fellow Steubenville High School student Evan Westlake picked up his Samsung Galaxy and hit record. This shit was too good to miss.

Nodi was soft and plain-faced. At this point in the night, though, the tables had turned. The football team—amped from winning their preseason scrimmage, swole from working out at five a.m. practices, pumped from a summer of chasing Facebook likes and hoes—were the spectators. Usually relegated to the stands, Nodi became the main event. For once, *they* were watching *him*.

This classic wood-paneled rec room—hoodies tossed over recliners, bare legs stuffed into gym socks and sneakers, the stench of sweat and pack proximity—was the closest Nodi would ever get to the locker room, and he knew it. He had to keep this going.

"She is so dead!" he chirped. "She's deader than OJ's wife."

He was rewarded with laughter again. He was so wrong, he was right.

Other teens were still arriving, ducking into the dim subterranean den. One by one, they left their quiet Ohio neighborhood behind—front porches tied with birthday balloons, mailboxes in neat rows, Dodge Rams and Chevys parked in driveways.

Nodi sipped from a super-size McDonald's soda. He tugged at his boxy Buckeyes t-shirt, taut around the middle. "They raped her more than the Duke lacrosse team," he tried, referencing an old assault case the other boys didn't seem to know. "She's deader than Caylee Anthony," he quipped, invoking the infamous killing of a two-year-old girl. "She's deader than Trayvon Martin!"—the Black teenager shot to death in Florida earlier that year.

"You're a sick fuck!" one of the boys yelped, but they were cracking up again, disembodied voices beyond the camera's shallow depth of field.

Nodi kept it coming. "Her puss is about as dry as the sun right now!"

Out of the darkness, a dissenting voice threatened Nodi's roll. "Yo," said Shawn McGhee, one of the school's top wrestlers. "This shit is not funny." His voice was deep and definitive.

Nodi seemed to panic. He doubled down. "It's not funny," he sniped, doubt registering for an instant on his face before his expression morphed into a smirk. "It's hilarious!" But the magic was lifting.

"You didn't see how they carried her out…like she was Jesus Christ back from the dead?"

"What if that was your daughter?" Shawn challenged.

"If that was my daughter, I wouldn't care." Nodi shrugged. "I would just let her be dead."

Shawn's judgment had changed the tenor of the room, power dynamics shifting like plates in the ground. Even Evan's laughter faltered from behind the camera, if only for a moment. "I'm sorry," he mumbled, "but Nodi is funny. *That's* not funny, but…"

Nodi's glow was fading. Time was ticking down. His moment in the spotlight was almost up.

———

While Nodi performed his comedy routine, at another house just a short drive away, a sixteen-year-old girl was being sexually assaulted by some of his classmates. "Trained," as the boys liked to say. She was passed out—"dead," as Nodi described her. The source of his best stand-up material.

Before Nodi's younger but more popular pals, Trent Mays and Ma'lik Richmond, left the house party with the girl, they and their fellow athlete friends had already started to openly violate her, snapping pictures of her unconscious body to post on social media. They carried her, limp, out to their friend Mark Cole's car, stepping on her hair as they walked. No one made a decisive move to stop them. Now they'd started sharing photos of the assault in real time with their buddies in the basement. And apparently it was hilarious.

"It isn't really rape because you don't know if she wanted to or not," Nodi snickered, shaking his head and grinning, back in the basement. "She's dead! That may have been her final wish."

"That's like rape," said Shawn abruptly. "It *is* rape. They raped her. Trent and Ma'lik raped someone."

"This is the funniest thing ever!" tittered Evan, his momentary shame seeming to fade.

At dawn, Evan uploaded the video to his personal YouTube channel for his thirty-eight followers to watch. Its audience would balloon into the millions.

Nodi's fifteen minutes were not quite up.

## CHAPTER 1

# THE CRIME

ON AUGUST 12, 2013, a year to the day after the assault, I arrived in Steubenville for the first time. It was nearing twilight. The highway was lined with oak trees. I could hear crickets singing and smell the remnants of a recent rainstorm on the breeze. Having read the news stories, I expected an ugly place, gritty and unforgiving, but the landscape was lush and serene.

We entered on a beautiful mini–suspension bridge over the Ohio River. For a moment, I was transported to my teenage years outside of Philadelphia and the liminal melancholy that accompanies the end of the summer, the lead-up to school starting. The surroundings felt familiar to me. I sighed. Then, out of the corner of my eye, I spotted a sign directing visitors to "Lover's Lane, Steubenville," and I was jolted from my memory into this very real moment. There was nothing romantic about this place or what led me here.

---

*ONE YEAR EARLIER*

"DEATH VALLEY! DEATH VALLEY! ROLL RED ROLL!" A packed crowd roared Steubenville High School's "Big Red" rally cry. Coach Reno Saccoccia called a play. The squad huddled behind the line of scrimmage. They fell into formation and charged. A crush of bodies leaned in from the stands: students, teachers, townspeople, and parents, so many parents. Moms with slashes of dark lip liner and frosted highlights pumped fists in the air, then yanked up their low-rise jeans. Dads hunched forward in nylon sports jerseys, alert to every signal and stutter-step on the field, their breath rising and falling with the rhythm of downs. "GO BIG RED! ROLL RED ROLL!"

There was a sense of something riding on this game, above and beyond a few casual bets. In fact, one local man would soon be arrested, charged, and forced to forfeit $1,526,104 by the FBI for running an illegal gambling operation, a recurring reality of the culture's fiber here. But no salaries or contracts were on the line. The fans were not drunk and belligerent. In fact, there was no alcohol except perhaps for a few tallboys snuck in by brash students and recent grads, slinking around the bleachers. Although the lights shone bright from the six-figure jumbotron and the stands were rocking, this was high school football.

Yet the laser focus in the eyes of the spectators suggested an investment beyond the outcome of the season's second scrimmage. Big Red was coming off of a 10–1 season the previous year, with promising young players rising up the ranks. These boys were the soul of the town; its mood rose and fell with each play—elation, devastation, success, failure. This was *Friday Night Lights* without the Texas sparkle and Hollywood tune-up. This was rust belt Ohio.

The multi-million-dollar stadium, known regionally by the nickname "Death Valley," demonstrated something larger at work too: deep pockets supported the football program and left Steubenville's South 4th Street, its "Main Street," and downtown to fall into disrepair. Originally completed in 1930 for $45,000, Harding Stadium (its official name) enjoyed regular upgrades. In 1948, the Big Red Booster club improved the lighting system. In 1966, they expanded capacity from 4,800 to 10,000 seats. In 1977, even as the town's economy began to falter, this became the first Ohio high school stadium to have miked referees. In the 1980s, there was a notable lull as Steubenville felt the full brunt of the steel mills closing and unemployment rose. But, by the 1990s, they were back in action, adding updated irrigation, lighting, and sound systems, as well as a new scoreboard with video replay capacity. The aughts saw almost yearly renovations, including the addition of their new Daktronics video board. This year, in 2012, they had just laid down new elevated AstroTurf and upgraded the lighting again. The unpolished but state-of-the-art facilities boasted an extensive weight room, cryo tanks, and massage tables. On top of the jumbotron reared a giant fire-breathing horse called "Man o' War," first erected in 1970. The notably well-endowed stallion erupted into flames with every touchdown. Local ads adorned the edges of the board, supporting the town's heroes—"The Pride of the Valley." *Pell's Hardware salutes Big Red's #1 Team.* These players might have been teenagers, but their stadium was fit for an elite college program.

On the field, the boys were soldiers on display, aware of the spotlights that followed them as they fought toward victory, looking to their leaders for guidance and reassurance. The coaches shouted commands from the sidelines: *Hold them! Tight D!*

The preseason game ended in victory, and the fans exhaled. Big Red was obviously going to have another great run. "We had a hell of a scrimmage," Coach Reno later recalled. "We beat the shit out of them." The crowd said casual goodbyes, friends and neighbors sure to see one another tomorrow at the Kroger grocery store or in the carpool line. And the next day too. The adults streamed out to their cars. They headed home or to the McDonald's drive-thru—some up the hill to the suburban sprawl of split-level homes and mowed lawns and some down toward the dilapidated main drag and public

housing projects behind it. The players tumbled off the field as win-
ners, primed to blow off steam. The air was thick, the energy electric.
It was going to be a sick year.

But the moment, however victorious, was fleeting. This particular
game marked summer coming to a close, signifying a sense of opportunities narrowing, of last hurrahs. For many of these boys, glory
days were already numbered, dwindling in the face of limited college
prospects. Everything was riding on this season. Playing well could
mean a scholarship and a ticket out of town to a school with more
opportunity. In Steubenville, starting when Wheeling-Pittsburgh
Steel first filed for bankruptcy in 1985, the steel mills faltered and
closed, making jobs scarce. Almost three decades later, the town
had not yet found a way to compensate for that loss or to propel its
offspring toward hopeful post-college careers and futures. Most of
these players would cling to every remaining second of high school
prestige before joining the ranks in the stands like their parents.

———

Shortly after, on an average suburban street peppered with American flags, cars pulled up outside an unsupervised house party hosted
by Kamy Belardine, a student from the rival high school, Catholic
Central. Teens piled out of passenger and driver's seats, exchanging nods, hugs, and ritualized high-fives. The Big Red boys made an
entrance through the back door. It was a familiar crew: Trent Mays, a
white kid with dark hair, was an incoming sophomore and promising
quarterback, who had the swagger of an upperclassman. He walked
in cocky, sharing pounds and jabs with buddies. Also in his group
that night was Ma'lik Richmond, six foot four and fast as lightning,
a rising star and the only Black teen traveling with the group that
night. He played wide receiver, tight end, and linebacker at points
and had just won the scrimmage for Big Red. Anthony Craig was the

social butterfly, an olive-complected, small, Italian kid, who was a confidant for many, especially the girls. Their friend Mark Cole was an already broad-shouldered champion wrestler, white with buzzed dark hair and plans to join the Marines. The other two, Cody Saltsman and Evan Westlake, were tall, white, and blond—like siblings—though Evan, a future Sigma Phi Epsilon fraternity brother at the University of Toledo, was known more as a follower. He had a prominent brow, a stretched smile, and the phone that would document Nodi's comedy riff on video.

Inside, they were greeted by the thump of bass. Drake's album *Take Care* was a favorite in the rotation. They joined the fray. At ten p.m., Kamy's twenty-six-year-old brother, Matthew Belardine, Big Red's volunteer assistant football coach and the only adult present, returned home from having a drink with a friend. He turned a blind eye to the drinking, a violation of Ohio state law and football team rules, and headed upstairs to hang out in his bedroom.

8/11/12 @TrentMays_12 Huge party!!! Banger!!!!

The night ramped up. Alcohol flowed freely. According to eyewitnesses via a trail of texts, tweets, and digital breadcrumbs that would guide the resulting police investigation, the gathering (later labeled "Party A") started small, with around ten to fifteen guests. At its peak, it swelled to between thirty-five and fifty teenagers. Circulating among the regulars was a new object of interest: a high school sophomore, sixteen years old, from just a few miles down the road and across the border in West Virginia. The girl had planned a sleepover at her friend Julia Lefever's house, who lived right across the street from the party. She and Julia had been friends since they were in gymnastics together as little kids and had reconnected that summer. Giddy and acting their age, the two teen girls had snuck out with big plans for the night. The new girl, though out of her element, drew focus. She was notably pretty; like the Ohio Valley's very own Ariana Grande.

After tonight, she would be known to the world as "Jane Doe."

Somewhere in the midst of this bedlam, as she sipped Smirnoff Vanilla from a Speedway slushie cup, the new girl started hanging out with two of those popular Steubenville athletes, Trent and his tagalong, Ma'lik. Though these boys weren't the stars of the team yet, everyone seemed to know that was where they were headed. Ma'lik was towering already and unstoppable on the field, though soft-spoken. He'd scored two touchdowns just that night. Although smaller, Trent, with close-set eyes and heavy brows, was the more obvious alpha.

Though Jane Doe was out of her element, the surrounding schools in the Valley were part of one big social scene. She had a romantic history with their buddy Cody Saltsman, including a breakup so ugly and dramatic that Big Red's Coach Reno knew about it. Saltsman was so gutted that it negatively impacted his playing on the field, cementing Coach's desire to keep his players away from girls as much as possible. Jane Doe was now friends with Anthony Craig and had been "talking" to Trent for a little while, flirting over text. It appeared as if everyone had moved on.

"Our victim…remembers clearly meeting Trent Mays at the party," said Detective J. P. Rigaud, the lead investigator on the case. A father to teenage girls himself, he was a trim Black man with glasses and a kind face. "[Jane Doe] remembered meeting and maybe having talked to Ma'lik, as well."

This unspectacular initial interaction was the tipping point, the moment a single thread was pulled and a supposedly close-knit town began to unravel.

———

Later in police interviews, Farrah Marcino, a Steubenville High School student, athlete, and cheerleader with long, thick brown hair and an enviable tan, would remember seeing Jane Doe across the room at "Party A" and waving to her. Both outsiders at this gathering, they knew each other a little from social media and rival girls' soccer games. "There was a bunch of Central girls and I was the only one from Big Red at that point," Farrah later described, "so I was kind of uncomfortable and she was like the only one who said hi to me."

8/11/12 @luckymcclurg134 holy fuck its about to be a night of reckoning.

Soon, many of the kids moved on to "Party B," as it would be labeled by the police: they gathered in Steubenville student Jake Howarth's basement rec room, the one where Evan and Nodi would later make their video. This time, the Howarth parents were home and supervising, so the drinking was at a minimum—in theory. It was a typical suburban setup: adults upstairs, teens in the basement congregating on couches and in dimly lit nooks. Jake's house was a regular hangout for some of the Steubenville boys, but tonight it was a bigger crowd. Teens roamed in and out through a side entrance without inspiring so much as a raised eyebrow. They hung out, sipped spiked Cokes, and waited for whatever would come next. This was a stopover party, a deep breath before the exhale of last hookups, late-night Taco Bell runs, and broken curfews.

Farrah Marcino was there and, as an eyewitness, remembers noticing Jane Doe again. "By the time we got to Jake's, she was getting worse," Farrah recalled. "I could tell that she was getting more drunk." By then, Jane Doe was so intoxicated, she could barely stand. She was, for all intents and purposes, alone. Before she left Party A, her friend Julia had realized how drunk Jane Doe was and tried to talk the boys out of taking her with them. She ran inside the house for reinforcements. The group of partiers outside watched Jane Doe stumbling as she was dragged toward the car. No one intervened. By the time Julia got back outside, breathless and searching, Trent, Ma'lik, and their group had driven away with Jane Doe in their car. Julia would be unable to reach her friend for the rest of the night. The police later filed and then dropped kidnapping charges against the boys for taking Jane Doe from location to location without her consent.

She'd arrived at Party B after midnight with Trent and Ma'lik. "From the time I seen her at Kamy's—and Jake's—it was completely different," Anthony Craig, a member of the boys' group and a key witness, later recalled in police interviews. "Like she couldn't respond, even." He described the transformation of Jane Doe from upright, "talking," and being social at Party A to staggering drunk and being dragged around Party B.

Later on, people, including the victim herself, speculated that Jane Doe had been drugged, citing telltale gaps in memory and the alarmingly rapid onset of intoxication. Within moments of arriving at Party B, Jane Doe ran to the bathroom to throw up—kneeling, head in the toilet, long hair falling around the bowl. But the other teens looked on with disdain instead of empathy, as noted in later trial transcripts, calling her "a mess." Jake Howarth and his girlfriend, Elayna Andres, watched Jane Doe sway on her feet, conscious of how unstable she seemed. Soon after, Jake's parents yelled down, "Anyone not sleeping here has to go home!" It was nearly one a.m.

Jake later testified that, at that point, he told Jane Doe she had to leave. She tried to comply, but when she got up, she collapsed. Unable to ignore the situation, Farrah Marcino pleaded with Trent to take Jane Doe back to Party A. "I kept trying to say, 'Take her to Kamy's, take her to Kamy's,'" she later lamented. She even followed up with a text to Trent, asking him to listen to her. When Jane Doe could form words, she insisted to Farrah that she was fine. But Farrah knew that was the alcohol talking, and the girl from West Virginia was alone and possibly in danger. "We kept trying to tell her, you don't want to go with them," Farrah would tell detectives, staring hard at her lap. "You want to go back with your friends where you're gonna be more safe…and you won't [be safe] with the boys."

————

"Let me just say something here," pressed Detective John M. Lelless, who was backing up the lead detective, J. P. Rigaud, during filmed interrogations and questioning later. "What made you use that phrase 'safer with us' versus Trent and others?"

"Well, I mean…'cause I put myself in her situation in my head…If she was my friend, like if she was my close friend, then I would take the extra step and make her stay, but you know I can't do that, so I just let her do what she wants." Farrah put a hand over her heart, a kind of reflex. "Which I understand was wrong."

————

If Jane Doe had been taken back to Party A, which was eventually broken up around midnight by Kamy's brother, the volunteer assistant football coach Matthew Belardine, she could have stumbled back across the street to Julia's house to sleep. But Trent had a different plan. Assuring Farrah he'd "take care of it," he physically picked Jane Doe up and began to carry her out of Party B to the car. Farrah, Elayna, and some other girls protested about how Jane Doe was being handled because Trent was trampling on her hair. So Ma'lik stepped in and grabbed her ankles while Trent held her arms in what Detective Rigaud would later call "a dead man's carry."

Jane Doe's ex-boyfriend, Cody Saltsman—laughing and pointing—snapped a photo of her passed out, head thrown back, and posted the photograph to Instagram.

@CodySaltzman Never seen anything this sloppy lol

Less than a week later when pulled into the police station, a chastened Michael "Nodi" Nodianos, the gleeful commentator from the YouTube video, told police in a taped interview, "As I was walking in, they were helping a girl out."

"Who was helping the girl out?" Detective J. P. Rigaud asked.

"Trent and Ma'lik. I saw them."

In the arms of Trent and Ma'lik, outside Party B, Jane Doe was barely responsive. She would eventually have vague memories of throwing up by the curb, surrounded by mowed lawns and paved streets. Ma'lik held her hair, witnesses later testified. Having thrown up on her shirt, she stripped down to only her bra and jean shorts. A crowd of boys were heckling and making jokes, daring someone to "piss on her." It was noisy outside. Headlights illuminated Jane Doe, sick, on an otherwise sleepy street. At any point, the parents supervising could have looked out the window to see her slumped over, in need of help. At any point, one of the teens could have stepped in to help her. No one did.

With Jane Doe in the car, Trent, Ma'lik, Evan, and Mark were ready to bounce to a new, more private get-together. Bass-heavy music blared as they headed to Mark's house (eventually labeled "Party C") over county lines because his mom was out of town.

In the back seat, Jane Doe was sexually assaulted for the first time.

In a moving car, Trent Mays unzipped her shorts and penetrated her with his hands, while she dipped in and out of consciousness. The boys in the front of the car laughed. Mark took a video with his cell phone.

Throughout the night and during the incident, Julia was still trying to reach her friend, frantically calling. But Jane Doe wasn't alert enough to answer her phone.

"I'm comin with you guys," their friend Anthony Craig texted Trent.

Anthony hopped into his car alone, leaving Party B for Party C at Mark's house. Vibrating with excitement, he texted another buddy:

> Bro...there gonna rape that girl!

He seemed to live for the drama.

Once at Mark's house, the boys dragged Jane Doe down to the basement. The space was crowded with hefty couches and an indestructible coffee table organized around a flat-screen TV. Police photographs of the scene also showed a little sister's dollhouse and toys.

The group set Jane Doe on the floor, in the narrow passage between the coffee table and the couch. "She was sitting there for a second and then she just leaned back and fell to her side, and that's when she threw up on the floor," Mark later admitted to police. "She wasn't in any state to make a decision for herself."

Surrounded on all sides by a giddy gang of teen boys egged on by Trent Mays, seemingly eroticizing her humiliation and their power over her, Jane Doe was stripped naked. Exposed, bare skin to the carpet, she was assaulted while blacked out. The boys snapped photos, stepping over her slack body for better angles.

No one did a thing but lean in for the close up.

———

"What is the conversation that's taking place in regards to either Trent, Ma'lik, Evan, and you?" police officer John Lelless later pushed Mark. "Don't sugarcoat nothing. Those guys put themselves in this jackpot. In your fucking house, in your *mom's* house! And here you are, what, seventeen? You're a fucking man. You said you're a football player. Fucking man up."

Nine days after the party, Mark Cole sat in the cramped interrogation room at the police station in soccer shorts, a tank top, and Adidas slides, his muscular frame slumped. He paused for several seconds before answering. "I think they were talking about 'training' her…"

"'Training,'" explained Detective Rigaud, staring straight ahead through his glasses in a later interview, "is a slang term for gang rape or 'running a train' on someone as a form of male bonding to humiliate and dominate another."

"Ma'lik was very much following the lead set by Trent Mays," then-Ohio prosecutor Marianne Hemmeter later noted, reflecting on her time on the case. "[Trent] knew how drunk she was; she knew him and thought she could trust him. He played on that. He used her like a toy."

———

Wait for me lol!!!!

Anthony Craig arrived late to Mark's, but in time to witness the assault. He took pictures and ferried them back in person to Jake's house, "Party B." He passed his phone around to the guys in the basement like he'd found some hilarious meme. Elayna wouldn't let Jake look, he later revealed, but she couldn't, or didn't, stop the others. One photo showed Jane Doe naked below the waist and facedown, Trent standing over her with his pants down, his hands on her buttocks.

That's what seemingly inspired Evan to press record and, surrounded by an eager audience, Michael Nodianos to begin his comedy routine.

"She's so raped right now." Nodi laughed. "Dead body!" The boys were in hysterics.

———

"Everyone was shocked as to what was going on," Jake Howarth later testified in court. "There was a mixture of jokes going around and people being scared." But no one seemed scared, or put off, in Michael Nodianos's twelve-minute video, a real-time record of the teens' reactions to the realization of Jane Doe's rape. Shawn McGhee was the only exception.

"This is the funniest thing ever!" giggled Evan Westlake.

Later in the night, Mark Cole went back out to go meet Farrah. After leaving the house, he texted Trent, discouraging him from taking it "too far," for fear of getting in trouble.

> Seriously dude don't fucking rape her

Shawn McGhee also warned Trent.

> You are dead wrong … you can go to jail for life for that if she says something

The fact that rape seemed like a probable outcome to Trent's friends was telling in itself. As Farrah had predicted, Jane Doe was unsafe, and now she was a victim of assault.

The next day, Jane Doe woke up naked under a Steelers blanket, bewildered.

———

"Pictures, text messages—social media's role in this case was documentation," Detective Rigaud reported with a shake of his head. Rigaud had lived in Steubenville since graduating from Franciscan University, the conservative Catholic institution on the hill above town. As the lone member of the juvenile unit, the onus fell on him, with help from the state Bureau of Criminal Investigation (BCI), to piece the case together. "I had never seen a case constructed like this…with that many elements in play, that many people who had some information about my victim's process from A, B, C. [The posts] provide evidence for that span of time our victim has no memory of."

With so many eyewitnesses and fragments of evidence to compile, it was easy to lose sight of what the bigger picture suggested. There were more than fifty witnesses throughout the night, and not one person stepped in to stop what happened. The lack of intervention pointed to something more disturbing. As Detective Rigaud commented, "There definitely were marked moments during that night where you hoped for some kind of a hero or someone to step in."

———

The next day, on the afternoon of Sunday, August 12, Trent Mays texted with a buddy:

Bradley: Did you fuck her?

Trent: Yup

Bradley: Yeah boiiii

It didn't occur to Trent to censor himself, that by admitting to "fucking" or even digitally penetrating an incapacitated girl, he was admitting to the legal definition of rape in his home state of Ohio. He never imagined that there might be consequences to both his actions and his flippancy. In August 2012, he didn't yet understand that Twitter was not private and that what he posted could never truly be deleted, or that the cell phone in his hand would be his indictment, setting a precedent for future cases. He couldn't fathom that his texts and tweets, and those of his complicit teammates, might wind up as evidence against them in a court of law—or go viral on the world stage.

He would find out the hard way.

## CHAPTER 2

# THE MORNING AFTER

JULIA LEFEVER WAS looking for answers.

It was the middle of the night. Her house was electric with quiet. Her parents were asleep—unaware, for now, of the trouble brewing. Soon enough, they would wake up and realize that Jane Doe was not dozing peacefully in their daughter's bedroom.

The plan was to get a little buzzed on vodka, hang out, then sneak back home—Jane Doe was *supposed* to be sleeping over. But instead, she had gotten drunk very quickly, in a way that Julia had never seen happen to her before, and was coaxed into a car by a bunch of Big Red football players. Now she was nowhere to be found.

Was she okay? Should Julia have done more to stop the boys from taking her?

But Jane Doe wasn't answering her cell phone. The one time Julia got through, Trent had answered and refused to pass the phone. Now Julia's calls kept going to voice mail; her texts went unanswered. It was enough to make anybody panic. She scrolled Twitter for some hint of where her friend might have ended up, a way to reach her. Suddenly at three in the morning, she saw it: a photo of a teenage girl. Naked. Possibly covered in urine.

*Jane Doe?*

Where was this photo taken? *Where was her friend?*

It was 3:12 a.m. She texted Anthony Craig, Ohio Valley's unofficial information trader. Maybe he would know something about the picture and her friend's whereabouts. Julia had seen him at Kamy's earlier, but then he'd also disappeared.

> **Do you know where [Jane Doe] is though?**

No response. All around Steubenville as parents sank deeper into REM cycles, their teenagers were still awake, trading illicit pictures, damning rumors, and outrageous stories. They were posting videos on YouTube before passing out on couches. Texts zipped back and forth, deepening the grooves of an evolving evidentiary map. Yet Julia couldn't find out a thing.

Finally, overcome by fatigue and her own vodka consumption, she too fell asleep.

———

The next morning—Sunday, August 12, 2012—the late summer sun rose in the sky, a diffuse yellow haze hanging overhead. In downtown Steubenville, the light settled over the town's beloved murals like a sepia filter. There was imagery of Manifest Destiny, rugged pioneers, steelworkers from the days when the economy buzzed, and of crooner Dean Martin—the local hero made good—suavely lording over the Kroger's parking lot. Historic Fort Steuben stood, a bastion of past glory, by the glimmering river. The air smelled of burning refinery and morning buns.

WTOV-9—the local Fox affiliate TV news station with a signal that stretched from northern Sharon, Pennsylvania, to southern Sistersville, West Virginia—was broadcasting evangelical programming and local stories about the winning scrimmage the previous night. Big news in Steubenville. Everybody was amped for the season to begin. In the early morning hours, Big Red's Death Valley arena was dead quiet. Nearby at Scaffidi's Restaurant, owned by Anthony Craig's family, the sign in a font chosen to evoke *The Godfather* trilogy glinted in the sunlight.

As the morning progressed, some mothers readied to drag their kids up to the Macy's at the Fort Steuben Mall for back-to-school shopping. The department store would shutter two years later, leaving a faltering cluster of shops: Claire's, GameStop, JCPenney, Lucky Duck Discounters, and an Armed Forces Career Center. Families who could afford it planned to stop at the shiny Dick's Sporting Goods to grab team uniforms and athletic gear. Others with less disposable income perused Goodwill or the Dollar General on Hollywood Boulevard, thousands of miles from its famous namesake strip in Los Angeles. Some families, like the Nelsons, who owned a religious iconography factory and storefront called Catholic to the Max, were jostling for mirror space before services, all ten of them in one shared bathroom. The churchgoers donned their Sunday best and headed to their respective sermons, settling next to longtime neighbors in pews at congregations from Holy Name Cathedral to First Baptist. Still others made last-minute grocery lists to stock up on family-size bags of chips, dips, soda, and beer before the first NFL game aired at one p.m. Eastern.

Early that morning, Julia's phone finally rang: anxious for answers, she picked up a call from Mark Cole. Ready to clean house before his mother returned home from the camping trip that had freed up the house, he asked Julia to come pick up Jane Doe. She took down his address, got dressed, climbed into her Pontiac convertible coupe, and pulled out of her driveway onto the still quiet road.

———

In the light of day, Jane Doe's eyes fluttered open. Naked and dazed under an unfamiliar football blanket, her gaze darted around Mark Cole's basement. *Where was she?* She had lost the last seven hours of her life. She had no idea what had happened the night before, but it obviously wasn't good.

"Her next memory is waking up…Sunday morning of the twelfth of August. And [she] can't find her phone," Detective Rigaud recalled. "She's, uh. She's not wearing any clothes. She's under a blanket. And in the room were both Trent Mays and Ma'lik Richmond. She was really kind of disturbed because she couldn't remember much."

Frightened and confused, Jane Doe got up and began searching for her phone—her lifeline, something that might give her some sense of context, connection, or control. Where had she left it? Without it, she was isolated.

Hearing Jane Doe moving around in the other room, Farrah Marcino woke up and came in. She had met up with Mark (with whom she had recently broken up) around two-thirty a.m. for a tearful relationship talk and then had come back to his place where the others were sleeping. By the time she arrived, the group of boys had scattered from the basement. She'd seen Trent and Jane together under one blanket and assumed they were just sleeping after hooking up. She'd seen Ma'lik on another couch across the room. Things seemed innocent enough to her.

But now Jane Doe was disoriented and woozy, possibly shaking off the effects of GHB, as she would later speculate via text (though it was too late to tell once she eventually visited the hospital). Anthony Craig would also later ask Trent:

> Did you pull some *Hangover* shit and roofy [*sic*] this woman?

Something was not right—that much was clear. Farrah had to help Jane Doe get dressed, even hooking her bra, as neither she nor Trent could manage it. Jane Doe's underwear was missing. She was in distress, and her anxiety was building. How did she get here? *What happened? Where was her phone?*

Trent called her repeatedly in an attempt to find it, he said. He called once, twice…nine times. It was obviously gone—dead, hidden, or stolen. Overcome by fatigue and still not quite sober, both Jane Doe and Farrah fell back asleep.

Not long after, Julia pulled up to an unfamiliar house with its front porch lights still on from the night before. Later in courtroom testimony, she described arriving to find her friend looking "like a mess"—confused, and with her shirt on inside out. Julia asked Trent and Ma'lik for an explanation about the night before. Fidgeting, they claimed nothing had happened. She didn't buy their story, but didn't have time to debate as Mark pushed her to drive the boys home, as well as Jane Doe. Julia, put in an awkward position, agreed, packing the victim into the back seat with her assailants yet again.

Julia dropped Trent at his house and Ma'lik with his guardians, the Agrestas, who had stepped in when his own parents were unable to care for him. As soon as she and Jane Doe were alone in the car without the boys, Julia turned around, wanting answers: *What happened? Where were you?* The stress of the night before came rushing back to both of them.

Jane Doe curled up in the back seat. "I don't remember," she murmured and began to cry.

She wouldn't need to remember in a court of law. In fact, the prosecuting attorney would argue that Jane Doe's memory loss proved she was incapacitated and unable to make decisions for herself. And thanks to the unabashed online bragging from the boys, the police would soon piece together what happened. Still, despite the legal strength of what would become the *State of Ohio versus Trenton W. Mays* and the *State of Ohio vs. Ma'lik Richmond*, Jane Doe would never have her own truth about that night; her memory would always remain cloudy.

"[Jane Doe's] mom ends up picking her up from her friend's house here in Steubenville," said Rigaud.

At the same time, the boys were still exchanging graphic messages recounting the night.

> **Anthony Craig: lol . . . they were feeding her alcohol like it was water all night.**

> **Cody Saltsman: I wanna see the video of you hitting her with your wiener lol**

> **Michael Nodianos: That girl got pissed on and pretty much raped! Dude, she may have been dead. There was a pic of her butt naked laying on the ground.**

> **Trent Mays: Yeah dude she was like a dead body haha I just needed some sexual attention lol**

Mark Cole tried to call Jane Doe twice, perhaps trying to find her phone as he cleaned up the crime scene for his mom's imminent arrival home. Then he texted Trent Mays, and though they'd sobered up, Mark continued to make fun of Jane Doe's situation: "It's about peeing on her for money lol," he wrote, referencing an inside joke from the night before as the victim stooped outside Party B, throwing up.

As news spread among the teens, people started asking questions. Some of Jane Doe's girlfriends, in particular, began texting the boys asking for details about what had actually happened. Soon Jane Doe's parents began receiving photos and screenshots of social media chatter, painting a horrific picture of their daughter's experience the night before. The victim herself began hearing bits and pieces too, and she texted other girls and the boys, expressing outrage and looking desperately for answers.

Coach Reno, who was quickly informed of any incidents involving his players, also started hearing rumors. Evan Westlake's father called, claiming that Jane Doe's cousin threatened to beat him and his kid up. What should he do? Information began to swirl among the teenage boys too, not nearly as cavalier as earlier in the day. Coach heard from a now worried Trent Mays, who seemed to be trying to get ahead of the story and looking for reassurance. As adults got involved and Jane Doe demanded answers, locker room talk began to muddle with fear of getting caught, as that possibility—of consequences—began to dawn on some of the players. Stories were already changing, allegiances shifting.

Mark Cole sent a stern text to Trent:

> Why are you sending those pictures around? Dude quit sending it that'll get in deep shit.

Right away, Anthony Craig positioned himself as a key intermediary, going back and forth, texting Trent Mays and Jane Doe, who still hadn't found her phone but was using another device. He even initiated a graphic fact-finding text exchange with Ma'lik, who was notably absent from most of the social back and forth:

> Anthony Craig: So you eat ass?

> Ma'lik Richmond: Fuck no. I licked the cat lol.

Anthony feigned friendship with and sympathy for the victim in order to get a clear picture of what Jane Doe actually remembered and who would be implicated. He assured her that he was horrified by what he had witnessed—disgusted, really. He described arriving at Mark's house and yelling at the other teen boys to stop. He claimed that he tried to help, but was powerless.

Meanwhile, he texted Trent Mays in a very different tone:

> Anthony Craig: U wana be real wit me for a sec? Did you have sex with that dead body last night? Lol.

> Trent Mays: No. But would I? Yes.

Via text, Trent told countless contradictory stories that day, demonstrating how some teenagers navigate the truth as the center of attention. He bragged to buddies that he "fucked" Jane Doe. He told others that they obviously didn't "hookup" because "she was dead." He followed up with a claim that he got a hand job when she woke up temporarily at three a.m., a difficult feat for "a dead body." He said he didn't "give a fuck" about her. He said he "took care of her." Despite all the wild inconsistencies in his recounting, either born of braggadocio, teenage panic, elaboration, or just old-fashioned dishonesty, law enforcement would eventually find and test a sample of his semen on the Steelers blanket from the Coles' rec room. Clearly something had happened.

As the day went on, Anthony continued to badger Jane Doe for information, feigning distress and then bringing his findings back to the guys. "If you remember anything at all then you need to tell me," he texted her.

That evening he texted Jane Doe again, all concern. "Are you alright?"

When she didn't respond right away, he texted Trent Mays: "Send me that pic!!"

She finally answered with a question: "What happened last night? I don't know who to ask or believe."

"You were like dead. They took you to marks. I went there and left after I saw you completely naked on the ground…I seriously felt so fucking bad for you and I couldn't do shit about it. I'm so sorry. I flipped out on them," claimed Anthony, "and they said they were just going to put u to bed."

In reality, he had scurried back to Party B with naked photos of her for the remaining boys to ogle and share.

"One of the young men, who was at all three locations, actually saw what was happening to the victim and was able to testify to that," Detective Rigaud explained to me in a filmed interview, detailing how Anthony Craig at first misled law enforcement when he described the photos he had seen, but didn't admit to taking them. "He had come back from the house where the victimization was happening and was actually telling them some of what was happening."

Anthony Craig lied freely, including to law enforcement. He collected information in order to protect himself, but also as a form of social currency, common in teenage dynamics.

> **Anthony: You okay??**

> **Jane Doe: Not at all**

As other teenage boys on the periphery found out what happened undeterred by a fear of consequences, they too reveled in the comedy of Jane Doe's humiliation. "I walk into my house and my brother and Brenton already knew about [Jane Doe]," a teen named Lucas texted Trent Mays. "People told them she got trained…that girls life is ruined lmao."

Reality apparently started to set in for Mark, who had a video on his phone of Trent assaulting an underage Jane Doe, filmed in the back seat of the car on the way to *his* house. Though the legal details had not yet been explained, he clearly understood that he was in possession of something damning.

Trent Mays: Send me the video

Mark Cole: No

Trent Mays: Why

Mark Cole: Bc I ain't sending that shit.

Trent Mays: That's dumb

Mark Cole: Dude I will when I'm with you

In wanting the video, was Trent claiming a prize, shaming his victim, collecting a fetish object of his conquest, or participating in "euphoric recall," deriving heightened pleasure from the memory of a sex act? Trent also texted photos of Jane Doe indiscriminately to boys who didn't even request them.

"I mean, these other boys weren't asking for the picture," said prosecutor Marianne Hemmeter. "He was sending that out to make fun of her, to degrade her even further. And that gives you some insight into his personality. You talk about predatory nature, and then you see it like that in such a young kid who has so much promise otherwise on the outside. And it makes you stop and wonder, how does that happen?"

As tensions among the other boys rose, Trent's mood began to sour:

[Twitter] Some of these "nice dudes" need ta shut the hell up

Trent appeared enraged by those who had come out in support of Jane Doe, criticizing the Big Red players for their behavior and the way they talked trash about the victim. He was defensive, of course, as he was at the heart of the conflict, but also seemed to see those who defended a girl as flaccid and weak, not to mention hypocritical.

When he wasn't lashing out online, Trent also texted with Jane Doe directly that day. To her, he denied that anything happened between them that wasn't consensual, though she couldn't remember a thing. He was almost affronted, maintaining the claim that he acted as her caretaker, deserving of gratitude instead of derision.

> **Jane Doe: Why would you or whoever the fuck it was take off my clothes in front of everyone? Why wouldn't you try to help me?**

That evening, Jane Doe was still piecing the previous night's events together, checking in with other teens to fill in the blanks. As she cried in her room, some of the boys convened at Anthony Craig's house for an old-fashioned Sunday supper with his family. His mother loved the boys, whom she'd known since they were small. That night over Sunday sauce, it was like nothing in the world was wrong.

———

The next day, on Monday, August 13, Julia tweeted at Jane Doe:

8/13/12 love youuuu! Cheeeeer up

Trent Mays retweeted her message.

Then, in a barrage of tweets, he swung between defensive, angry, and above it all:

4:51 PM Ya see, what had happened was...

4:53 PM But forreal, #TeamFuckThemHaters

4:56 PM Karma? #💩

7:11 PM #shutup

7:20 PM Nothing even happened ppl seriously need to shut up

7:42 PM Ima snap

8:06 PM I hope guys actually finds out what happened...

8:07 PM #Can'tWait

9:51 PM Let's have a good practice tomorrow red 🙏 🏈

That evening, Trent also texted his friend and Jane Doe's ex-boyfriend Cody to report that Coach Reno's brother had seen Jane Doe's father arrive at her school and walk her off the softball field, that his and Mark's names had come up during a discussion about what happened. He knew, he said, because Coach Reno called and told him.

Whether because they were still in the dark or because they didn't see a reason, Trent's parents hadn't taken his phone away.

By late Monday night and early Tuesday morning, Jane Doe's parents had collected a trove of photos and screenshots, many sent by concerned relatives. They had taken Jane Doe to the hospital, though it was too late to retrieve evidence of drugging. At 1:38 a.m., compelled to take action on behalf of their daughter, they arrived at the police station with a jump drive full of evidence and filed a sexual assault complaint. The next day, on Tuesday, August 14, Detective Rigaud met with the family at the Child Advocacy Center. "It's where we interview children involved in any kind of alleged case involving abuse," Rigaud said. "I interviewed her that afternoon. It wasn't actually very long when it comes down to it because she couldn't remember much. She knows she had been drinking and others had been drinking as well." Fortunately, Rigaud took a trauma-informed approach to investigating this sexual assault by choosing a safe and neutral location and not treating Jane Doe as if she were under investigation. He knew that a gap in a victim's memory was not an indication that the victim was lying, but a possible result of drugging or trauma.

News travels like lightning in a small town, and it wasn't long before the parents of all the Big Red high schoolers knew there had been an incident over the weekend involving Steubenville football players and a sixteen-year-old girl from West Virginia. Chatter began in an online Ohio Valley Athletics forum for adults. Phones rang, tweets chimed, whispers were exchanged over instant coffee and during Monday morning Shop 'n Save runs.

The immediate public nature of the case troubled Detective Rigaud, who preferred to keep this kind of investigation quiet. The kids "left it all out there on the line, like dirty laundry." He frowned. That meant the case could not be worked privately, as it normally would, with the goal of "preserving the dignity of the child" and of all the children who might be involved. "I had to work it like any other case," he told me. "But it wasn't."

By Tuesday afternoon, those associated with the high school knew some version of what happened. Jake Howarth's older brother Zach, who would become a Peace Corps volunteer, shot a text to Anthony Craig:

> Shame on you craig. I heard about that girl. That's fucked up. You shoulda stopped it.

For the boys who were intimately involved, what started as low-level unease began to spiral into full-blown alarm. Evan Westlake deleted his YouTube account and the twelve-minute Nodianos video, which still had only a few views. Others deleted their tweets and posts.

At first, Trent Mays acted like he was covered. He told his friends to "chill." Once back at school that week, Coach Reno had called the boys in and said he was there for them, but only if they were honest with him about what had happened. "Every day after practice, I would say to the kids, 'If you have anything to say, tell me. I'll help you out. I won't defend you if you're wrong, but I'll support you.'" They all insisted that they were innocent and were thus absolved. In fact, Trent texted one friend,

> IDGAF [I don't give a fuck] I got Reno he took care of it ain't shit gonna happen.

He texted another:

> I shoulda raped her now that everybody thinks I did.

And yet another:

> She was so in love with me that night.

But rumors swirled that Jane Doe said she was drugged and was tested to prove it. The boys amped up their harassment, texting and calling her. They wouldn't leave her alone. She'd started ignoring Trent's messages badgering her about whether she was pressing charges, and even eventually responded, "Fuck you. Stop texting me."

"He's going to kick you off the team," one friend texted Trent, raising concerns about the ultimate punishment—being banned from playing football by Coach Reno. "I lied and said you weren't involved."

Trent texted Mark:

> Listen if we get questioned, she was real drunk and we let her stay at your house an [*sic*] took care of her. Just say she came to your house and passed out.

He texted Cody Saltsman, "You gotta back me up."

Cody was receptive, texting back, "I got you man. I'll say they were just trying to take care of her."

To Evan Westlake about Nodi's video, "We just gotta tell em that we gave her a safe place to stay." And, "Delete that off YouTube seriously that girls dad knows about it. seriously you have to delete it!!! I'm so fucking scared."

"Don't drag me into it!" said Anthony Craig, who also denied to Trent that he'd taken any pictures that night.

Trent wrote back, "Seriously I need as much help as I can get."

He even texted Jane Doe's father, using a phone number shared by Cody Saltsman.

> Sir this is Trent Mays. this is all a big misunderstanding... She was at the party and her and I talked at the time. Mark Cole, Ma'lik and I were about to go home and she was really drunk so I took her with me and let her sleep at marks...I never once tried to do anything forcefully with your daughter but I'm sorry for all the trouble this has brought you.

Her father responded, "What is on video?"

But Trent was too late to stem the flow. The evidence was already laid out across YouTube and Twitter, no matter how the frantic boys attempted to cover their tracks online. What Jane Doe's family collected on their jump drive and submitted to the police was only the tip of the iceberg.

Over the next week, the police called witnesses into the station one by one for interviews. Some lied, like Anthony Craig, until they got caught. Some told the truth and demonstrated what appeared to be authentic regret, either for what happened to Jane Doe or the repercussions for them and their male friends. Most stared at their feet and wrung their hands, rubbing their foreheads and fiddling with their fingers.

"You were there," said Detective Lelless to Farrah during her interview. "None of us were there. You saw things. You heard things. You understood things."

For Detective Rigaud, and Jane Doe by association, the uphill battle was trying to make a case in Steubenville, a small, entangled town. "This was a tough enough investigation already because it involves people who all know each other," he'd later note during our interview, sipping from a Steelers mug and wearing a blue button-down and tie. "Trying to get the truth from kids who are maybe telling on friends is the biggest obstacle."

A week later, enough of the stories lined up. Trent Mays and Ma'lik Richmond were arrested and charged with rape.

## CHAPTER 3

# THE PLACE

O N ALTAMONT HILL, the highest point in Ohio's Jefferson County, looms a 900-foot tower that sends a signal from the local Fox affiliate TV station WTOV-9 to anyone with an antenna in eleven surrounding counties. The station also feeds its broadcasts to cable networks and satellite platforms like Dish Network and DirectTV. Within twenty or thirty years, according to veterans of the station, that newer technology will likely render the transmission tower defunct, transforming it from a powerful conductor and modern-day megaphone into a rusting relic overnight, much like the mills.

Bought from Cox Enterprises by conservative conglomerate Sinclair Broadcast Group in 2013, WTOV-9 stands for "We're Television for the Ohio Valley." The Steubenville station aired local programming like pre-recorded Big Red high school football games, but it was also known as a stepping stone for on-air reporters, attracting young hopefuls with aspirations of cracking the regional TV market. In fact, they sometimes ran "Where Are They Now?" profiles on former reporters who moved on to larger markets like Cleveland and, for some bright stars, even Seattle and Los Angeles.

At home, most Steubenville locals tuned in to Fox News on this channel. But during the day, as they drove around in their minivans, trucks, or sedans or helped customers at their shops, they were likely awash in the amplified musings of longtime local radio DJ David Blomquist, known as "DJ Bloomdaddy." His booming voice ruled the waves on news radio 1170, WWVA "The Big One," out of neighboring Wheeling, West Virginia. Owned by iHeartMedia, formerly Clear Channel Inc., the station's national programming in 2012 included conservative "shock jocks" Glenn Beck, Rush Limbaugh, and Sean Hannity, and overnight shows like *America's Truckin' Network*.

On August 22, 2012, Bloomdaddy's standard teaser about football or the weather took a more serious turn. "I'm working on a story out of Steubenville that is very, very disturbing," he said, his usual bravado seeming to falter. "I can't give you many details right now. It's just one of those stories that—you know, you're talking about underage kids and just have to cross a couple more t's. For Paul Morgan, I'm Bloomdaddy, [Glenn] Beck coming at you next. Stay tuned. I'll see you tomorrow, same time." The story was officially about to become news.

After Trent Mays and Ma'lik Richmond were arrested, information about what happened on the night of August eleventh and into the morning of the twelfth began to spread beyond Steubenville's inner circle of students, football parents, and school officials. Rumors and facts circulated as if via a massive game of telephone, resulting in divergent versions on the other end. WTOV-9 minimally covered the arrest on their website, posting a lightly reported article with the headline, "2 juveniles arrested in connection with alleged sexual assault in Jefferson Co." The outlet chose not to name names, although identifying accused minors in lawfully obtained, truthfully reported, newsworthy stories is legal as of a 1979 US Supreme Court decision concerning journalistic freedom of speech. Notably, the comment section was locked.

"When I first read this story, there wasn't a lot of substance to the article," recalled crime blogger Alexandria "Alex" Goddard, who would play a significant role in the amplification of the case. "Two high school football players had been charged. Just a couple of paragraphs about these two boys and that was it."

Alex, known ironically as "Prinnie" for "princess" or by her Twitter handle, @PrinnieDidIt, was hanging out at home that August 22, scrolling online for intriguing stories. She was living in San Rafael, California, with her dogs, Wilson and Winnie, working as a consultant for an attorney. She'd never been to law school, but had worked at law offices starting at fifteen years old, as well as taken myriad adult education courses post-college. The responsibilities were in alignment with her left-brain talent for creating order and organization.

Distance or no, Alex knew Steubenville like the back of her hand—its skeletons and its backdoor deals. When she was two years old, her mother and stepfather had moved the family from Germany to the small West Virginia town of Meadow Bridge, where she grew up without running water. Her stepfather was an army veteran who raised her with a strong sense of justice. When she was a teenager, she got into heavy metal, hair bands, and sneaking out to see shows. She later showed me old photos of her younger self with sky-high teased bangs, heavy eyeshadow, and a studded jacket, saddled up to Bret Michaels, front man of revered 1980s rock band Poison. Alex Goddard did not grow up going to football games.

She was tough and a hard worker; she didn't take shit from anybody. "I worked a part-time job in a law office, which I started in the tenth grade," she recalled. "The week after graduation, I started a full-time job in another law office, as well as waitressing part-time on weekends at the Al Rosa Villa, a Columbus bar with live entertainment." It was there that she met a lot of rock band members, including Michaels. "I am proud that…I could allow myself to have fun in an era when women were expected to be getting married and having babies," she added, "instead of putting themselves first." Though it was the mid-1980s, which meant a kind of liberation for women in certain sectors of the country like big cities, in this area, gender roles and expectations were slower to change.

In her twenties, Alex moved to Steubenville, where she began working two jobs and cultivating a circle of eclectic friends. It was during those years that she became acquainted with the town's underbelly. She dated cops and tended bar at a private after-hours club that required a special key for entrance, working into the morning hours surrounded by a seedier element. Steubenville may have presented itself as a family town, but this spot was populated with its late-night crowd, including the mayor, who notoriously received multiple DUIs.

Steubenville has a complicated backstory. For one thing, the area has a long-standing gambling history. During prohibition, it was a swamp of speakeasies and brothels, drawing lost and nefarious souls. Judy Jordan, infamously known as "The Steubenville Madam," represented a legacy of everything from prostitution to mafia ties, though she was not convicted of those crimes. The FBI had raided the town, targeting numbers games and other criminal behavior, more than once. Corruption was something of a given as a result. Somehow, that dark undercurrent never quite lifted.

The population peaked in 1940—just before private Catholic institution Franciscan University was founded, looming over the town in pious stature—and has since been in demographic decline. Not surprisingly, that drop-off was most marked in the 1980s, when the steel industry collapsed, dragging the town down with it and creating a cocktail of anger and resentment. This was in large part because Steubenville, like many of its rust belt counterparts, was constructed around an unsustainable industry: turning coal and iron into steel takes a tremendous amount of capital, so the Ohio River Valley's mills—originally built from the 1870s to 1890s—had much the same operations 100 years later. This meant that only wealthy economies across the world had steel industries, and many were destroyed by the end of World War II. "The US steel industry had a kind of global monopoly," said Gabriel Winant, assistant professor of history at the University of Chicago and author of *The Next Shift: The Fall of Industry and the Rise of Health Care in Rust Belt America*. "Domestically, they were organized into a kind of cartel. So, the major steel companies would fix prices together. There was almost no competition. They had over-expanded quite dramatically in the 1940s and early 1950s for war production because the federal government paid them to do that. You can think of it as a big sleepy Goliath that isn't used to coming under much pressure.

"What that meant was…as new steel industries were built in Germany, Austria, Japan, and South Korea [after the war], they were built with newer technology and were more efficient. Over the course of the 1950s and '60s, they began to be able to outcompete American steel." The Ohio Valley and its peers were being outpaced in productivity and out-priced in labor costs. Once the domestic steel industry in Steubenville and elsewhere began to update their technology in the 1960s and '70s to answer the competitive threat from overseas, it meant the beginning of job loss. "The machinery makes some groups of workers obsolete within the mill," explained Winant.

Mini mills began to pop up in the American South with a much lower overhead. They specialized in turning scrap back into usable steel, which ate into the bottom of the market. By the 1970s, the industry got stuck in a "wage–price spiral," which meant that the union was powerful enough to win salary and benefit increases and force the steel companies to offset the costs by raising their prices. Simultaneously, a phenomenon called "stagflation" arose, which meant that, counter to standard economic theory, inflation and unemployment both increased. "By the late seventies, this is seen as a very, very serious problem," said Winant.

In 1979, President Jimmy Carter appointed a new chair of the Federal Reserve, Paul Volcker, who testified before Congress that in order to combat inflation, "The standard of living of the average American has to decline." To do that, the Fed raised interest rates to induce a recession, deliberately, "and that recession will, in particular, punish big capital-intensive industries," explained Winant. "Basically, it's a way of choking it off."

When interest rates went high, people didn't borrow as much money to build houses, other real estate developments, or infrastructure or buy cars—essentially, everything made of steel went quiet. "Managing steel became a way to manage the larger economy," said Winant. "Across America, this is a serious recession but not the end of the world, but, in what we now think of as the rust belt, it's a second Great Depression." On top of this, by 1980, more than half the remaining steelworkers were over forty-five. There was a regional aging effect, a "very rapid out-migration," where young people stopped seeing opportunity and left, leading to population decline. Over the course of several years, unemployment reached 17 to 18 percent in nearby Pittsburgh, reflecting numbers in Steubenville, as well. By 1983–1984, the big steel mills had almost entirely zeroed out employment. Any that eventually reopened did so with new owners and skeleton crews.

When the bottom fell out in the 1980s, during Ronald Reagan's heyday, the area experienced a kind of collective loss and unbalancing. Their culture took a massive hit. "Virtually every indicator of social distress that you could come up with—infant mortality, home foreclosure, people seeking spots in domestic violence shelters—spikes," said Winant. "There's generalized social distress. The population gets sicker and poorer very fast. Suicide rates go up. And that's a genuine kind of trauma that people then just kind of live with and gradually climb their way out of. And my general impression is that the lesson of the trauma is a deep sense of lack of agency." This was the anger on which nationalists like Donald Trump would later capitalize.

In 1989, a Steubenville Steelworkers Memorial, depicting an oversize man in full garb laboring over molten steel, was erected in remembrance of generations of workers. But it also felt like a gravestone for industry itself. In 2015, the statue was moved to a prominent position across from the Steubenville Library. An era had ended for the town. The now disenfranchised steel workers, majority white men, and their offspring express a feeling of being forgotten and misunderstood here, often making statements like, "My dad built this country" and lamenting better days when that work was not overlooked. "I've heard so many people describe lying in bed at night imagining their dad's fingerprints on a bridge or something [in that vein]," said Winant. "If you just try to picture twentieth century America, you imagine skyscrapers, you imagine highways, you imagine cars, maybe the military industrial complex—it's all steel. Twentieth Century America is made out of steel."

While the sense of loss is real and palpable in Steubenville, memories of the good old days don't generally factor in women's realities or rights or the rights of Black people and other marginalized communities at that time. Many had to suffer a long history of systemic abuse and oppression as their birthright. Even in the best of times, when the men in places like Steubenville were gainfully employed and even unionized, cyclical strikes and layoffs were the norm almost annually during the postwar Golden Age, according to Winant. The jobs were dangerous. There were constant injuries and deaths. Many of the men worked shifts that let out at midnight or even eight a.m. Alcoholism ran rampant, with a ring of bars built up just beyond the mills' gates.

The 1950s were positioned as a model era, and there was pressure to live up to that impossible standard. Many of the difficulties trickled down to women, who bore the brunt of this sense of impotence and frustration in the form of everything from unachievable house-hold responsibilities to domestic violence. "This creates intense dis-sonance between this idea of how people are supposed to be living and the fact that they can't really make it work," said Winant. "And then all of the pressure that generates inside the family. The wife who has to make sure that even though they're actually not bringing in enough income, they have to try to fake it. All the pressure of keeping the house clean in this filthy environment under a giant smokestack. The husband comes home in clothes covered in industrial grease every day; she has to make two dinners. And is he going to have had a drink? Think, what's that going to be like when it all falls apart?" As Winant pointed out, "There's nostalgia for the way things used to be, but it's more like the ruts of life are just so deep. It was disorienting [when it collapsed]."

In Winant's book, he included observations from a number of steelworkers' wives. The women spoke directly to the rampant alco-holism, inequity, and the resulting both subtle and blatant abuse they experienced even in steel's heyday. For women in places like Steubenville in the 1950s and '60s, life was no picnic. One woman talked about how she stayed silent, despite feeling rageful about her husband's relative freedom, because it made her life harder if she spoke up. Concurred another, disagreeing with your husband only brought trouble. "I let him be the boss. It makes us all happy," she said. One woman said it bothered her when other wives spoke poorly about their husbands, even when they were mistreated. The ground-work had been laid for a culture of silence among women that would persist and solidify over generations.

The women talked about feeling belittled for expressing opinions or ideas. Some said they were left alone with the kids, unable to go out or take breaks. One woman talked about how her husband liter-ally threatened to murder her if the children didn't behave and the household wasn't under control. As Winant noted, "A thread of fear ran through these assessments."

Winant referenced *Striking Steel*, a memoir by onetime professor Jack Metzgar, who grew up just two hours from Steubenville. In the book, which takes place in 1959, the writer recalls his mother's early subservience to his steelworker father, who "abused her good nature" and, as Winant notes, "how his father took pleasure in performing bodily dominance over" his mother.

In these mostly large Catholic families, sex was a source of shame and even more silence, as the women said they were forbidden to discuss the act before marriage and even after. As one woman said, "I was so shamed…I'm still shamed." There was also a resounding silence around how much moonshine the men would consume, which often led to violence. One woman argued that it was better to have a career outside the house if possible as a wife, simply to avoid getting beat up. "I saw some marriages where the men were rather brutal—some of the men would really beat their wives," she said. "One man in particular I remember during the night he was beating his wife out between some houses there, and we woke up with all this screaming and carrying on about it…A lot of people that I thought were pretty nice were not."

The culture of abuse, of oppressive and rigid gender roles, and of silence continued to grow, fester, and root throughout the years. By the time the local economy tanked in the 1980s, the rust belt was embroiled in this deeply ingrained imbalance along with the loss of their way of life. It was a recipe for disaster. Winant cites a 1984 study that found that alcohol-related offenses and domestic violence incidents both spiked after the mills closed. From 1983 to 1985 in the neighboring Pittsburgh area (so close that some saw Steubenville as a bedroom community), the Women's Center and Shelter of Greater Pittsburgh experienced a 37 percent rise in victims served. The alcoholism, the patriarchy, the silence, the violence, the shaming—all of these factors so rooted in the fabric of a rust belt town like Steubenville, contributed to what allowed Jane Doe's assault to happen amid cheers and taunts so many years later. This rust belt history was a foundational precursor to the rape culture that seemed so callous here.

While crime blogger Alex Goddard held her own in town when she arrived a few years after the economy went belly up, brewing a bubbling unease, she didn't always like what she saw. "I developed a sense of what the community was like," Alex told me, her long hair framing her strong bones and striking green eyes. "To me, it wasn't a very woman-friendly environment."

Football, always male-dominated, became something for the town to hold onto amid a dwindling sense of identity. Alex's day job was as a ward clerk at a hospital ER, where she observed how the nurses' locker room "was adorned with both Big Red and Catholic Central colors," pendants and flags everywhere during football season. Even adults without children seemed deeply invested in the high school team's success and failure. That hero worship was rumored to win the players small and large perks, from free cookies at the bakery to much more. "The community loves this team," said former Big Red football player Jeno Atkins, who was an incoming senior when Jane Doe's rape occurred and was friends and teammates with the teenagers involved. "They loved it then and still love it now. So our meals and small things were usually covered by a random Steubenville citizen. If you struggled in classes, the coaches got you tutors." The team had to thrive at any cost.

"Football IS the Ohio Valley," Alex wrote on her blog, "and the players are treated like sports royalty. To an outsider, it seems a bit over the top."

That was how Alex knew the story of Trent Mays's and Ma'lik Richmond's arrests was significant, despite the short write-up on the WTOV-9 news website (which was later expanded as a "developing story"). She wasn't surprised by the crime itself, had kept in touch with locals, and had heard rumblings about a "rape crew" since April. But if two football players were actually being *arrested* and held accountable for their actions, the crime had to be impossible to ignore. "I thought, 'This is nuts!' because that town is so entrenched in their football team," she recalled. "This was big news." She took a long drag from her Newport and tapped the ashtray with a knowing smirk.

CHAPTER 4

# THE INVESTIGATION

I N 2012, ALEX GODDARD was consulting in law offices by day. By night, she was a true-crime blogger who brought a fact-driven lens to salacious cases like the killing of Caylee Anthony and of a twenty-one-year-old Illinois woman by a group of fellow Juggalos (fans of the horrorcore group Insane Clown Posse). Alex poked around for new evidence and chased down leads, raising the profile of small cases and constructing theories based on court documents and records to post on her blog, Prinniefied. She also worked to weed out corruption, particularly exposing "Stolen Valor" scams where military imposters defrauded people by pretending to raise money for veterans. This specifically enraged her because of her stepfather's service. "Not everything is as it seems," she said, sipping from her Mountain Dew. "If something stinks, I'm going to be the first person that calls it out." Unlike many armchair sleuths, Alex had skills. She was an early adopter of new technologies and was well versed in the ways of the internet, including its darker corners, boards, and chat rooms. She had the courage to poke around forums I was too intimidated to approach despite my tech background.

Alex made it her business to be aware of exactly where the lines were drawn in terms of legal investigation. All of the information she dug up was publicly available. Though she never dipped into it herself, she respected the power of white hat hacking, the perils of doxing, and was fluent in the language of boards like Reddit. She understood how grassroots viral movements and internet beefs were born.

So, when she scrolled through the WTOV-9 article about the football players' arrest and saw that the comments section had been locked, her antennae shot straight up. She understood the practices of the town, the way they liked to bury their bodies quickly and without apology. "It's like a rotten onion," she said. "You peel one layer back and there's something equally rotten underneath it." News of the arrest of two Big Red football players was too big for the station to completely ignore, but the site managers were local. It seemed as if they wanted to protect the players by discouraging discussion. For Alex, who believed strongly in freedom of speech, shutting down the comments felt like suppression. WTOV-9's decision sparked her outrage, sending her down a rabbit hole.

She went deep. Her pups at her side, Alex settled in with menthols and a mission. After all, dredging skeletons up in the name of justice was her passion, and this crime had happened in her childhood backyard. "I went to the high school's website, pulled the roster of all the football players, and started searching for any social media that they may have had online," she explained. "Facebook, Twitter, Instagram—everyone had their full legal name." All she had to do was begin searching Twitter to uncover the trail of what had happened to sixteen-year-old Jane Doe ten days before. "I determined that, after a scrimmage game for Big Red high school, there were several end-of-summer parties that all the kids were attending," she said. "There were tweets going around about how everyone was having a great time, but then something changed." Like most people—and even the parents of the boys themselves as they sat in the courtroom months later with slack jaws, listening to the content of their own children's tweets and texts—Alex was horrified by what she read:

the celebratory, cavalier, and aggressive tone of their messages and posts, the way they reveled in the girl's degradation. When she saw Cody Saltsman's photo of Jane Doe being carried out of the Howarth residence unconscious, she was shocked.

All night long, Alex dug through the bowels of the digital universe, following the trail left by the football players and their friends and, with the help of Google Cache and Tweet Tunnel, uncovering evidence they'd tried to erase. "I used some archive tools to track deleted information," she explained. "It was all out there." She created a folder for each teen, in order to keep track of the players and the timeline, since she didn't know any of them directly. They became like characters to track in an unfolding teen drama. She was up until dawn the following day scouring and screen-capping their social media accounts, resurrecting photos and video posts. As she worked, she could practically hear the boys' hearts thumping with fear as they hustled to delete the images. Their cover-up was no match for Alex's drive once she got started. "I sat up for hours and hours and just followed the timelines, fanning out who was retweeting what at a certain time," she remembered. "So it was almost like watching this in real time. The complete lack of empathy; that's what was so frightening. By the end of the night, a young girl from across the river had been sexually assaulted." Suddenly, the perpetrators seemed less Teflon.

Though she was no stranger to men's bad behavior, what was so shocking to Alex was the blatant nature of the boys' commentary. They put their actions in writing and broadcast them. This was a public demonstration of rape culture: the minimizing and normalizing of sexual violence and the cognitive dissonance around the public nature of social media. Through the lens of teenagers, who thought they were acting in private, rape became a big joke full of typos.

The next morning, Alex called and left a message with her then friend whose husband was a member of Steubenville law enforcement. Alex didn't claim to have criminal evidence or a "smoking gun," as she wasn't sure what portion of this new social media was admissible by police, but she had dug up a lot of material. "I wasn't sure what they had," she said, "and before I wrote about it, I wanted to make sure that my information wouldn't compromise the investigation."

No one called her back.

————

At the same time, at the Steubenville police station, Detective Rigaud and his team were working to piece together their case. Before the arrests, they had consulted with town prosecutor Jane Hanlin, who was able to identify the boys in the Nodianos YouTube video. Hanlin had already begun to come under scrutiny for not immediately recusing herself from the case, as the mother of a teen who was close friends with the accused and witnesses. "She's lived here her whole life," said the detective, of her close relationships with those involved, which allowed her to identify the players and also rendered her unfit to try the case. There were people who defended her decision not to recuse herself right away and many members of the town supported Hanlin, though some would come to see the benefit of a neutral investigation. But to many outsiders, her intimacy with those involved put her in a compromised position, one that did not bode well for Jane Doe. In a later *New Yorker* article, she was quoted as saying, "'If you do anything to say, 'Wait until we get to the truth,' you are 'pro-rape'—whatever that means…You are part of a conspiracy, a cover-up.'" She otherwise avoided defending herself, stating that it wasn't appropriate to discuss an open case.

"The day following the interview [with Jane Doe] was really [about] trying to dive into other media we'd been given, to make sense of it," said Rigaud, referencing the jump drive of evidence that Jane Doe's family had collected and delivered by hand to the police. "And we could see that, most of the time, [the tweets and photos] were being posted through a cell phone." With assistance from his team, Rigaud had worked to identify the relevant individuals and get search warrants for their phones. "On August sixteenth, just before we executed those search warrants, we received a phone call from one of the moms," he said, referencing Mark Cole's mother, Angie Paterra. She was the owner of the house known as "Party C," where Jane Doe was assaulted in front of multiple eyewitnesses. "[She] calls us and says, 'I think something happened here. I don't know what. I'm scared.'" Paterra cooperated with the police, allowing them to scour the house and collect any remaining evidence. The police also talked to Mark himself. That's when he made his initial statement.

Paterra's willingness to come forward was not the norm. While the school did cooperate in the beginning, sharing requested contact information with the police, local parents were a different story. They closed ranks, reticent about coming forward and fearful that even if they were only adjacent to what happened, their sons would be labeled as rapists. The adults, in a position to set an example about taking responsibility and creating transparency, chose to protect the teenage boys and the Big Red football program. Coach Reno said he encouraged his players to be honest—with him. In general, there was a definite sense of keeping things quiet. And, especially in a small town like Steubenville, steeped in mafia lore, nobody liked a snitch.

This phenomenon has repeated itself over and over again, at every level of football, as coaches and institutions like universities, the NCAA, and the NFL prioritize wins and star players over legal action to protect women from sexual violence. In fact, for example, spanning from 2011 to 2015 at Baylor University, fifty-two accounts of rape by members of the football team were recorded and suppressed, many committed by known perpetrators who transferred to the school to play. Once outed, these allegations led to the termination of head football coach Art Briles (with a $15 million separation agreement), the resignation of Baylor president Kenneth Starr, the resignation of athletic director Ian McCaw, and the firing of others. It also led to convictions of multiple football players, who were found guilty of sexual assault. Before there began to be consequences, the message had been clear: speaking out about rape is verboten if it disrupts a winning streak or a shining football program that brings pride and money to a school.

While the silence in Steubenville continued, Rigaud and his team realized it was essential to get the boys' phones as soon as possible—the data could be erased. Apple had just introduced software that rendered deleted items gone for good. The department obtained warrants to seize devices from Trent Mays, Michael Nodianos, Mark Cole, Evan Westlake, and Cody Saltsman, as well as another friend, Anthony Commisso, who had received naked photos of Jane Doe the night of the assault and said Trent often sent him nude pictures of girls.

On August 16, the deputies went to collect the phones at the boys' homes. But when they arrived, the teens had already left to play a scrimmage. The officers rushed to the stadium to seize the devices for fear that the players could receive warnings from their parents and erase essential evidence. "The parents were told, 'Well, there's a search warrant for your son's phone, so you know, be certain not to have him change or touch it, because we'll be able to see anything that you've done to manipulate or change it,'" explained Detective Rigaud, who awaited updates back at the station.

The uniformed officers crossed the green, manicured football field to approach the relevant boys and claim their cell phones as evidence. Coach Reno, a formidable figure with a stout frame and barrel chest, the prototypical coach with a whistle hanging around his neck, stepped forward to intercept them. He frowned as an officer explained their presence and demanded the teenagers' tech. Coach Reno crossed his arms. He wasn't their parent, he said. It didn't feel right to hand over their possessions. He and one deputy exchanged words. Later, he angrily recounted to Detective Rigaud that the officer threatened to arrest him for obstruction of justice. "I really didn't expect them," Coach Reno said in his police interview. "If I had been ready for them, I wouldn't have minded it." His objection seemed in line with his perceived role as the boys' protector and the town's real authority.

Detective Rigaud was not accustomed to pushback from the town. After all, he was a local. These were his peers. Plus, he was an Eagle Scout and a former DARE officer who had visited schools to teach kids about the dangers of drugs. He had always loved working in the community. But the tension between his deputies and Coach Reno, who seemed to represent the voice of many powerful townspeople, was only the beginning. Though a portion of the Steubenville population was supportive, others were not. At junctures, Detective Rigaud would not only meet with resistance, but would find himself under personal attack by his own community. At one point, a mother of an involved teenager approached him as he shopped at Walmart to assert that Jane Doe herself was to blame for the assault. "I had no more energy in me to argue that it should not be put on her," he sighed. At another point, a rumor circulated that his own daughters, who attended Catholic Central High School where their mother was a teacher, were at Kamy's house party and that he'd somehow been covering that fact up. In reality, the family had been away on a camping trip that weekend. Rigaud was not only frustrated; he was wounded. "That was one of those that hurt," he said. He would have recused himself immediately had his daughters been witnesses, he promised.

He and his team had no choice but to push ahead against

resistance. With paperwork in hand, the deputies refused to take no for an answer. Ultimately, Reno did call the parents. Once some arrived, the boys handed over their devices. They were about to be in a world of trouble.

That day, the one smartphone police were not able to confiscate was Ma'lik's. They couldn't get a warrant because he wasn't named in the tweets. But once a large number of phones were seized and text messages could be analyzed, the situation changed. "We went after his phone the following week," said Detective Rigaud. By the time they got to Ma'lik's house, the device was long gone.

"If it was my kid, I would have thrown it in the river," one towns-person told me, echoing what many were thinking.

The phones the police collected had been sent to a cybercrime analyst at the Bureau of Criminal Investigation office in neighboring Youngstown, Ohio, a state rather than local investigative body. It was a sign that the case was becoming more complicated and required sophisticated evaluation. Sheriff's departments in neighboring Ohio towns and even in West Virginia were also collaborating on the case, as several of the witnesses were based outside the boundaries of Steubenville and Ohio. The findings were about to blow the investigation sky high.

Before the phones were fully analyzed, Detective Rigaud called Michael Nodianos, the amateur comic from Evan Westlake's cell phone video, in for some classic grilling. "Trent Mays was always the primary suspect, and Ma'lik Richmond was always [known to] have had some involvement," said Rigaud, but law enforcement needed to collect as much information as they could about that night. Though Nodi seemed to have little to do with the rape itself, he was at the center of the controversy and also, based on the YouTube video, privy to information about Jane Doe's assault in real time. "Michael Nodi-anos's video is not a crime," prosecutor Marianne Hemmeter told me when I interviewed her later. "It shocks your conscience. It, in a very odd way, became the backbone of our investigation because we could tell who was in the room and who was saying what." Using his good-cop tactics—a kind and gentle voice, active listening, offering the benefit of the doubt—Detective Rigaud coaxed Nodi to spill.

———

On August 17 at 4:03 p.m., Michael Nodianos, clad in soccer shorts, settled uncomfortably into his seat for the case's first official hard interview. As he was a legal adult now, his parents weren't present. Going by official protocols for interrogations, the detectives read Nodi his Miranda rights and he consented, feverishly gnawing on bubble gum. Right away, he seemed afraid of getting his buddies in trouble and nervous about saying the wrong thing. Nodi wasn't a regular with the popular crowd, and although he was out of school and off to college, he didn't want to be the one who ratted out the Big Red football team. He would have to show his face in town on school breaks, and his mom lived in Steubenville.

"I need to know, from you, everything from your Saturday evening through Sunday," commanded Detective Rigaud, referencing the weekend of Jane Doe's assault.

"Uh, do you need names, if they're not involved or anything?" Nodianos asked.

"I need *everything*, Mike."

"Everything?"

"Everything."

In his interview, Nodianos, who was three years older than Trent and Ma'lik, described arriving at Jake Howarth's house as the boys were depositing Jane Doe into the back seat of a car. To cast doubt about Jane Doe's character in defense of his pseudo friends, he said he'd heard that "She had kind of got around before." Nodi's insinuation is an age-old one, which gets to the heart of gender, class, and racial bias and becomes even more pronounced when victims find themselves defending their stories in court. Jane Doe was not a true victim in the eyes of the culture unless she was deemed pure, checking the boxes of what assault activists call "the myth of the perfect victim." "I see the same story play out time and again," wrote Amanda Rodriguez, executive director of Baltimore's rape crisis center, TurnAround Inc., in a recent op-ed for the *Baltimore Sun*. "To be a perfect victim of sexual assault, human trafficking or intimate partner violence, you cannot also struggle with addiction, poverty or mental illness. To be a perfect victim, you cannot accept a drink, engage in commercial sex or walk alone at night. You cannot wear tight clothes or have a criminal record. You cannot be human."

Jane Doe was a high school student, like many others. She was white, came from a two-parent home, went to church, played sports, and did well in school. Her crime in the eyes of her fellow students was that she was pretty and popular, boys liked her, and she wore trendy clothes (deemed provocative after the assault by many on social media). She had boyfriends. What Nodi was really suggesting was that, because of her sexual history, Jane Doe was asking for it.

Instead of taking the bait, the police floated the possibility of pressing child pornography charges against Nodianos, as he was in possession of at least one photograph of an underage, exposed Jane Doe on his phone.

"What are we going to find on your phone?" the detective asked.

"On my phone?" Nodianos replied. "You will find the picture."

"What picture?"

"It is her laying on the couch, and then, um, nothing else on that phone besides that."

"Why would that picture be on your phone?"

"Because Trent sent it to me."

The charges against Trent and Ma'lik were beginning to take shape: sexual assault, child pornography, possible kidnapping because the boys had transported the victim while she was unconscious.

Things had turned serious. The teens stopped carelessly texting each other. Their virtual chatter quieted, though others took to Twitter to argue in defense of one side or the other. Many of their fellow students were convinced that their male friends and teammates had been wronged, including Jeno Atkins. "Sad to say, but at that time, in 2012–13, I didn't believe the victim and was ready to go to war for the boys," he said. "I had to step out of my element to realize what happened, that the boys needed to answer for the crimes. I didn't believe at first 'cause [I thought that] false sexual harassment claims ruin guys all the time, but after years of maturing and not having a crazed football town in my ear, I was able to assess the situation better." A study conducted at one major northeastern university by renowned clinical psychologist Dr. David Lisak and peers found that only 5.9 percent of rape allegations over a ten-year period were false. The re-victimization of assault survivors after reporting and pressing charges makes false reporting an unappealing option.

Five days after Nodianos's interrogation, six days after cell phones were seized, eight days after Jane Doe's parents filed a police report, and ten days after the assault, the police drove to Ma'lik's home and rang the bell. He emerged dressed in a red t-shirt, cargo shorts, and slip-on sneakers. The officers ushered him to the police cruiser. Next, they drove to Trent's home and rang the doorbell. He too was dressed for an average August day—t-shirt, shorts, white gym socks straight up with rubber slides.

At the station, Detective Rigaud repeated their Miranda rights and asked each teen if he'd like to make a statement. They both declined, likely having been counseled by lawyers. After the arrests, they were remanded to the local juvenile detention center and remained there until several weeks after the probable cause hearing in October. Then, following that hearing, Trent was permitted to go home under house arrest, and Ma'lik went to stay with his guardians, the Agrestas, where he had lived on and off since he was eight years old. While they were in juvenile detention, the police started to call in other witnesses, including Coach Reno.

———

Alex was losing patience fast. Law enforcement didn't seem interested in her help, despite what she had uncovered. "All I could do at that point was to blog and try to bring attention to it using social media to amplify the case," she said. Meanwhile, the community was already forming opinions about who was *really* the victim. Many sympathized with the boys. Though some rallied behind Jane Doe as a symbol, intent on bringing the perpetrators to justice, others expressed more compassion for the teenage boys and the way their lives could be ruined and their futures threatened by the actions of a single night. "A lot of people would say, 'Oh, you should see the photos she posted on Instagram; you shoulda seen the outfit she had on,'" recalled Michele Robinson, a local resident. "Everybody was talking bad about Jane Doe." Apparently, Jane Doe was not a perfect *enough* victim.

On Facebook, Alex also saw comments from friends of friends beginning to victim-blame Jane Doe, referencing her "reputation." "I had seen some local forums where the discussion was already escalating, [implying] that she was not raped," Alex recalled. "The victim-blaming was starting, by adults. If these kids were openly calling it 'rape' [on social media the night of], they obviously knew it was rape." Alex was aghast at how quickly the Steubenville community circled its wagons.

Many women and girls were vocal about their disapproval of Jane Doe on these forums, despite the gendered allegiance one might expect or at least hope to find. In fact, the compartmentalization of identity in these circumstances and the desire to side with the more powerful entity even if it doesn't include or recognize you is common in these situations. "In 'separate sphere ideologies'—societies and cultures where men and women are thought of as different species, where roles are complementary but are actually always hierarchical [such as] institutionalized in patriarchal religions, single sex education, and sports culture like football—rape myths and stereotypes tied to gender norms flourish," explained Soraya Chemaly, activist and award-winning author of *Rage Becomes Her: The Power of Women's Anger.* "Girls are no less likely to act in ways that are deeply sexist, misogynist, and racist. Girls police other girls. It's learned behavior early on, and includes slut shaming."

On the popular WWVA news radio airwaves, DJ Bloomdaddy echoed the online skepticism, suspicion, and blaming of Jane Doe to listeners, suggesting that she'd probably invented the whole story to protect her reputation: "This is the latest on the incident out of Steubenville," he said. "All I can tell you is this: it's a she-said/he-said right now, without a doubt. You know, anybody can make an allegation. These girls at these parties sometimes maybe drink a little bit too much, sometimes they get a little promiscuous, all of a sudden they're being called, you know, 'a whore,' what have you, and it's real easy to all of a sudden say you were taken advantage of rather than own up to the fact that, 'Hey, look, I did what I did.'"

"Who seduced who, yeah," agreed his DJ counterpart.

"It's easier to tell your parents you were raped than, 'Hey, Mom, Dad, I got drunk and decided to let three guys have their way with me.' That's all I'm saying, based on who I've spoken to."

Alex had had enough. "It was at that point that I decided to post what was out there," she said. In a series of posts on her blog, Alex took a slow crawl toward full disclosure of the assailants' and bystanders' identities, republishing their social media posts word for word. On August 23, she posted her first story about the crime on Prinniefied. In it, she condemned the boys for their behavior, flagged special treatment of football players, questioned why the WTOV-9 article didn't mention the names of the teens charged and instead locked the comments. She expressed revulsion at the offensive photos and videos the boys posted on YouTube and Twitter. She noted that Jane Hanlin, whose son was friends with the teens involved, had said she would step aside as prosecutor, but still hadn't asked the Ohio attorney general's office to take over. In the post, Alex also defended Jane Doe when people criticized her for posting "happy shit" online after the fact and used hashtags like #dumbbitch. Further, she asked, "Do they think because they are Big Red players that the rules don't apply to them?"

Alex waited three days before posting again, after conducting more research, and this time she didn't hold back. She wrote that she was "utterly disgusted" not only by the boys' tweets, but also by the community's response. "Tweet after tweet has been filled with support for the boys who were arrested, as well as vowing…support and willingness to stick together because they are #SteubenvilleStarsForever," she raged. "No, you are not stars. You are criminals who are walking around right now on borrowed time." Alex was setting a tone on her blog. If you wanted the nitty-gritty details, this was the place. She called out the bystanders who were still "suiting up for football," but also the adults like volunteer assistant coach Matthew Belardine, who had permitted the teens to drink and had not been charged. She knew it was within her rights to post her opinion based on what she had found, even if some people didn't like it. "I know their names and *for now* I will not post them," she warned. Noting that she had screenshots of all the posts, she described how some of the boys had tried to erase the evidence. When Nodianos joked on Twitter that "The song of the night is 'rape me,'" and another teen tweeted the Nirvana music video in response, it was proof, she argued, that they understood they were witnessing a rape from afar. She summed it all up by saying, "To the other boys that were involved who are still free to go to class tomorrow morning, I can only hope that their time walking around as free men is limited. Tick tock."

Alex's local following had begun to grow. The comment section on Prinniefied was fast becoming a hub for discussion, especially since comments were still locked on WTOV-9's website and their Facebook page. Those who sided with Jane Doe shared the blog posts with each other in solidarity. Those who disagreed read, shared, and commented in anger. There was no doubt that Alex was offering, and teasing, more intel than other sources, including the police department and traditional news outlets.

By the next time she posted, two days later on August 28, Alex was ready to share some of the more disturbing and damning content. People needed to judge the truth for themselves. Maybe then they'd stop defending the boys. She included a screenshot of a choice tweet from Michael Nodianos and didn't hide his identity:

Some people deserve to be peed on #whoareyou

"I will let the words of its author speak for themselves," she concluded. The mocking tweet inspired vitriol against the boys, inciting hundreds of comments.

Alex's blog became a forum for locals who wanted to voice their distress and discuss the evolving situation anonymously. With each post, more people joined the conversation, hiding their names, with handles like Concernedmomof2 and Mamabear. It was important to Alex, as host, to provide a safe space where people could express themselves not only about this case, but about the former steel town's rampant culture of violence against women. Protecting the anonymity of victims and those who commented on her blog was nonnegotiable.

Whether or not Alex was building a criminal case, she was presenting stark evidence of a rape culture—one in which boys laughed, joked, and tweeted about assault—that was becoming hard to deny. She was raising questions: What motivated these boys to behave as they did and to believe there would be no consequences? How did the dynamics of football contribute to rape culture? The high school athletes and their friends were so sure they were untouchable that they'd posted photos and videos of the actual act. Their parents defended them. Was it football that made them feel so entitled? The enabling by adults? She called into question the notion of bystander accountability, as well. What is our responsibility as witnesses to step in and prevent harm? The fact that so many stood by and did nothing was as noteworthy as the assault itself. She named the bystanders and those who took the videos and photographs. She named the tweeters and the retweeters. She named them all.

Reception was divided, to say the least. Some people were grateful for her contribution, while others were furious. Alex became a lightning rod. Detractors poked at her online, and she poked back, uncensored. They hurled everything at her from morbid curses, like the hope that she'd contract AIDS, to death threats.

Even DJ Bloomdaddy weighed in on her involvement. "I'm going to read you a couple of emails. Let me start with this one: 'If you Google this Alex Goddard, she is indeed a cyberbully. What she's doing now, posting screenshots of tweets made by innocent kids, is a sin. Just because a kid retweets a post or replies to a post doesn't mean that kid had anything to do with the rape. It's just creating more victims. Prinniefied.com is not doing this community any favors. Continue to cover this news in a fair, balanced way; that's what separates the journalists from the others.'" Everyone was a victim—except Jane Doe.

———

A little over one hundred miles away in Cleveland, a comparatively big city known for its rivers, the Rock & Roll Hall of Fame, and hometown hero basketball legend LeBron James, a staff reporter at the flagship American newspaper the *Plain Dealer* got an anonymous tip. Rachel Dissell, a decade-long veteran of the newsroom with a pixie cut, impish face, and pragmatic manner, sat at her desk at the bottom of an active staircase where people often convened for big announcements. Dissell regularly covered sexual assault cases in Ohio and, at the time, was collaborating with a colleague on an investigative series about the proliferation of untested rape kits in the city. They were surrounded by boxes filled with sexual assault reports and sex crimes detectives' personnel files.

In the midst of this bustle, she received an email, one long message with no paragraph returns, from an unnamed source in Steubenville. The message alerted her to the crime and pleaded with her to investigate for fear that the story would otherwise be swept under the rug.

"The person suggested I look into the story of football players drugging and raping a girl because it wasn't being taken seriously," Dissell remembered. "I did a little digging and found a few paragraphs online, the chatter on the Ohio Valley Athletics page, and Alex's blog." Her interest was piqued, but at first she wasn't sure that the Big Red assault, in a small town miles away, should be covered by a big Cleveland paper. "On its face, the Steubenville case was not that much different, unfortunately, than other cases you might hear about in local suburbs," she said. "What felt different was the reaction, the public displays of defensiveness, victim-blaming, and the social media element. I wrote an email to my boss at the time, Debra Adams Simmons, the first Black woman to lead the paper, with the pros and cons of taking a trip to Steubenville to check it out." The two debated and agreed that Steubenville was far away and that the story was, unfortunately, not rare. But some of the details, or lack of details, nagged at Dissell. Ultimately, she and Adams Simmons worried that if they didn't cover the story, perhaps no one would. That was reason enough. Given the green light, Dissell set off on the 135-mile drive to a different world.

On Monday, August 27, Rachel Dissell spent the day making the rounds and talking to key people in town. Her first stop was to the stadium on Sunset Boulevard. As she walked down to Death Valley's field, an older man tried to dissuade her, but she kept on. "The team was practicing and it was raining," she remembered. When she asked to speak to Coach, who was on the field pointing and barking plays, they said he was busy, so she went to wait under some bleachers. Her hair was plastered to her face; she had a notebook and a pencil instead of a pen (a tip for rainy days from a journalism professor). "Eventually, Reno strode over. He mentioned he didn't want me out there getting soaked," she said. "He didn't want to talk about the case, so I started to ask him about the social media posts, some of which came even after the arrests. He wanted me to know that the 'boys' were like his own kids and that [this type of] behavior wasn't acceptable to him. When I started to read some of the language—the actual words his players used on Twitter—he got frustrated, said he didn't know anything about social media and walked away." Taking cues from Rachel months later, when I too was in Steubenville, waiting for Coach to talk to me by the same set of bleachers, he lamented agreeing to speak with Dissell that day, saying he'd been sucked in by how young and unassuming she appeared, standing there in the rain. He had underestimated her. Just like he would underestimate me.

Dissell also talked to school superintendent Mike McVey, whom she remembered as defensive, evasive, clearly annoyed about all the attention to the district, and surprised to find reporters showing up to talk to him. He appeared uncomfortable in his suit, his face red and sweaty. "He tried to draw some imaginary lines between what happened on the field, what happened outside of school, and what happened inside the school building," she recalled.

The reporter also met with police chief William McCafferty at his office, whom she remembers as "compact and tan with hair that looked lightened," and who seemed to convey as much openness as possible. "He was the kind of chief who wore his uniform all of the time," she said. "He said to call him 'Bill.'" He expressed frustration with all the gossip and false stories and disappointment at local parents for not encouraging their kids to come talk to the police. Most of all, he wanted to refute the rumor that law enforcement was not thoroughly investigating the crime. He insisted that there was no cover-up, despite what some people had been claiming online. Dissell returned to Cleveland with a stronger sense of what had happened and of Steubenville itself.

On September 2, she broke the story in the *Plain Dealer* with her comprehensive article, "Rape charges against high school players divide football town of Steubenville, Ohio." The feature exposed the fractures in the town, including quotes from people like McVey, who said in response to criticism that the school hadn't truly investigated or taken Jane Doe's claims to law enforcement, "We're not going to be witch-hunting everyone down." This language implies the victimization of the accused despite the improbability of guilt. The expression "witch hunt" has origins in the actual murders of an estimated 40,000–50,000 women accused of witchcraft, and yet the school's superintendent McVey appropriated it in defense of the boys, not Jane Doe. The idiom would later be embraced by the likes of Donald Trump, when he himself was accused of sexual assault. He tweeted the expression "witch hunt" hundreds of times during his time as president—forty-five times in thirty-four days at one point, according to *The Nation*.

Dissell cited Alex's research in the article, bringing it and Jane Doe's story legitimacy. "I was very happy that a known media outlet was picking up the story," remembered Alex. "Back then, the mainstream media wasn't too happy with 'bloggers' reporting the news. It did inspire me to keep going." Alex forged ahead and began trading information with Dissell.

As the school year got into full swing, three days later on September 5, Alex shared the photo of Jane Doe being carried unresponsive out of Party B, snapped and posted to Instagram by Cody Saltsman. She wasn't interested in keeping what she'd found to herself anymore. Careful to protect Jane Doe's anonymity, Alex blurred out her face and body. That, combined with the screen captures of the boys' tweets, set readers aflame on another level. "Once I posted, it was mayhem." She shook her head. "It got to the point that I couldn't even read through all the comments. People were upset; they were mad. It was crazy, the amount of traffic coming from Steubenville. When people actually saw…what these kids were saying, it caused a very visceral reaction. People have a right to know."

The tenor began to shift for some townspeople. Mark Nelson, a father of ten and owner of religious swag factory Catholic to the Max, later commented during an interview with me, "It seemed as if it hit social media and just exploded. There were photos circulating already and deleted texts. And the earliest photographs were very disturbing. The idea of an incapacitated girl being drug around is horrible. The last thing you want to do is imagine your daughter in that type of situation—or your boys." Mark Nelson was a leader of the home-schooling, highly conservative Catholic sect in town and considered something of a moral compass, but he had his own dark past. As an anti-choice activist in 1990, Mark Nelson had spent time in prison for violating clinic boundaries in attempts to block women from seeking medical care. Everyone brought their own complicated lens.

On September 14, Trent and Ma'lik appeared in court to assess whether there was enough evidence to proceed. The county judge ruled in favor of the prosecution; there would be a trial. Jane Doe and her family weren't driving the process anymore. It was the state of Ohio. "That's a hard prosecutor's call," said Marianne Hemmeter, who was now representing the case on behalf of the state. "Do you go forward when your victim doesn't want to? There was a point when [Jane Doe's] mom did go down to the police station and say, 'We don't want this pressure. We don't want to go forward.' And that was early on in the investigation. And the discussion was, 'We've already filed charges. We can't back down now.'" There was a mountain of evidence. They had to move forward.

On Friday, October 12, there was a chill in the air. Any vestiges of the humid summer were gone. The long Ohio winter was coming. For now, wary, the teens were keeping parties specific to their local Steubenville friends. Big Red football wasn't feeling the absence of Ma'lik and Trent too acutely. They were good players, but they were "only sophomores." And the town's support never wavered. The season was going just fine, but the team felt the strain in other ways. "We got taunted and called 'rapists' at every game," remembered Jeno Atkins.

At Ma'lik and Trent's probable cause hearing, in which the lawyers had to prove that the defendants reasonably could have committed the crime, Trent and Ma'lik sat in front of the judge and watched as three of their friends, now witnesses, took the stand to testify against them. The case was deemed viable. A court date was set for March 2013. And this football town was officially split in two, whether people wanted to acknowledge it or not.

"[Reno] is talking X's and O's," reported Dissell in her article. "The rest of the town is talking rape." And that was just part of the problem.

## CHAPTER 5

# THE COACH

THIS IS STEELERS COUNTRY.

Located less than an hour from the city of Pittsburgh, with its beautiful arching bridges, Carnegie libraries, and industrial edges, Steubenville bleeds black-and-gold. Branded mugs crowded messy desks at the local police station, "Steelers Nation" bumper stickers graced the back of trucks, entire families wore Franco Harris and Terry Bradshaw jerseys to the grocery store on game days. God forbid Ravens fans showed their faces.

The Steelers were led by "Big Ben" Roethlisberger, who was drafted in 2004 and who, in 2006, became the youngest quarterback to win a Super Bowl in NFL history at twenty-three years old. He led the team to victory again in 2009, dominating the Arizona Cardinals.

Shortly thereafter, the unsavory details of Big Ben's personal life went public. In July of that same year, a woman filed civil charges against the pro athlete for an incident that reportedly took place in June 2008 during a celebrity golf tournament in Lake Tahoe. According to the complaint, Roethlisberger lured the woman—a Harrah's Casino employee—to his hotel room under false pretenses about the mechanics of his in-room TV, then cornered and sexually assaulted her. Afterward the woman quoted her boss, who was friendly with Roethlisberger, as saying, "That guy can have anyone he wants," suggesting both his willingness to deliver Roethlisberger whatever he desired and also questioning why a famous quarterback would bother raping her. The football player denied the allegations, and the case was settled out of court without admission of wrongdoing.

In early 2010, Big Ben found himself on the wrong side of media scrutiny again when another young woman accused him of coaxing her into a Georgia nightclub's VIP room and then to the adjoining bathroom—with help from his off-duty policeman bodyguard—where he cornered and raped her. She went to the hospital afterward, where an ER doctor and two nurses reported finding mild bruising and lacerations "in the genital area." Local police sergeant Jerry Blash, who had posed for a photo with the quarterback earlier that day, was the first officer on the scene and griped, "We have a problem. This drunk bitch, drunk off her ass, is accusing Ben of rape." Blash later resigned.

In the end, no charges were filed because the prosecution declared that there wasn't enough evidence. Roethlisberger and his legal team denied the allegations, but the woman never backed down from her story. Most of the fans never backed down from their support of "Big Ben" either. Under pressure from national media, the NFL suspended the quarterback without pay for six games for violating their "personal conduct" policy. When the attention died down and the national press focused elsewhere, they reduced his punishment to four games. It wasn't until years later, at a virtual ManUp Pittsburgh conference with head coach Mike Tomlin, that Roethlisberger disclosed how his Christian faith had since helped him combat an addiction to alcohol and porn. No mention of a problem with sexual assault.

Unfortunately, Big Ben wasn't the Steelers' only problem. Their controversial one-time wide receiver Antonio Brown was accused of sexual assault by his trainer as well. The charges arose after he'd left

Pittsburgh, but dated back to his time with the Steelers. Brown and his legal team denied the allegations, but a civil suit was settled out of court without admission of wrongdoing. Despite this, and the fact that there were so many domestic disturbances later at his Florida home that the local police department disinvited him from participating in their youth league, the Tampa Bay Buccaneers signed him as a free agent. He and Tom Brady would go on to win Super Bowl LV together in February 2021.

For most of the football-loving boys in Steubenville, Steelers players like Big Ben were, and are, heroes. When it came to their own football futures, the Big Red players dreamed of being scouted by Ohio State and Penn State. Those schools were the ultimate destination, almost as major as getting to the pros, though only a few Steubenville players had ever reached the NFL. Diehard Penn State fans could be identified around town by their bumper stickers proclaiming, *If God weren't a Nittany Lions fan, why'd he make the sky blue and white?*

Penn State fans had confronted their own set of systemic sexual misconduct revelations and their hero's painful fall from grace when, in December 2011, assistant coach Jerry Sandusky was arrested and charged with fifty-two counts of child molestation of young boys, perpetrated through his organization for at-risk youth. Stretching between 1994 and 2009, some of the assaults occurred in the Penn State locker rooms. "Part of the issue with Sandusky was that he had exalted status as a rescuer of children," said Dave Zirin, political sportswriter, sports editor for *The Nation*, and the author of ten books, most recently *The Kaepernick Effect*. "You could not have picked someone who was more horrific. He was helping because of his own predation. This was someone held up as a savior of children, particularly children at risk, children of color, poor kids, the most vulnerable. The very demographic that plays college football." Ideally, football can provide structure, purpose, camaraderie, joy in the game, precision, focus, and feelings of accomplishment. Instead, these children were preyed upon.

By and large, the community of fans condemned Sandusky for his actions—a no-brainer, as he'd molested young boys. "With Penn State, because of the history of homophobia in the locker room, the idea of men having sex with boys inside that space generated a degree of outrage that was just—and I recalled wanting a similar amount of response to gendered violence in sports," said Zirin. "There is a 'boys will be boys' edge to how violence against women is looked at, especially at high school and collegiate levels, and there is a culture of cover-ups. We saw the cover-up at Penn State, but it's just about the reaction when the stories meet the oxygen. Reaction is quite different depending on who the survivor is in the case."

In June 2012, Sandusky was ultimately found guilty of forty-five counts of sexual abuse. But the real challenge came when fans learned that longtime head coach Joe Paterno, a revered, iconic father figure, had known about and ignored assault allegations against Sandusky, going as far back as 1998. For thirteen years, he had looked the other way. Paterno was fired, and countless alumni and local fans were devastated. Condemning Coach Paterno for his role as an enabler and bystander was a harder pill for Penn State fans to swallow. This kind of cover-up seemed to mirror similar institutional negligence in the Catholic church, another powerful force in this part of the country.

Big Red's players looked up to Coach Reno Saccoccia in much the same way Penn State fans adored Joe Paterno, which is why Trent Mays assumed that "Reno" would be able to protect him from the state of Ohio's rape charges. Reno Saccoccia was born and raised in Steubenville, attended Catholic Central High School, and studied education at the University of Akron. He returned home to coach junior high school football before joining the Big Red staff, under a different coach, in 1981. Reno took the reins at Steubenville High School in 1983. In 1984, the school won their first state championship. After two years of coaching, his record was 23–1–0. "When I was younger, I used to wear number 84, so I figured that 1984 was our year," he was quoted as saying on the Big Red website. "Now I don't believe in the stars, but I do believe in the person who makes the stars." By 2007, the school had renamed the arena "Reno Field at Harding Stadium." During this time, he had three kids and eight grandchildren. To say he was a fixture of the community was an understatement.

The first time I met Coach Reno, I was watching him from the stands during a grueling summer scrimmage. He was shouting at the boys as they trained, barking encouragement, corrections, fine-tuning their form and focus, his eyes on everyone at once. He was so in his element; it was kinetic and intimidating to watch. He reluctantly spoke to me off the record, and let me tag along into his office, a converted gym next to the field. I saw a teenage boy asleep on the floor, napping because his mother had dropped him off at dawn before she went to work. Another teen approached to seek advice about what classes to take for the upcoming semester. Coach found ways to help his players, especially those from households that were stretched thin, and was known to help girls at Steubenville High School too, slipping them a few bucks for gas to get to appointments. He "took care" in the traditional sense of the expression.

"Kids look at their relationship with their coach as a second father or mentor figure," said Valencia Peterson aka "Coach V," a football coach at Pennsylvania's Penwood High School and the founder of an anti-violence program for youth, Open Door Abuse Awareness & Prevention (ODAAP). "They see the football team as a family that's functional, that's structured. The dynamic [involves] having each other's backs, fighting for each other, and they find a great deal of identity in that." For many, after graduation, losing that guiding, protective hand can feel unmooring.

Coach Reno's power didn't end with the students. One could almost hear the *Godfather* theme song playing as he made his appearance at the annual Christmas parade, working his way down Main Street, kissing the men and women of Steubenville on both cheeks. The parents revered him too, as did the superintendent and governing bodies of the high school that put him in charge of disciplinary action when the rape was first reported.

When rumors initially materialized about a probable assault, on August 14, just two days after the rape, instead of calling in law enforcement, Superintendent McVey sent the school principal, Michael Crosier, to talk to Reno. They kept the dealings internal. The two men empowered Coach to investigate the crime, determine guilt or innocence, and mete out any disciplinary action based on the word of his own players. These boys knew there would be acute punishment for alcohol consumption and were incentivized to deny drinking and other wrongdoing to stay on the team. The teen boys vehemently denied everything, and Coach let them go with a warning. No one in the school's leadership saw this as a conflict of interest, and no one thought to consider the well-being of the teenage girl involved. "[McVey] was most agitated when asked why Reno was allowed to decide punishments for players," recalled Rachel Dissell. Coach was at the center of it all.

"He low-key rules the town," said Brendon Sadler, a former rival athlete from neighboring Weirton, West Virginia. "It all gets swept under the [rug]. The football players in Steubenville get away with murder." Accusations of special treatment for football players swirled after news of the rape began to spread. Police chief William McCafferty expressed frustration, telling reporter Rachel Dissell for her *Plain Dealer* story, "It's ridiculous for people to even think that. Other people might put football first, but we [as the police] don't."

After years of unchecked behavior within Big Red, kids from other valley schools reveled in schadenfreude when the players faced repercussions. "Before the situation went down, Steubenville was already not liked around the area," said Jeno Atkins, not long after the incident happened, before he had time to reflect. "Even since I've been born, there's always been some type of weird tension between Steubenville and other cities. After that situation [with the rape] came about, that just gave people a reason to be extra vocal about it. It's not like we weren't used to it." Many in the Ohio Valley found Big Red players cocky. Later Jeno noted, "Steubenville is hated in this area because of our sports dominance, so when that case went down that added a surplus of fuel to the already burning fire."

In town, however, as Alex noted, there was an outpouring of support for the players and anger at Jane Doe, who received death threats on Twitter from local girls. " 'Bullying' is homophobia, racism, ableism, and sexism," said Soraya Chemaly. "We don't want to name these things when children behave in these ways, but the older they get, the less useful it becomes to homogenize the behavior that way. Bullying needs to be named for what it is, like slut shaming or racism." In the days following the teens' arrests, as Alex looked on with scorn, Big Red fans took to Twitter with hashtags like #SteubenvilleStrong and #SteubenvilleStarsForever. Dissell's article quoted one football player opining, "Were not gonna let dumb shit [*sic*] like this mess up our state championship goal." The team did not make the state championships that year.

In general, the Steubenville football players were discussed in terms of their "blood, sweat, and tears," language usually reserved for soldiers. "Sports are huge in Steubenville, so that always brought the community together," said Jeno Atkins not long after the rape. "Like every Friday you see ten thousand fans in the stands, cheering us on. It's like a brotherhood that you'll forever be a part of, like a fraternity that you can never get out of." The town had fewer than 18,000 residents, down from 40,000 during their boom years. On any given night, more than half the residents of Steubenville might potentially be in Harding Stadium, aka Death Valley, watching the game.

————

On Big Red's website, as the music swells, an in-depth history of football in the region starts with a rhyming ode:

> *Way back since the days of old,*
> *when the coal and steel was our gold,*
> *were the men who sacrificed and bled,*
> *for the mighty Steubenville Big Red.*

The website—which features the team's signature red stallion, Man o' War, galloping across the words "Roll Red Roll"—goes on to detail everything from the team's first recorded season in 1900 to the history of the stadium and their rivalry with nearby Catholic Central High School. It covers the reigns of various coaches, including the "controversial" hiring of Coach Reno in 1983 over more seasoned candidates. According to legend, Reno triumphed over all obstacles, shutting dissenters down. As of 2020, Big Red had made it to the postseason more than thirty times and won the state championship four times. This was an extraordinary accomplishment for a tiny town in the football-obsessed state of Ohio, where they had to compete with big city programs in Cleveland, Cincinnati, and Columbus.

Steubenville's longtime mayor was Domenick Mucci Jr., a Democrat who would ultimately serve six four-year terms in a row (including one three-day prison sentence for drunk driving in 2011)—proof of Steubenville's reluctance to change. But Jerry Barilla, considered by many to be the unofficial mayor of Steubenville as its historian and biggest cheerleader, came to the defense of his hometown, arguing that valuing their football team didn't mean devaluing rape. "It was portrayed that we were covering up the [crime]," he complained. "We had many emails that came through, 'We're never coming to Steubenville. You people are nothing but supporters of rape.' Hey, we're a little town. We have good high school football teams, so we rally around that. Who doesn't rally around their football teams? We get wrapped up in it."

Yet the intersection of football and rape culture is long and storied. According to a 2019 *Miami Herald* article, hotlines and shelters see increased instances of assaults on women on football game days. A study by the National Bureau of Economic Research found a 28 percent increase in rape reports by college-age women on days when Division I football teams played. The increase was greater when there were home games (41 percent) versus away games (15 percent).

The perceived relationship between sexual assault and football is so widely accepted on a cultural level that, on her show *Inside Amy Schumer*, the actress and comedian aired a skit in 2015 spoofing *Friday Night Lights* called, "Football Town Nights," in which a new maverick football coach played by actor Josh Charles meets resistance when he tries to institute a "no raping" policy. "You don't like it?" he shouts. "Don't let the door rape you on the way out!" The players posit multiple scenarios in which they should surely be allowed to rape a woman, including, "What if my mom is the DA and won't prosecute?" (That was a familiar scenario for Steubenville.) Ultimately, the parody pointed to parallels between football and assault and the conflicting messages teenage players receive when Charles says, "How do I get through to you boys that football isn't about rape? It's about violently dominating anyone who stands between you and what you want! That other team—they ain't just gonna lay down and give it to you. You gotta go out there and take it!" It brilliantly underlined the disconnect between what our culture teaches boys about how to behave on the football field as men versus how to behave in their lives.

The video hit a nerve and went viral, garnering millions of views on YouTube and extensive coverage by media outlets from *Rolling Stone* and *Entertainment Weekly* to less expected platforms like *Business Insider*, the *Washington Post*, and *Texas Monthly*.

"A lot of times, the reason why you see an intersection between rape culture and sexual violence and athletes is because of two words: privilege and entitlement," said Coach V. "We have created a culture where, if you're an athlete and you're making a name for yourself, you're entitled to certain privileges. And, unfortunately, that's trickled down into, yes, you can rape a woman or treat anyone badly and you'll just get a slap on the wrist." Among players on a team where negative values (or no particular values) around gender, sexuality, and respect are embraced, demeaning women can even be a show of strength and dominance or camaraderie, a way to fit in. As Jeno mentioned about being a player with Big Red, while looking back, "The main rule was to be humble, no drugs or alcohol, and so help you God if you were not home by eight-thirty p.m. [the night before a game]." And yet when it came to Jane Doe's assault, for the Big Red players, any positive lessons got drowned out by notions of supporting the brotherhood at all costs, loyalty over ethics, boys over girls, football over all. What's different about the approach of someone like Coach V, and also in theory programs like ManUp, is a linking of positive masculinity and teamwork on and off the field. There's a conscious integration around ethics and relationships, elevating the humanity of all, not just "the boys."

On October 10, 2012, Reno walked into the police station with Superintendent Mike McVey at his side. Coach was fired up, taking an aggressive tone in the recorded police interview, and demanding to know why Detective Rigaud waited so long to call him if it was so important that he come in. But Rigaud would not be goaded; he responded calmly and clearly—he'd been sorting through the evidence and waiting on the text messages from the phones, some of which pointed to conversations with Coach about what happened.

For the most part, Coach Reno denied knowing anything about the details of the assault, short of receiving a worried text from Trent Mays on that Sunday evening and also a call from Evan Westlake's father about the threat from a member of Jane Doe's extended family. On Monday, August 13, having begun to hear rumors, he called Trent, Ma'lik, and Mark Cole into his office and asked them what happened. "They said, 'Coach, we never did that. We didn't screw her, blah, blah, blah,'" he recounted. "I said, 'If you don't tell me the truth right now, I can't help you. If you tell me the truth, we'll do what we have to do.'" Judging by Trent's text about Reno protecting him, at least one of those boys took that to mean "by any means necessary."

According to Coach, the boys continued to deny any wrongdoing, even after the prosecutor filed charges, particularly with regard to the kidnapping, which they kept interpreting in traditional terms. What the prosecution meant by "kidnapping" was carrying Jane Doe from place to place without her knowledge or consent, versus a more dramatic Hollywood ransom kidnapping. "They says, 'Coach, we never kidnapped that girl. We never screwed that girl. That girl wanted—we, we left the party and her girlfriends told her not to come with us. We didn't want her to come with us,'" he said. "And I said, 'Did you rape her?' They said, 'No.' I said, 'Did you fuck her?' They said, 'No.'" At times, Coach was parroting the words of the teens, but he also flippantly and liberally used expressions like "screw" and "fuck" to talk about this violating sexual act with a sixteen-year-old girl. The use of aggressive sexualized language toward women and girls seemed so ingrained that it was nearly unconscious and spotlighted a normalization of sexism and rape culture.

Normally, the players were automatically suspended from the football team if they were caught drinking alcohol. In this case, though, Coach Reno made a conscious decision *not* to suspend them because he thought it might cast them in a negative light, and he didn't want to make them look guilty of the rape. He also admitted to urging the team, before their phones were confiscated, to be careful about what they texted to one another. "All the texts from the football players should've really slowed down after the fourteenth or fifteenth 'cause I was pounding it in them, you know, 'Watch what you say on your phone,'" he said, seemingly unaware that he may have been coaching the boys on how not to get caught instead of examining the content of the messages and their behavior. But Coach Reno did express concern because he talked to Mark Cole about his probable cause testimony in advance and gave him some advice: "I go home and I'm saying, 'Fuck. They might get me on tampering with a witness.'"

His dedication to protecting his players at any cost, what he saw as his responsibility, came through loud and clear, especially when he talked about those kids who didn't have strong foundations at home. "If I'm going to go to a banquet with them, then I'm going to hell with them too," he said, like a weathered general leading his troops into battle. "I'm not going to defend them if they're wrong, but they need to see me there. I [expect them] to give me their heart and soul every day. And I've got to give mine in return."

And yet his protective instincts didn't extend to the other teens involved, the girls—or in this case, one girl—whose lives were also impacted. He accused the prosecutors of pressuring Mark Cole into testifying against his friends and saying what they wanted to hear. He said the local judge was avoiding him—"He hasn't said a word to me since this happened. Not one word. He's avoided me like the plague. And every other year he's calling me every other week for a ticket." Then Coach Reno told Detective Rigaud a story, a kind of local legend, about another Big Red football player who, according to him, returned home to Steubenville to visit in the mid-1970s and had his life derailed when he was accused of assault by a girl he was dating. "She said, 'rape,'" Coach Reno said. "I'm not saying he was a saint, but he's forty-seven years old today and he's a mess. And he was on full scholarship to Miami of Ohio. And that's what's going to happen to these kids. There's pressure on these…prosecutors to get these kids guilty because that's what people want. Number one, because they're kids, they're boys against a girl, and number two, because they're from Big Red and they're football players." As Coach Reno's police interview progressed, it became clear that he and, by proxy, the entire football program was steeped in rape myths, primarily the idea that women make up these stories to ruin men's lives. In his retelling, the boys and men were the real victims. The authorities always believe "the girl." Not long after this, the "rights of the accused," prioritizing the concerns of men who were wronged by women who claimed rape, would come to the fore when Betsy DeVos was named the head of the Department of Education under Trump.

Back in the interrogation room, Coach Reno signaled that the victim was in part responsible for what happened to her. "We've been dealing with this girl since March," he said, alluding to the fact that she had dated Cody Saltsman, who got upset when she broke up with him. "She's been a problem since March."

Detective Rigaud remained calm as he reminded Coach, "They would not have been arrested if there wasn't strong evidence to say that they raped her. Now, realize rape isn't necessarily a forced situation we're talking about here. It can be they fingered her, and any kind of penetration on any part of her body, is what's under rape. And now, we realize that. That's another thing the public is really stupid on." Rigaud showed himself to be highly skilled at engaging with witnesses and building trust through a variety of tactics.

In interrogations with the players and with Coach, he employed patience and compassion.

Steubenville is a small place where everyone knows one another. Suddenly, through the lens of this case, an entire community was being forcefully educated on the laws defining consent and assault, and Rigaud faced the uphill battle of being their translator. As a filmmaker scouring these police tapes later, it dawned on me that Rigaud, a detective investigating a crime, was functioning as the town's consent-based sex educator. Unfortunately, that education was happening in the interrogation room, in the aftermath of a horrific and preventable sexual assault. In Steubenville, this comprehensive education had never been available for or from coaches, clergy, teachers, or any adults in leadership positions.

In fact, evidence-based and in-depth sexual education, including lessons about consent, rape myths, and inclusive sexuality, is still not mandated in the United States. A state profile of Ohio's sex ed policies in 2007, just a few years before Jane Doe's assault, notes that schools were only obligated to teach about "venereal diseases" as part of the health curriculum and had to stress that "abstinence from sexual activity is the only protection that is one hundred per cent [sic] effective." Schools were required to teach students to refrain from sexual activity until after marriage, "teach the potential physical, psychological, emotional, and social side effects of participating in sexual activity outside of marriage," as well as stress the "harmful consequences" of having children out of wedlock. With regard to assault, they simply had to "advise students of the circumstances under which it is criminal to have sexual contact with a person under the age of sixteen pursuant to section 2907.04 of the Revised Code." Meanwhile, in the same state, 44 percent of female high school students and 45 percent of male students were having sex, regardless of what the doctrine preached. In young people ages fifteen to nineteen, Ohio ranked twelfth in the country for cases of syphilis, eleventh for cases of chlamydia, and ninth for gonorrhea. And yet, in 2009, community-based organizations in Ohio received $4,948,806 in federal funding for abstinence-only-until-marriage programs. Evidently, this approach wasn't working.

"There is still a widely held, and widely disproven belief, that providing info about sex and sexuality somehow increases sexual behavior and will cause someone to change their identity, as though it were something fleeting and that easily influenced," said Anne Hodder-Shipp, CSE, a certified sex educator and founder of Everyone Deserves Sex Ed (EDSE). "That's partly because sex ed is so sexualized, as is sexual identity. We do have research that shows access to accurate and affirming sex ed can lead to teens waiting longer to have their first sexual experiences, decrease STI rates and unintended teen pregnancy rates, teach valuable decision-making skills related to romantic and sexual relationships, and also has a powerful effect on mental health."

And yet the teens in Steubenville weren't privy to this type of comprehensive and tolerant education. In the dawning age of social media and internet culture, they were likely looking mostly to pornography, movies, memes, and one another for signals about how to behave. Perhaps they were also looking to their coach, who may have believed he was promoting respect, but used words like "fuck" and "screw" in reference to a teen girl. This lack of consistent and clear guidance is exactly what can inflame rape culture. "Withholding information, making it difficult to access, or controlling what *is* accessible creates gaps in understanding, which means that key pieces of information about bodily autonomy, relationship dynamics, and sexual expression are missing and disempowering young people," explained Hodder-Shipp. "They end up having to navigate situations through trial and error (lots of error) without anything to tether them to what's realistic or reasonable to expect from ourselves and others. Patriarchy and white supremacy are at the foundation of rape culture and give it the power it needs to thrive."

Now, in the interrogation room, Coach Reno, one of the town's primary male role models, was grappling with the notion of digital penetration as a definition of rape. He faced Rigaud, sputtering with barely masked frustration. "So, can't they use another word from, from 'rape'?" He leaned in, crossing spacial boundaries, and touched Rigaud's leg, signaling either a sense of camaraderie or, worse, dominance. He was a man accustomed to getting what he wanted—just like his players. But the law in Ohio is clear, and the case would spiral beyond Coach Reno's sphere of influence.

## CHAPTER 6

# THE PLAYERS

**A**T STEUBENVILLE HIGH SCHOOL, the social hierarchy was a picture of separate-sphere ideology on steroids. Rigid gender norms and social policing came in the form of slut-shaming, monitoring each other's social media for excessive "thirstiness" or promiscuity, and evaluating a boy's perceived homosexuality. These codes favored hyper-masculine athletes over everyone else, giving them an out-sized sense of entitlement. It demanded conformity. With regard to gender and rape myths, "By the time you get to high school, you are already in the realm of having to unteach people," said Soraya Chemaly. At Big Red, the football players were seen much like the popular athletes portrayed in old school movies like *The Breakfast Club* and *Revenge of the Nerds*. They ruled the school in opposition to teens like Nodi, suggesting that while notions of cool might have been changing elsewhere, Steubenville was still the land of jocks and geeks, with other categories, according to Jeno Atkins, like "gangsters, suburban kids, and kids who were a little country." "I got along with anyone," he said, as though that was the exception. "Football wasn't my identity."

Cheerleaders were talented athletes in their own right, but they were window dressing in this environment. Few fans paid attention to their tumbling skills on the field or court. At one game I later attended, there was a lead cheerleader, a stunning blond girl with a glittering smile, who did back handsprings across the entire field. Like most cheerleaders, she wore a spangled and skimpy outfit in the biting Ohio cold. As we watched her, some of the men behind me in the stands commented on her looks, as they seemed to do regularly at the games. An older man grunted, "Yeah. But does she do laundry?" She was sixteen.

One notable exception to the celebration of hypermasculinity was the marching band, where less athletic types could get their groove on with drums and clarinets in enthusiastic, though atonal, fight songs.

"You know, they took God out of our schools," one woman told me, conspiratorially, at a game, perhaps mistaking me for a religious student from Franciscan University. I was carrying a Catholic to the Max tote bag that Mark Nelson had given me after our interview. This was my soft attempt to disguise myself as a local and not a snooping filmmaker. "And they won't let us pray on the field anymore. Then they wonder why we have all these problems."

By "problems" she meant negative attention about the football program in the local news and underage sexual activity. She did not mean the problem of rape or rape culture, which few in town had ever paid attention to despite a long history of systemic violence against women. All that changed with the assault of Jane Doe, when the police made arrests that were suddenly impossible to ignore.

Unfortunately, the town seemed so busy defending itself and placing responsibility elsewhere that it didn't see its own complicity in perpetuating the boys' sense of entitlement or the opportunity it had to educate its children about harmful sexual behavior. As police chief McCafferty explained, "The police are called after the fact. In this case, we came, we got the evidence, and solved the case. That's our job." He wouldn't say if it was the parents' or the school's job to put violence prevention into place.

As the town struggled to reckon with its own social decline, there was a lot of talk about the children of "single mothers" and all that implied about women, race, and economics. When I asked townsperson Jerry Barilla whether he thought that kids were being taught to respect women in their homes because of a lack of curriculum in school, he talked about a dearth of discipline and too much freedom, which he attributed in large part to divorce rates. "I think a big breakdown in society is that we've broken the home up," Barilla said. "The words *respect* and *responsibility* and *manners* are of the past. The attendance of churches has gone down. Divorce, single mothers, guys living with girls—what are they teaching? It's a society issue." Yet these teenage boys, who would come to be dubbed the Steubenville "rape crew" by some after whispers of additional incidents that predated August 11, 2012, were mostly from white, middle-class, two-parent homes.

So what dynamics *did* perpetuate this rape? Each Big Red teenage boy played his specific part in Jane Doe's assault, exemplifying common roles in cases of high school and college sexual assault. A rape doesn't only involve two people—or even the multiple people immediately entangled. There is most often a climate that fosters such behavior.

This is what enabled rape culture to flourish within the Steubenville football program. As the teenagers were called in for police interviews at the end of August and into September 2012, they seemed to perpetuate their same roles in the interrogation room as well.

The players in Jane Doe's story fit the basic archetypes that I've noticed often emerge around sexual assault discourse, many of which are versions of "The Bystander." The original notion of the bystander effect—that people are less likely to intervene and help a victim if there are other people present who are also not acting—was posited in 1964 based on the Kitty Genovese murder during which thirty-eight bystanders supposedly watched a violent crime occur and did nothing. That particular story proved to be inaccurate, but it inspired a significant examination of the role of witnesses and their likelihood to help based on power dynamics, group sizes, relationships, and more.

A 1968 study by American social psychologists John M. Darley and Bibb Latané determined that the degree of responsibility a bystander felt was dependent on three factors:

1. Whether they felt that the person was deserving of help.
2. The competence of the bystander.
3. The relationship between the bystander and the victim.

Intervention or assistance could range from directly stepping in to help or simply calling the police.

Like many, Alex Goddard felt that the social media from the night of the assault told a story of disregard for a young woman in distress. "They humiliated her," she said of those who joined the online fray. Even those who did nothing did something. Echoing back to the film *The Accused* starring Jodie Foster, when people cheered on a gang rape, it begged the question: what does it mean when the online discourse is so callous? What does it mean that no one, in person, helped Jane Doe? Beyond the rapists themselves, who is also complicit?

Often in these cases, boys beyond the direct perpetrators play roles in assisting, egging on, or passively observing the violence. This bystander effect (also known as "bystander apathy") was especially troubling to Chief McCafferty. He noted that what bothered him most about the Steubenville case was the silence, both on the night of the incident and after the fact, when his plea for witnesses to come forward was largely ignored. "That night [of the incident], not one person stepped up and said something," he was quoted as saying. "Whatever happened, not one person stepped in to stop it." To another media outlet, he later commented, "The thing I found most disturbing about this is that there were other people around when this was going on. Nobody had the morals to say, 'Hey, stop it, that isn't right.' If you could charge people for not being decent human beings, a lot of people could have been charged that night."

Since, as the townspeople kept insisting, Steubenville was not only populated with rape apologists who wanted Jane Doe to suffer, the question was: where were the good guys? Why did observers that night seem to believe that a show of ethics somehow signaled disloyalty? Why were so many adults afraid of being ostracized for speaking out too?

In the bystander effect, the relationship of the bystander to the perceived victim is key. Jane Doe was an outsider from across the river. Was she chosen for that reason? Did her past relationship with Cody Saltsman and the jealousy she may have inspired in other girls because of the attention she attracted make her less deserving of help in their eyes? If even one bystander had acted on her behalf, Jane Doe might never have been raped.

That's why violence prevention organizations like Green Dot focus on bystander intervention training as key to reducing sexual violence and to educating youth. This idea is embraced by Tyrone White, formerly known as "Coach Ty" at Cleveland's St. Ignatius High School, one of Ohio's most competitive football programs. Inspired in large part by the Steubenville case, White has educated many football players, including Miami Dolphins linebacker Jerome Baker. Thanks to White's teaching, Baker now uses his platform to speak out about violence against women in sports. He has even shared a personal story about stopping the potential assault of an intoxicated young woman on one occasion.

Tyrone White demonstrates the positive impact a coach can have on his players. "The Green Dot program has a curriculum, so individuals know how to respond when confronted with situations [like this] because, many times, there's a whole flood of other thoughts that are in a person's mind [as they react]," explained White, likening bystander training to being taught to make snap decisions in sports. "If [teenagers and young adults] don't have the experience of training in and cultivation of how to respond instinctively in the moment, they go to complacency, passivity, and say nothing."

White, who now teaches criminal justice courses, knows from experience as a former college football player who is ashamed to have once stood by as his teammates violated an intoxicated woman in a nearby dorm room. "Sexual assault awareness [has] three different domains of prevention," he explains. "The training: what do you do in the moment when you're seeing your boy, your dog, is getting ready to do something horrific to violate another individual? How do you stop that? Then distraction, getting other people involved, say, so that you can maintain personal safety, but [still] intervene to stop someone from being victimized. And then the third domain is suppression. After it's already happened, what are you going to do now? And that's where there's cognitive restructuring [learning to label and combat irrational thoughts], and getting people who had been involved in these kinds of situations [can] be helpful." The striking difference between Coach Ty's takeaway from having been a bystander and the collective reaction in Jane Doe's case is that nobody seemed especially disturbed by the violence against Jane Doe as it was happening. Shawn McGhee, the wrestler, expressed concern and raised a moral objection during Nodianos's video, but no one else in proximity to the victim, or tracking via social media, seemed to have a twinge of guilt. Instead a kind of "groupthink" or "pack mentality" took over, where people adopted the same mindset as one another, accepting, even celebrating, actions that they would normally have viewed as wrong. "'Groupthink' refers to the social pressures to agree with members of your 'clan,'" explained Dr. Sherry Hamby, research professor of psychology at University of the South and director of Life Paths Research Center. "It can be very costly to be expelled from a group, even a group of friends or colleagues, and so people will not say what they really think in order to avoid those social costs."

In order for the "groupthink" to take hold, each individual had to play his role. And these roles are ones that I've seen emerge again and again in assault situations. First and foremost, in these cases, there's the *ringleader.* Trent Mays was responsible for setting the ball in motion. It started with "talking" to Jane Doe beforehand and manipulating her into thinking he liked her or, at the very least, was a friend. "Around town, I heard nice things about Ma'lik; no one had a kind word for Trent," recalled prosecutor Marianne Hemmeter, who spent fourteen years focused predominantly on sexual assault cases. Trent seemed to be a more classic predator, known as assertive and unkind even by other classmates. "What we saw as we investigated the case, on the part of Trent Mays, was that he had really singled [Jane Doe] out," Hemmeter continued. "She was the most vulnerable person that night on a lot of levels. He knew she was an outsider. He knew how drunk she was. He showed absolutely no respect for her, not only by sexually assaulting her but then by taking those pictures and sending them to his friends as a kind of joke. He was sending that out to degrade her even further. That gives you some insight into his personality."

Trent, like all the teens involved, was the product of his environment. He came from a white, middle-class, two-parent home, where his father was a football coach and his mother was a stay-at-home mom. People couldn't blame their usual bogeymen like "broken" or "godless" homes. He was embraced by peers and Big Red fans, even if his behavior was at times bullying. But perhaps there were less obvious problems at home. It is alleged that his father had resigned from his position at Indian Creek High School years before due to statutory rape allegations. Around town, this was a widely discussed rumor; however his resignation documents make no mention of sexual misconduct and he was never charged nor made any admissions of wrongdoing. When I dug around in town to get more information about Trent, some people muttered, "The apple doesn't fall far from the tree."

Trent may have had other motivations and conditioning as well. "When people like this enjoy high social status with other kids, but especially adults, there's an implicit message that they are above the law, and it happens from the time they're little, little messages that come all the time," explained Rosalind Wiseman, *New York Times* bestselling author of *Queen Bees and Wannabes* (later adapted by Tina Fey into the film *Mean Girls*) and *Masterminds and Wingmen* and co-founder of the organization Cultures of Dignity. This dynamic is age-old and repeats itself over and over and over again to the point where Wiseman said she's saddened but never surprised by these kinds of stories. "When young people are in a cultural position of power, it becomes difficult to have a moral compass because they aren't held responsible for their actions with consequences. They become very good at justifying that what they're doing isn't bad and, even if it is bad, assigning responsibility to the victim, so that they can escape the sense of moral obligation to treat another person with dignity."

Trent's elevated status and his sense of entitlement likely cemented this mindset, especially the unbridled praise and enablement by adults. They placed him in a position of power from which he could act without fear of repercussions.

Some of these impulses can also be traced back to a definition of masculinity that teaches boys to believe they must dominate in order to be considered strong. "There are complicated and intersecting motivations," said Dr. Sherry Hamby. "Masculinity panic drives a lot of the behavior: the incredible pressure on young men and boys to 'prove' themselves sexually. In most crimes, there is some calculation of perceived gains and losses. A lot of sexual violence is motivated by efforts to gain social status and, unfortunately, being sexually aggressive can improve status in some groups. There are so many distorted ideas of what real manhood is and, unfortunately, the cultures of some sports teams make these worse."

In contrast to Trent, Ma'lik was soft-spoken and likeable. Steubenville loved him. "As much as we see the predatory nature of Trent Mays exploiting the victim's trust, what we see in Ma'lik is that he's a *follower*," observed Hemmeter. "You didn't see Ma'lik try to manipulate the victim. Once the cat's out of the bag and everybody is talking about what happened, Ma'lik doesn't do that."

Starting when he was eight years old, Ma'lik Richmond, who grew up with a father in jail and a mother who had her own struggles, was raised on and off by his youth football coach Greg Agresta, and his wife, Jennifer. The Agrestas were white, economically comfortable, and prominent in the community: he worked as an executive vice president at a bank and was on the school board; she was a teacher. Recalling a problematic story like *The Blindside*, when a savior white family scoops up a talented Black football prodigy, the Agrestas became Ma'lik's legal guardians and, in high school, helped as football coaches began scouting him. "I think that definitely created a different kind of pressure for Ma'lik," said Tyrone White. "The Agrestas didn't realize or didn't accept that they [as white people] were playing by a different set of rules than Ma'lik was."

Wiseman agreed that many influences, from race to economics to athleticism, could impact a teenage boy's perception of his tenuous social status among peers and influence his behavior. "I've dealt with many boys who, after the fact, couldn't believe what they did,"

Wiseman said. "People need to be held accountable to the extent that they're accountable, but their ability to speak out [in defense of a victim] is very much influenced by the social dynamics around the boys. It has very little to do with the girl. The girl was a pawn. Young men in situations like Ma'lik's are constantly having to make decisions about whether to step up or go along with what's happening; he was groomed to be a follower. He needs to be held responsible so he can learn from this situation and become a more honorable man, as a result, but the only way we do that is to acknowledge the complexities of the situations that people are in."

Many people expressed surprise about Ma'lik's involvement in the rape. He wasn't the kind of kid who got into trouble. He was a Black kid in a majority-white town, accepted into elite social circles because of his athletic prowess. He worked hard at football and didn't want to blow his future. Perhaps aware of his fragile acceptance, he followed Trent's lead to flex this growing social currency. Being part of the Agresta household provided a level of community acceptance and a false sense of protection or impunity. The *follower* is someone who is trying to fit in and not interested in making waves.

On the other hand, Anthony Craig, the *gossip*, was a classic information trader, all about stirring up drama. His family had a kind of legitimacy in Steubenville as owners of the favorite Italian restaurant in town; his Facebook photos boasted travel to Sicily. He was on the tennis team and he wrestled—a different kind of jock. In the police interrogations, he was cooperative and solicitous. Belying his gleeful texts from the night of the rape, he told law enforcement that what he witnessed "scared" him and made him want to tell his dad.

Anthony Craig was one of two teens who were called back for second police interviews because they omitted key facts the first time, in his case that he had taken at least one photo of Jane Doe naked and shared it back at Jake's basement. "They seemed to be pretty animated, telling us things, and then you find out, oh, they did that, too?" recalled Detective Rigaud. When Anthony came in for his follow-up interview, the police did not pull punches:

"Anthony, you seem like a nice guy, and…you seemed to be at least mostly cooperative with us on Friday," said Rigaud. "But you realize this is an ongoing investigation, so the more we keep getting stuff, it can come right back and knock you silly…At any point, did you touch her?"

"No," Anthony said. "I promise on it."

"Well, but you realize that…you didn't give us this information, so that's why I'm asking you this question, Anthony, because it's going to come back and it's going to really haunt you. We're going to want to be able to say, 'Well, this guy's reliable. He told us everything,' and then, all of a sudden, damn it, here's this."

"I want to apol—I'm going to apologize for that…"

"I forgive you. But you gotta be straight with me from now on. This is damn serious."

Rigaud recalled, "[Anthony Craig] was everywhere. He was at all three locations [and] actually saw…what was happening to the victim. There's always that person who knows everything—who *wants* to know everything, maybe more so—and, in this case, he knew a lot. His cooperation was crucial to coming to understand the truth. There were others who were at all three places, as well, but he seemed to have literally captured more of what happened—and, eventually, he was willing to share it. Not at first, but eventually he was." Trading information is a play for power. Anthony had to rely on his relationships, his access to facts and details, to compete in the ring. He also significantly contributed to Jane Doe's humiliation, spreading images and rumors about his supposed friend like wildfire. Had he not circulated gossip and photos, the infamous Nodianos video might never have been filmed. There would have been much less to talk about.

Anthony Craig collected information in order to try to protect himself, but, as both Hamby and Wiseman said, in situations like these, information also becomes social currency. That's likely why Anthony took pictures and ran back to Jake Howarth's basement to share them. He wanted to be first to offer that up, the most in-the-know. And, as Wiseman noted, Jane Doe's humiliation itself became a kind of currency, which is where Nodi came in. "Our culture condones the idea that when you're in a position of power, someone else's embarrassment becomes your entertainment," said Wiseman. "And that makes you not see that other person as a human being. When you don't have to respect other people, you don't have to treat them with inherent worth. I ask the kids I work with all the time to consider the idea that it might be a mistake to get drunk, for example, but it's not unethical. What's unethical is to humiliate someone for those mistakes."

Anyone who watched Michael Nodianos's twelve-minute video posted to YouTube, in which he skewered the victim and the act as it was happening, will understand what I think of as the role of the *clown*. The clown seizes the opportunity to humiliate someone else for their own gain, and that night, Nodi's face glowed pink as he riffed on the victim's physical and mental state, trying to get and keep the laughs. "I wouldn't call it simple joking," said Dr. Hamby of the shared laughter between boys leading up to and during an assault. "It's grooming perpetrators. Joking about sexual assault or encouraging impersonal attitudes toward sex or lack of empathy for others contributes to the likelihood of sexual perpetration. A lot of sexual assault prevention programs are targeting exactly these kind of broader features of the social environment because these attitudes and behaviors can encourage sexual aggression."

Also, making fun of someone as they are being victimized creates a kind of psychological barrier, a distance that makes people feel like they're less likely to become victims themselves. "Dehumanization is what makes it possible to laugh at victims," said Dr. Hamby. "That and fear. People like to believe in a 'just world' [where] bad things only happen to bad people. So it can be soothing, even on an unconscious basis, to ridicule a victim because it helps them believe there was something wrong with the victim and that they are not in danger of a similar assault."

Nodi was eighteen at the time of the incident and on his way to college, yet he still seemed desperate for approval from high school sophomores like Trent Mays. A slightly geeky non-athlete, his low social status was elevated when he landed jokes. That night he had his moment. It was brief, but he took it. Later, as his hard-earned academic scholarship to Ohio State hung in the balance due to his actions, his attitude sobered. But in his police interview, he still remarked on Jane Doe's reputation, downplaying the photo the other teens circulated, despite having described it in the video, while laughing, as depicting "a wang in the butthole."

"There was a picture. I think; I'm not sure who had it," he told the police, a chastened version of himself. "You couldn't really tell what was going on, but I thought it—it just seemed like a joke…from the way I saw it, like, his pants were still up and stuff and she was just laying on the ground." Grasping at straws in front of the cops, he was still trying to cover for the team.

The *bystanders*, Mark Cole and Evan Westlake, participated as voyeurs, recording videos of Trent assaulting Jane Doe and of Nodianos delighting in Jane Doe's downfall. "It tells you what that peer pressure can do," said prosecutor Marianne Hemmeter. "There are all those studies…coming out on college campus assaults, where, really, it's the male peer pressure that can turn a case one way or another." Hemmeter and her prosecutorial team dubbed Craig, Cole, and Westlake "the three musketeers"—eyewitnesses to the assaults who did nothing to help the victim.

According to Wiseman, what many don't understand as they question why bystanders didn't step in is that after being conditioned to accept progressively bigger examples of immorality from alphas like Trent and even adults in power over the years, the teens likely didn't see what was happening as wrong in the moment. It was part of the stew of the culture. "In these situations, where everything is a joke and is entertainment, then it is absolutely not clearly wrong to the teens," she explained. "They're conditioned from years of being silent when smaller things have happened. If you speak up, you're ridiculed, effeminized." This is the culture of not only their peer group, but their society, so they're accustomed to these kinds of attitudes and actions.

Many girls witnessed what was happening to Jane Doe from afar and acted as passive bystanders too. Farrah Marcino voiced her reservations but ultimately did not intervene too aggressively. She lamented later that, had Jane Doe been a close friend, she would have done more, but did not risk her social status with her on-again/off-again boyfriend Mark and his friends for a stranger. Jake Howarth's girlfriend, Elayna, was also concerned, but didn't do much at Party B to help get Jane Doe home safely. In the end, Elayna was critical of Jane Doe, as were many other girls, underlining the notion of perceived worthiness. This kind of girl-on-girl mistreatment and bullying is common, not just among strangers, but even among friends. Doing the right thing can mean sacrificing social capital.

Also, according to Wiseman, there's a tendency for teen girls to justify what happened to other girls in their minds: "They tell themselves, 'That girl deserves it because she did something before. She just wants attention.' Our culture is constantly telling us to seek attention, yet somehow we justify not treating girls as human beings if they're labeled that way. If you're somehow vulnerable in front of other people, you deserve it. As a girl specifically, you should know better. It absolves the other people of responsibility for their part in whatever happened to you."

That's why going against the grain in these situations is rare and requires a very particular kind of character. "It takes a lot of personal strength to speak up against the crowd, and a firm sense of your own principles, as well as a deep capacity for empathy and understanding of how other people would feel," said Dr. Hamby. "A lot of young people are afraid of the price they will pay for standing up for others. Being an active bystander or upstander comes with real risks of getting hurt yourself, whether socially or physically. Educating young people about [upstanding] and helping them practice these skills should be [part of curriculum] in schools." Even the term "upstander" has begun to fall out of favor because kids find the expression uncool and are therefore less likely to subscribe to the ideas around it.

There was a lone dissenting voice in the Nodianos video that broke through the hilarity with a moral indictment—the voice of Big Red wrestler Shawn McGhee. While he wasn't able to stop what happened, as the *upstander*, he did express distress about what Trent and Ma'lik were doing. "That's rape. They raped her. This is not, like, funny," he said, trying to reach Trent via text. He attempted to snap a room full of boys, who were either laughing or apathetic, into consciousness without success. "I had just got there, walked in, everyone was intoxicated, saying stuff," he later recalled in an interview with me, "so I reacted off of that." Shawn may have known better. As a young Black man and the son of a corrections officer, perhaps he understood the potential consequences on a different level. Unlike Ma'lik, he had likely been prepped his whole life for the potential real danger out there in the world and the bias and racism he would face as a Black boy and then a Black man. "We have to play by a different set of rules," said Tyrone White. "And we're often, as young African American males, taught that right up front from our parents that, if you're going to be competitive out there, you can't just be equally good because you won't be chosen. If you're pulled over by the police, you have to handle yourself differently. Keep your hands on the steering wheel. Yes, sir. No, sir. Don't make any sudden moves. There is a level of fear that is much different for a person of color." Due to his close relationship with Trent, in interviews with me, Shawn seemed more worried about the repercussions for his buddy than harm to Jane Doe, which is also typical in social dynamics, but he at least understood the gravity of the situation.

When trying to reason with Michael Nodianos, Shawn asked, "What if that was your daughter?" According to Joe Samalin, a violence prevention specialist and founder of MenChallenging, this is a common default for those who are bold enough to speak out and try to reason with other men about issues like violence against women. "'What if it was your sister, mother, girlfriend?' can be a very powerful tool and a lot of people go to it as a default tactic for bystander intervention," he explained. "When I do trainings, [men] come up with that on their own because... they tend to learn about it, think about it in personal terms and start to see it as a problem when it happens to someone they know." Samalin himself first became attentive to these issues after his mother disclosed her own familial sexual abuse when he was a high school student. Though ideally men would come to allyship and develop empathy for women because of an innate sense of humanity, the personal connection can be a very important motivator and a good first step. But it's not enough. "The serious error is when we stop there," said Samalin. "When raising awareness and empathy and intervening becomes that line—and nothing else. Because then we are reinforcing and doubling down on the idea that a woman's value is only in relation to men. The ultimate goal is the natural assumption and belief that all people everywhere, especially women and girls, are worthy of respect, dignity, safety, and humanity regardless of who their fathers or brothers or husbands are."

In this case, though, Shawn's pleas fell on deaf ears. Why? How responsible were coaches and other role models to shape either a culture of civility and empathy or one of toxic masculinity and rape? How complicit were the adult bystanders, especially those who swept unattractive truths under the rug and endowed the boys with too much power? How had the boys learned this worldview?

The one factor that can mitigate the way a teen in power loses their moral compass, according to Wiseman, is if they have an adult in their life "who truly holds them accountable and is in real relationship with them." Otherwise, it's the adults' showering of unfettered praise and also their discomfort with broaching tough topics that perpetuates this cycle. "We are deathly afraid of actually giving children the education they need to be able to function in society well, an education that reflects the complexity of their lives," said Wiseman. "Our baggage is to do with the complexity of power, bigotry, and discrimination in our culture. People do not want to deal with it. They'd rather fight anyone who wants to talk about it. But no matter how we vote, we all have these dynamics that allow this to happen. I can say, well, adults weren't raised that way themselves. We've had generations of not talking about this, from the Catholic church to coaches, we silence the people. We cannot handle conflict because we've been silenced ourselves. But I would like for us at some point to be able to get some courage and face these directly. I don't see the will for substantive change. Instead, we blame, attack, mock, and deny the people who come forward."

Whatever forces shaped the boys' thinking, none of this would have happened if Cody Saltsman hadn't introduced Jane Doe into the fold and felt wronged by her. I call him the *fire-starter* because he both added fuel to the fire of the potential assault as it was brewing and then unintentionally brought the story to the national stage. Burned by a recent breakup with Jane Doe, we know he snapped the photo of her being carried by Trent and Ma'lik and posted it to Instagram with the caption #sloppy.

During one text exchange between Trent and Jane Doe after the assault, he told her that Cody still had feelings for her. "Oh so is that why he didn't help me?" she wrote. "Is that why he put a picture of me on instagram? Is that why he put a Youtube video on Twitter saying, 'she deserved it'[?] No one fucking deserved that. He has no feelings for me and he never did before. If he did, he wouldn't do all that to me. To this day I would never ever wish anything like that upon him and if he was ever in a bad situation I would try to help. I actually cared for him and I have a heart."

When Alex Goddard reposted that same photo on her blog after pixelating out Jane Doe's face and body and credited Cody for taking it, it pulled focus to him—and to her. Cody had skirted police interviews and wasn't a player at Party C; he almost escaped mention in the story. But when Alex posted the photograph and named him on her blog, she outed his participation to the townspeople. He and his family did not appreciate it.

On October 25, Alex found out she was being sued: the Saltsman family had filed charges against her for defamation of character. A friend was watching as WTOV-9 cut into coverage of Hurricane Sandy to break the story of the lawsuit against her, then called to let her know. Not only did the lawsuit seek to shut Prinnified down, but it sought to expose the identities of eighteen anonymous commenters on Alex's site, people who had criticized the Saltsmans' son. This was an affront to Alex's values of free speech. As moderator, she saw herself as the commenters' protector. There was no way she was going to let the Saltsmans take her down or expose the "Jane and John Does" who had anonymously responded on the site. So she continued to post, though not about the case itself.

In the meantime, a friend began tweeting about the situation with hashtags like #freespeech and #anonymous in hopes of drawing attention to the case and also perhaps attracting a lawyer for Alex. She was successful. In no time, Alex had representation.

Next, the ACLU of Ohio stepped in and offered to defend all of the John and Jane Doe commenters named in the suit. As the organization's press release read on December 14, 2012, "'We believe the real goal of this lawsuit is to discover the identity of anonymous online commenters so that they, and future commenters will be intimidated and discouraged from voicing their opinions,' said ACLU Volunteer Attorney Scott Greenwood. 'This is just an updated form of a classic Strategic Lawsuit Against Public Participation (SLAPP) which is typically used to silence speech that is protected under the First Amendment…If subpoenas are honored and the identities of these commenters are revealed, the First Amendment damage is done,' said Greenwood. 'Even if the lawsuit is ultimately unsuccessful, the Plaintiff will have discouraged others in this small community from engaging in online conversation which they believed to be anonymous. This would have serious implications for other forms of anonymous free speech on the internet.'"

The attempt to silence Alex backfired, calling additional attention to the dispute and Steubenville as a whole. The case between Alex and the Saltsman family would go back and forth for months.

———

On December 16, as the town attempted to ready for the holidays as if everything was normal, the *New York Times* took the Steubenville rape story national. Their extensive article, "Rape Case Unfolds on

Web and Splits City," reported not only on the assault itself and the town's response, but also on Alex's sense that her freedom of speech was being threatened by parents trying to suppress information and punish her for telling the truth. They quoted a statement from her lawyers, saying, "This case strikes at the heart of the freedom of speech and of the press. We intend to see those constitutional guarantees vindicated at the end of the day." Cody Saltsman's little fire was officially raging out of control.

I was in Florida visiting family over the holiday break when my father dropped the *New York Times* in front of me and said, "Look what's happening in Ohio."

I read the headline and sighed. "Dad, this is happening everywhere." I wasn't wrong. My father was likely taking note because a story about a high school football team committing rape in a small American town, *over here*, felt familiar and close to home. In fact, the brutal gang rape and murder of a young medical intern in Delhi, which would inspire mass protests across India, was happening across the globe as we spoke as well. That story would grace the front page just two days later.

But as I learned more about what happened in Steubenville, I felt stirred to action: this case offered an unprecedented window into American rape culture. I'd been seeking out the opportunity to understand perpetrators and dive into their language and thought processes. Because this was an assault in the age of burgeoning social media, when teens had access to platforms like Twitter and Instagram but had not yet absorbed the potential risks, they couldn't deny what had happened. The Twitter trail eliminated a he-said/she-said defense. It demonstrated how easily a seemingly average set of circumstances can become dangerous when the surrounding culture doesn't adamantly condemn this type of behavior.

The story exploded all over the news. Many focused on the use of social media and the vehemence of the town's response. The *New*

*York Times* article called not only the boys but the complicit adults into question. The town was reeling. Then on December 23, 2012, one week later, vigilante hacking collective Anonymous joined the conversation. They posted a video on social media and, later, on the Big Red football website, calling out bystanders and those who protected the football players: "This is a warning shot to the school faculty, the parents of those involved, and those involved especially," the masked vigilante said. "A preliminary dox is being released on some of those involved, while a full-sized dox of everyone involved including names, social security numbers, addresses, relatives, and phone numbers is being compiled as you watch this video, on every single member of the football team, those involved, the coaches, the principal and more. This dox will be released unless all accused parties come forward by New Year's Day and issue a public apology to the girl and her family."

Anonymous wasn't bluffing.

## CHAPTER 7

# THE VIGILANTES

**G**REETINGS, CITIZENS OF THE WORLD!" A ghoulish figure peered through the portal of the internet, his computer-generated voice stilted and uninflected. He wore a black-and-white mask frozen in a sardonic grin, eyebrows raised. "We are Anonymous," he boomed, a specter beaming in from YouTube. "Around mid-August 2012, a party took place in a small town in Ohio known as Steubenville. On this fateful night, a life was changed forever as a group of the football players of Big Red high school began taking advantage of an underage girl. The girl was sexually assaulted, raped, and dragged unconscious from party to party. The town of Steubenville has been keeping this quiet and their star football team protected. You can hide no longer. You now have the world looking directly at you. #OpRollRedRoll engaged."

On Christmas Eve morning 2012, the residents of Steubenville, still reeling from the *New York Times* cover story the week before, woke to yet another unwelcome surprise: a video had been uploaded by the leaderless hacker collective Anonymous to the Steubenville booster club website, RollRedRoll.com. (It had been "hacked" into, some would laugh, by guessing the password: RollRedRoll.) In the virtual proclamation, a masked vigilante threatened exposure—a "dox," or the dissemination of personal information—of anyone involved with the rape who didn't come forward, confess, and apologize for their role. With this threat of released social security information, phone numbers, addresses, incriminating photos, and maybe more, the town was forced to reckon with this more sinister and alien element. The rape case was having an uncontainable ripple effect, spreading far beyond the borders of Steubenville—and even Ohio.

"I knew a rape had happened over the summer," remembered former rival athlete Brendon Sadler, who was a family friend of Jane Doe's and knew she'd been the victim. He was just a few years older, white, athletic, with piercing blue eyes and dark hair tucked into a grubby Nike hat. He slumped on a well-loved couch. "It kind of got swept under the rug. Like nobody would talk about it for a while. And then, all of a sudden, some guy comes on, he's not even from the area, and he's like, 'I'm coming for you.'" Brendon marveled at the audacity of this entity who took action publicly in the name of the underdog. The man behind the mask seemed like a modern-day Robin Hood, swooping in and fighting injustice. *She was passed out; it's not okay—this is wrong*, Brendon remembered thinking. "As soon as Anonymous posted the video, I was like, 'I want to help.'" Brendon had long been incensed by the Big Red players' sense of entitlement and bullying, and liked the idea of them getting their due, but he was also titillated by this notion of futuristic vigilantes. Anonymous just seemed cool.

"No one in Steubenville talked about [the case] much until Anonymous hit," remembered Jeno Atkins, an indicator of the way the teens on the periphery of events viewed what had happened versus some of the more opinionated adults. The grown-ups may have been up in arms for one side or the other, but at least some portion of Big Red's student body was already consumed with other concerns—grades, crushes, games, movies, holidays—until the auto-tuned crusaders came on the scene.

"I don't think anything like this had happened in town before," said Sandra Lyons, a rape crisis counselor for the county, based in neighboring Weirton. Many people didn't know what to think. On top of everything else, for the older generation only beginning to get a handle on social media platforms like Facebook, it was a culture clash. Most locals didn't understand concepts like hacking or doxing or even how the Anonymous video had invaded the Roll Red Roll website. The last thing many residents wanted was to call more attention to this case.

"It's hard to get anyone in this area to discuss rape," added one local woman, who was initially nervous to be interviewed for my film, but was emboldened by Anonymous's outspoken stance. Once she began talking, she delivered her message with confidence, her straight strawberry blond hair tied half-up, baring her resolute expression. "And if they do, it's kind of a little bit and then, 'I've had enough. Let's put this subject away and move onto something else. I've had enough.'"

While I was in Steubenville on various visits, I interviewed women, many in their fifties, who had been silenced or ignored when they tried to report their assaults in town. This is the very foundation of rape culture and what allows it to fester in so many environments. The silence turns survivors into second-class citizens, always forced to watch their backs and their mouths, retraumatized every time they happen to run into their attackers at the local grocery store or on the street. Like many places, this community didn't understand that doing nothing and saying nothing was the crux of the problem, and wouldn't make the scourge of sexual violence go away.

"I don't think anyone really knew who Anonymous was," recalled Chief McCafferty from behind his desk. "There's never been a case like this in Steubenville." Rigaud and his team were tying up loose ends of the investigation before the trial, sorting through data from the Bureau of Criminal Investigation (BCI), while the chief found himself juggling the fallout in town. The police department had even created a web page called "Steubenville Facts" to help disseminate correct information about their discoveries and the case. Anonymous seemed to cast doubt on local law enforcement and insinuate that there was a cover-up by authorities. To some, especially the more analog locals, the message from the masked man felt not only threatening but also like a harbinger from the future. It was as if "the internet," this amorphous entity, was threatening to descend on their town.

The ominous cloak-and-dagger theatrics were no accident. Dramatic flair is a hallmark of Anonymous, which describes itself as "nothing more than an idea that can be appropriated for a common cause." The element of performance is a device to get the public's attention. As David Kushner reported for *Rolling Stone* in his November 2013 article, "Anonymous vs. Steubenville," which inspired actor Brad Pitt's film production company to option the story and Kushner to publish a 2020 book, *A For Anonymous*, "Anonymous is a purposefully chaotic and leaderless collective. Anyone can proclaim themselves a member or declare an 'operation' against a target. But getting others to give a shit is another story."

In this case, though the man in the video commanded authority as if in a veteran leadership position, he had only joined the ranks that summer after watching *We Are Legion*, a documentary about Anonymous by Brian Knappenberger. According to Kushner's article, for Deric Lostutter, a computer programmer in Kentucky who spent his childhood being bullied and witnessing domestic violence in his own home, the chance to play the vigilante role and take down the establishment was instantly enticing. All you needed to join was a plastic Guy Fawkes mask with raised eyebrows and an anchor goatee to mimic the seventeenth-century British rebel, available on sites like Amazon or Party City.

Adopting the moniker KYAnonymous, Lostutter began scrolling

for relevant causes online. He started with an operation he dubbed OpEducation, releasing the contact information of Clark County, Kentucky, school board members. He charged them with mishandling funds and putting monetary gain above the needs of children. Once he posted, he was rewarded with additional material as people forwarded him internal emails, expense reports, and more evidence. Posting that information on Twitter earned him a temporary suspension from the site. But, as David Kushner reported, eventually the Clark County superintendent retired after being "under fire from a citizen's group," and Lostutter saw that his vigilante work could have an impact.

After that, he successfully targeted the owner of a revenge porn site, as well as hate group Westboro Baptist Church, who planned to protest a vigil for the children killed in the Sandy Hook Elementary School shooting. According to Kushner, for #OPWestboro, KYAnonymous recorded a YouTube manifesto over a video of ominous storm clouds, railing against the church's "hatred." Though some Anonymous members complained that he was taking on too much, the collective ultimately backed him, doxing the church's members and taking down their website. Lostutter also successfully organized a counter rally, Occupy Newtown, "soliciting the help of plainclothes cops, as well as Hell's Angels, to form a human wall around the funeral." That won him attention, both good and bad, from some of his Anonymous predecessors and a reputation for establishing a new category of Anonymous acts—"Justice Ops."

More than one element made the Steubenville op feel different from others. "The hacker wasn't some European guy in a black turtleneck in a room," said David Kushner. "He was a turkey hunter in the middle of Kentucky. Anonymous as a sprawling international group had been making the news with their mass protests against Scientology, but Steubenville was different because here was this guy getting in the middle of this small-town 'cover-up' and terrible tragedy. He was like the masked avenger, riding his horse into this small Ohio town to help this individual girl. It was smaller, more personal. Like him or hate him…he managed to do something good."

At that time, Kushner said, "Anonymous was in its volatile and awkward adolescence. Anyone with a computer or smartphone could become an activist, could become a movement. White, Black, male, female. There was a freeing nature to it." In other words, Anonymous was still defining itself. And not every proposition or op won support. A proclamation or mandate like KYAnonymous's for Roll Red Roll would be posted on boards like Reddit or 4chan. The call to action needed to earn enough likes and interest to graduate from a gripe to an actual op.

It was after reading the *New York Times* article on Jane Doe's rape that KYAnonymous turned his attention to Steubenville. His outraged Twitter posts attracted Alex Goddard's attention. She was still intent on getting more eyes on the case, using hashtags that signaled a desire to amplify an injustice. The rape of Jane Doe was bad enough, but it was the Saltsman family's attempt to silence Alex that represented a violation of free speech and helped fuel the collective's indignation. Their goals dovetailed nicely.

Embroiled in the lawsuit with the Saltsman family, Alex was skittish about sharing her archive of evidence and imagery relating to the case. Instead, another woman reached out to the hacker via social media, arming him with deleted tweets, videos, and photographs. And it was that evidence that inspired KYAnonymous to post his video manifesto on YouTube—voice disguised by the text-to-speech program Cepstral David—hoping to light a fire under authorities and draw out Steubenville's guilty parties.

Even Lostutter was surprised by the resounding response to his video, in part because it was another Anonymous hacker—Noah

McHugh from Virginia Beach—who had apparently taken it upon himself to hack the high school football website and post Lostutter's message front and center. McHugh was later sentenced to eight months in prison for this act. By morning, the manifesto was being covered by TV news stations like Fox and news outlets from the *New York Times* to Jezebel. Officially, Steubenville was on warning.

The ball was already in play, and, while some townspeople were upset, others like Brendon were on the ground to help. "I was kind of the midpoint between Anonymous and Steubenville," he said proudly after the fact, fingering a Guy Fawkes mask in his hand. "It's like how Spider-Man puts on his mask or Superman changes into his costume. You're kind of a superhero. With Anonymous, I finally felt like I had a voice." As Kushner notes, hackers do often have origin stories with tropes like superheroes including past abuses or traumas that fuel them to become vigilantes. According to Brendon, the goal was "weaponizing the media" for massive viral attention to the case. A rally called "Justice for Jane Doe" was planned for December 29.

For women like Sandra—a rape counselor and survivor herself, who had lived in what felt like a brew of systemic misogyny her whole life—a rally like this had another level of significance. She felt she had to be there as a show of support, for the cause and Jane Doe, and for the countless other victims who had remained silent. While statistics were available in bigger cities like Columbus and Cleveland about the prevalence of sexual assault, rape, and domestic violence, transparency around sexual violence in Jefferson County was a different matter. The rule of thumb when it comes to rape is that higher numbers (meaning instances of reported assault) actually indicate that a community feels safe reporting and victims feel safe coming forward. Thus, higher numbers can be seen as a positive sign about the environment. Steubenville averaged about four reported rapes a year from 2010 to 2015, in the years before the reporting included male victims and non-forcible rape. With numbers of reports so low, it can be implied that speaking up was frowned upon. It was as if the complaint was the problem, not the violence.

Although warned by her bosses not to attend the rally because Anonymous was seen as a group of reckless vandals who flouted the law, Sandra was intent on supporting the cause. She brought pamphlets from the Rape Crisis Center to disseminate. As an empathic person, she wanted people to know that help was available and most importantly that survivors were not alone, as she had been when she too was assaulted as a teen. "My husband was like, 'You're absolutely not going. It's too dangerous,'" she recalled, with a hint of triumph in her eyes. "That morning, I decided that if my husband wasn't going to take me over, then I would just walk! I…needed to be there." Garnering support and a ride from her husband, Sandra kept her identity secret at the rally, disguising her face somewhat ineffectually with a scarf. But afterward she faced professional repercussions for attending. Anonymous was seen as an anarchic force and not something with which the county institution wanted to be associated.

While Brendon and Sandra appreciated the increased focus on Jane Doe's case, much of Steubenville remained unhappy about the negative heat. "I got a lot of nasty phone calls," noted Chief McCafferty. "I got, I'm 'the chief of rape city.' How do I let this go on? How can I let people get away with it? As far as I was concerned, we didn't let anybody get away with anything. We had this case solved in the first two weeks." McCafferty and detectives like J. P. Rigaud acted quickly to identify and charge the perpetrators. They felt as if Anonymous was asking them to prevent rape instead of punish and prosecute it. In addition to the police, Anonymous was critical of Jane Hanlin, who they felt took too long to recuse herself and bring in Ohio's attorney general, demonstrating a possible failed cover-up.

Some townspeople, even outside of law enforcement, felt judged by the interference of Anonymous and the court of public opinion. "These are churchgoing people," Jerry Barilla later said to me earnestly in the front of his downtown appliance store decorated with Christmas lights and nostalgic paintings of Main Street. "We all got labeled like we're monsters here!"

Ultimately, that first rally was not the main event. "People just stood in solidarity and that's pretty much what happened," recalled "Hevvy Hearted," a soft-spoken local Anonymous member who adorned her mask with a red heart and lipstick.

"I just remember looking at it and thinking it needs production," agreed her fellow Anon member, "Master of Ceremonies." I met with them both in an abandoned elementary school in West Virginia. Organizing the interview via encrypted DMs felt like its own Anonymous op.

Master of Ceremonies felt strongly that this crowd needed to step up their #OperationSteubenville game. While Anonymous was anti-establishment and anarchistic, they were not a bunch of gamers messing around with World of Warcraft in their mother's basement. They were intent on making a legitimate statement with decent production value.

In KYAnonymous's original video, he had established a January first deadline for all those responsible to come forward and apologize. With that date looming and no one having accepted responsibility, Brendon stepped in as intermediary for Jane Doe. He got a message to KYAnonymous that she didn't want innocent people associated with the football team to suffer. She asked Anonymous not to release the personal information, as they'd originally threatened. The collective honored her wishes. Instead of the dox, KY decided to release something else, which turned out, intentionally or not, to be far more explosive.

First, the local Anonymous chapter got prepared. "I knew [what KY was going to drop] was gonna bring thousands of people," said Master of Ceremonies. "If it looked like [the first rally] when they got here, it was going to make news for a day and that's gonna be that." So, they began to set the stage for a larger event.

A day after the original deadline, on January 2, 2013, Anonymous posted the deleted twelve-minute Nodianos video on several platforms at once, including a tweet sent out by @YourAnonNews to more than a million followers. Previously, no one had seen the video except for Evan Westlake's thirty-eight followers, a few teens who had passed it around, and law enforcement. Even Alex Goddard hadn't seen the contents. In hindsight, a doxing might have been the gentler path, affecting some innocent bystanders with the leak of personal information. Instead, the Nodianos video—rape culture writ large— went devastatingly viral, smearing the entire town of Steubenville with the stain of misogyny, brutality, and entitlement.

"Once that Nodi video came out, all hell broke loose," said Master of Ceremonies, shaking his head and laughing.

"The video was a huge turning point in the public consciousness of the story," said Kushner of both KYAnonymous's arc and Jane Doe's assault.

*"She is so dead."*

Nodi's comedy routine got picked up by news stations and websites across the country, shocking in its callous language and lack of empathy. From Fox News to CNN, anchors were incensed. From a viral standpoint, the twelve-minute video proved to be a perfect storm because, while displaying emotional indifference, the video itself was not actually graphic, without much sexual imagery and profanity. As a result, clips of it could be shared widely without hesitation. And yet the impact was as horrifying and blatant as watching the video of Ray Rice punching his fiancée in an elevator. The boys' giggling in the face of Jane Doe's rape breached the audience's desensitization. Who could laugh at this? If Steubenville had thought things were intense thus far, they were in for a rude awakening. Views quickly soared to over a million.

As a filmmaker, when I saw the video, I immediately understood its impact—the shareability of it, the visceral revulsion it would inspire, the banal location, and the gleeful laughter that would haunt viewers. The difference between reading the language these teen boys used and actually hearing the disdainful, callous language would be immense. Nodi put their arrogance on display in a way none of us had seen or heard before. This was cruel and unusual and put the focus squarely on the perpetrators. No one asked what the victim had been wearing after they sat through that video. Instead, the country and then the world finally asked, "What is wrong with boys in America?"

The national media came down hard on Steubenville. The Anonymous organizers gambled and won: the ephemeral nature of a YouTube clip recorded almost four months prior had real-world repercussions for a brick-and-mortar town. The collective had successfully "weaponized the media" and, as a result, this was the first rape case ever to go viral in the United States. The internet demanded that people pay attention and even go to Steubenville to investigate. The national news media showed up on the courthouse steps.

"It was sort of surreal watching CNN pull into my backyard," recalled local B & B owner Scott Dressel. "At first I was really angry. It was a really negative thing to live through. I've invested my retirement here and built up this inn. This huge negative publicity was not good." Sure enough, two days later, Anderson Cooper profiled the case.

"NBC, CBS, CNN, Fox, ABC, Dr. Phil, Judge Jeanine, Piers Morgan, Dr. Drew, you name it—they were in Steubenville. And let me just say this: it was wrong what [the teenage boys] did," backpedaled DJ

Bloomdaddy on air, "so nobody out there starts misconstruing. That's why I almost hate...I can't wait for this story to go away."

"I don't like Anonymous," commented another townsperson. "How they came into our town and created havoc. Why won't they show their face?" There was a growing sense that Anonymous and their supporters represented a group of critical outsiders rather than the citizens of the area. That would soon be proven wrong.

By January 5, the date of the second Occupy Steubenville rally, people were fired up on both sides. Some seemed more concerned about the invasion of their privacy than what had happened to Jane Doe. These particular townspeople felt like the attention was over-blown. In fact, an opposition rally, "Stand Up for Steubenville," was planned for January 12.

"I have lived here for about forty years," shared a local woman during a filmed interview with me. "I was sexually assaulted. When I called the sheriff's office, I said, 'I want to see if I can prosecute.' The response that I got from the deputy who I spoke to was, 'Oh, I know him. And the prosecutor has decided that he is not going to take the case.'" She swallowed hard. "After that happened, I slept with a base-ball bat, making sure the doors were locked all the time. I would go places where he normally wouldn't be and there he would be. I was paranoid, and I couldn't depend on anybody else to look after me, so I had to do it myself. If the Anonymous group hadn't come in and brought national attention to this, I think it would have disappeared like so many others have."

The trove of evidence and the callousness of Nodianos's rant convinced others to get involved. Sexual assault "happens all the time, but it's never been brought to focus in our community," local resident Michele Robinson told me. She felt compelled to stand up for Jane Doe. "I was like, you gotta be kidding me. So I went to the second rally."

"Welcome to Steubenville!" an amplified voice echoed from the top of the Jefferson County Courthouse steps.

A crowd of about one thousand women was clustered together in Steelers jackets and Anonymous masks below, holding up signs with slogans that read, "Arrest the rest!" "We do not forget!" "Why didn't anyone stop it?" Anonymous's Master of Ceremonies was at the mic, riling up the crowd with vehement chants about justice, call and response.

Then something incredible happened, deeply unlikely in this rust belt town: a lone woman made her way to the front, ascended the steps, and told Master of Ceremonies that she had something to say. He stepped to the side. She turned and faced the crowd, cleared her throat, and began to give testimony, sharing her personal experience of being gang-raped at fifteen by four boys and then shamed for it "right here, in Steubenville." After she finished, the crowd, stunned and moved, responded with resounding support, shouting and clapping. Their chants got louder. Her courage gave others their voices. "If you have something to say, come up," Master of Ceremonies encouraged the women, as momentum began to build. The lectern with its waiting microphone became an invitation. One by one on that brittle winter day, women ascended, many slowly and purposefully removing their masks to give a face to their experience. At least twenty-five people told their stories that day, many for the first time. *We're real,* the act seemed to say. *You can't ignore us any longer.*

The stories were myriad and heartbreaking, each woman deriving the bravery and power to speak from the person before her. Even for someone like me, who was no stranger to shared stories of sexual assault, having participated in Take Back the Night in the late 1990s in New York City and marched on Washington for reproductive choice, it was incredibly moving to watch the footage of these women sharing their stories for the first time. Speaking out had always been a right for me; I was protected by the big city I lived in, by anonymity, by other activists who led by example. Speaking out was our norm. But for so many women at the Steubenville rally, this was a landmark moment. And you could feel the opening up, the breaking point. One thing was becoming clear: Steubenville was many things—a football town, a churchgoing town, a town with pride and community. But it was also a town that hid systemic violence against women and seemed unwilling to face its own reality. And no amount of Christmas parades would cover the problem.

"Before we even delve into rape culture, it's worth asking ourselves why we systematically demand that women adhere to cultural scripts that rob them of their sense of self-worth, instilling in them a fear of their own independence, and how this ties into the broader culture of dehumanization and violence that we experience as Americans," said Aditi Khorana, a cultural critic, novelist, professor, and former journalist for ABC News, PBS, and CNN, who focuses on exposing xenophobia and racism around the feminist myth. "A society sustains itself by telling and retelling the same story over and over again, and even before we get to a point in the broader story where rape is happening, accepted, and goes unpunished, we need to take the narrative apart piece by piece and ask ourselves a series of questions about what we demand from women and what we deny them. In doing this, we're not victim-blaming or placing the onus on women for preventing rape, but we are dismantling the cultural narrative that asks women to 'Lean In' without asking what exactly they're leaning into...or why we expect girls to be quiet and accommodating while we expect the opposite of young boys."

The root of why Steubenville was a breeding ground for rape culture was much more deep-seated than any kind of intentional or conscious tolerance for abuse. It started with the way women and girls were defined in the culture, the expectations for their futures, and their socialization from childhood. What does it teach girls about their value as women when we behave as if finding a husband, to protect and provide, is the ultimate goal? Who does that endow with power? What does it teach when we prize young women's physical appearance above all else or model "loyalty" to our boys and men without question, even to our own detriment? What does it teach when we make football—an activity that inherently excludes girls and women on every level except as eye candy or water girls on the sidelines—the central focus of an entire community? How can they grow up feeling like anything but support staff at best, and easy prey at worst?

This is also why the notion of women elevating other women is so important for change. If we don't treat each other as if our voices are important and worth honoring, why should anyone else listen? This second protest became an outlet, a supportive environment in which women could share their own experiences in solidarity with Jane Doe. Woman after woman soldiered her way up the courthouse steps.

"I had no intention of going up there and speaking, but as soon as I got there and I saw these people talking, I headed right up them steps." Michele smiled. "I wasn't even thinking. I just took off. And when the girl [before me] got done speaking, I said, 'I want to talk.'"

"I'm fifty-one years old. Sexually molested when I was eight years old. I never told anybody. And finally, in my forties, I decided to get help."

It was difficult to deny the reality of the collective picture these women were painting. "When the testimony came out, it hit me like a lightning bolt because it became kind of like a woman's movement," said Brendon. Anonymous offered a different way for disenfranchised young men as well as women to feel powerful and be "part of something," whether they were inspired by the cause, by the idea of being allied with something bigger than themselves, or were seduced by the proximity to some fame and excitement.

That rally became significant for the women of Steubenville who participated. "Some of the survivors had not gotten justice in any way, and this was their first time speaking about what had happened," Sandra said.

"It made me feel like a brand-new person," Michele agreed. "It's like I was set free. It felt good." Some of the women formed a kind of informal sisterhood or support group for one another, spending time together after the rallies, offering comfort and friendship.

"The town kind of came together, handing out [Anonymous] masks," Brendon recalled of this portion of the community. "I heard these women speak. And that was a game-changer."

Of course, not everyone felt so enthralled.

A week later, at the more sparsely attended opposition to Anonymous rally, locals took to a lectern with a different message in defense of Big Red and the town's love of football. "They say our city is divided!" shouted one middle-aged woman. "We must stand together and unite it. They say we should be ashamed to wear red and black. I say wear it proudly!"

"You want us to be ashamed of our tradition!" delivered one man, clad all in Big Red garb. "Ashamed of our success. Ashamed of our children. You want our children to be ashamed of the school they go to. This case is in the legal system. Let them handle it!"

The protests at the courthouse steps were about rape and rape culture, not about football. But the opposition was insistent that speaking out against Jane Doe's rape, and the boys who perpetrated and tolerated her abuse, somehow diminished Big Red football itself. The headline was that the safety and rights of girls couldn't exist in tandem with thriving boys and a successful athletic program, especially if having both meant examining root causes instead of moving on without analysis. The group seemed keen on pretending that Trent and Ma'lik were just isolated "bad apples," despite the mass testimonies at the courthouse steps. This zero-sum game or the lack of understanding that gender equity serves everyone is also at the core of rape culture.

"We're not convicting an entire team, and people need to remember that," said DJ Bloomdaddy. "There are a lot of individuals up there who are good students, good kids, good football players."

"We see those who try to shield or protect perpetrators; they're very resistant," said Tyrone White. "They see themselves as being the victim of unfair public attention. You know, 'You're not paying attention to all the good things we do here in Steubenville.' They put the focus on [themselves] instead of the person who has been hurt. We see that in racial issues, as well. It [takes] the emotional ability to be able to acknowledge, 'Yes, my thinking, my mindset, my way of interacting with other people is wrong and, therefore, I need to…change.' It's very uncomfortable." It's not possible to find lasting solutions if we close ranks before we admit that a problem exists.

In the end, Hevvy Hearted of Anonymous described her work as essentially neutral. "We just put the information out there," she said of calling attention to Jane Doe's case. "And then it's free for anybody to do whatever they see fit with that information." The public could draw their own conclusions.

"Whatever I can do, I'm going to do," said Sandra, of continuing the conversation about sexual assault in the Ohio Valley. "I hope that if someone is thinking of doing something wrong [now], that they're going to think, 'What if somebody found out?'"

For Sandra, Michele, and other rally participants, the idea of standing together to "unite" meant something different than it did to the crowd at the opposition rally. Coming together was not vowing "unity" in the face of criticism or blind allegiance to Big Red football or the sanctity of the town. "Yeah, I would like to see people rally together and support one another," Michele said. "The steelworkers do it when they're gonna lose their jobs. The coal miners just bused themselves to Washington. You don't want people to forget what happened. The talk needs to be about, 'Where do we go from here? And not only where do we go, but where does the whole country go?'" Once the truth was exposed, would there be justice for Jane Doe? Was there such a thing? How would the root causes be dismantled? Could they be? But first, a trial was looming.

These issues weren't only reaching a fever pitch in Steubenville. Towns across the country were grappling with similar divides. Though, unfortunately, cases of teenage girls being assaulted by classmates were nothing new, the proliferation of these stories online began to attract attention; headlines made it harder to look the other way. In Maryville, Missouri, two young white teen girls, Daisy Coleman and Paige Parkhurst, were both assaulted in January 2012, and the trial was upcoming. That case also drew Anonymous's attention when townspeople showed support for the perpetrators online and when charges were dropped against one teenage boy who was related to an influential former state senator.

Audrie Pott, a fifteen-year-old white girl in Saratoga, California, had been sexually assaulted on September 3, 2012, by teen boys she knew. While she was intoxicated and unable to consent, they drew on her body, took pictures, and posted them online. She died by suicide ten days later.

In July 2014, Jada, a Black sixteen-year-old from Houston, would wake up the morning after a party to find images of her unconscious naked body plastered on social media with the mocking hashtag #jadapose. Unwilling to hide in shame and bend to her attacker's cruelty, she posted a picture of herself in response with her own hashtag: #IamJada. The hashtag caught on, posted by others in solidarity. For the Black feminist website *For Harriet*, writer Michelle Denise Jackson wrote an essay titled, "In Defense of Jada: The Danger of Being a Black Girl in Rape Culture," which explored not only what it meant to be revictimized after a rape with the proliferation of images online, but also the particular experience around rape for a Black women. "While sexual assault and rape against any human being is an unfathomable…it is different for Black Girls," she wrote. We must remember the lies that have been told about our Black female bodies: they signal a sexuality that is both criminal and irresistible…We must remember that these lies are told to do one thing: make our bodies a commodity to be consumed, discarded, and ignored. We must remember that these lies help perpetuate a rape culture that denies us our right to be Black and Woman and human."

Thanks to the internet's power for good and evil, the stark reality of sexual violence among the nation's teens was becoming impossible to ignore, and people were enraged. Across social media, hashtags in support of Jane Doe and other rape victims began to trend:

#occupysteubenville #justiceforjanedoe #justicefordaisy
#justiceforaudrie #iamjada

It foreshadowed a much bigger hashtag movement to come.

In all this, Deric Lostutter, aka KYAnonymous, was keeping a low profile, according to David Kushner. Thus far, he'd successfully ducked law enforcement as well as angry individuals bent on identifying and outing him. He hadn't even told his girlfriend about his exploits. Despite helping to organize the rallies, he had never left Kentucky.

After he received an online tip that he was being investigated for hacking, he tweeted that he'd be "going dark" for a while, only to receive an ominous response from someone saying they knew his given name and location. He wasn't sure who knew his identity, but he was clearly vulnerable. As he told Kushner, "Everyone in Anonymous gets raided at one point or another if they're halfway good at what they do." He ran upstairs, grabbed his Anonymous gear, and burned it in a fire pit.

But the FBI was coming—and Lostutter would face more severe repercussions for his alleged hacking than did the football players he had outed in Steubenville.

In late December 2012, the Saltsman family dropped their lawsuit against Alex Goddard. As part of the settlement, she acknowledged that Cody had not been directly involved in the rape and allowed him to offer a written apology via her website, which recognized her work "to make sure the full truth about that terrible night eventually comes out."

On December 30, Alex was a guest on the *Roseanne & Johnny* show co-hosted by Roseanne Barr, beginning what would prove to be a significant role as a media pundit and expert on the case. She started posting links to livestreams of the continued rallies.

"#OccupySteubenville had another great rally today," she posted on February 3, 2013. "There were many times that I teared up listening to some of the various speakers. I applaud everyone who stood out in the cold to take part and show their support for ALL Jane Does. I do not believe that the world is hating on *everyone* in the city of Steubenville specifically. People are asking questions—not just about Steubenville, but perhaps about their own towns. Something magical has happened as a result of this case—rape culture is being acknowledged around the world as a real problem . . . It is up to the community to change and move forward from this in a positive manner."

Later that year, when I interviewed Alex, who by then had moved back to Ohio, she talked about the women who were brave enough to speak out, and her tough outer shell cracked: this was a movement she'd helped create. Recalling when she watched the women take off their masks and tell their stories, she began to weep. As a local, she knew intimately what it took to defy the norms in the Valley and raise your voice. It was an act of courage to take off your mask and show your face. She expressed her conflicting feelings about posting the imagery of Jane Doe online to garner attention for the case and justice, however blurred out. When the ripple effects of her determination to expose the story began to overflow, so did her guilt and shame. I suddenly realized—Alex was a survivor.

I knew because I was a survivor too. While I was living abroad in my twenties, I went home from a party with a co-worker whom I thought I could trust. I was nursing a newly broken heart at the time and was craving some comfort. We were making out, things progressed, and then, suddenly, without my consent, he forced himself on me and raped me. I screamed, but he didn't stop.

Afterward, as I cried and curled up in a ball, he lamented being a "bad man" and, maybe in an effort to improve my view of him, showed me pictures of his children. I was sickened and traumatized. I felt horrible and alone—guilty too, for what I had "brought upon myself."

It took me years to work through that experience, to name it, decipher it, hold it, and then decide how to release it. I chose to make a film about my experience because it was the only way I knew how to investigate my feelings and find meaning. Otherwise, the facts seemed impossible to pin down, and "the truth" would always be up for debate. Even after I interviewed my attacker with a hidden camera and wove it into my first documentary, *The Line*, there was no sense of catharsis or closure from the rape, just a painful fragment of harm and violence that was slowly finding its place in the larger narrative of my life experience. Making the choice to film him wasn't easy, but I wanted to record the encounter while also somehow keeping my distance. During that conversation, he was unapologetic and flippant, insisting that we both wanted what happened. Though his body language read guilty to me, as he was constantly shifting in his seat, avoiding eye contact, and looking over his shoulder, he ultimately argued that my version of the truth wasn't real.

The hidden camera I used gave me a thin veil of protection, but, as the scared young woman behind it, I wasn't ready for the interaction. It was demoralizing and painful to act "neutral" while inside I was screaming to defend my position, my memory, and my reality. My one bit of power lay in the video I had captured of him, and his cagey behavior and gaslighting language spoke volumes beyond any accusations I could have made. Ultimately, I decided to conceal his identity in the film when I released it because exposing him wasn't the point. Obscuring his identity made him a symbol, and let male audience members see themselves in his behavior—or not. I couldn't change the past; I couldn't undo what he'd done. But I could fight to change the culture by shining a light on these perpetrators and the victims they leave behind. I could start a dialogue with men and boys—potential allies—about the reality of rape culture and their role in it.

When I was assaulted, I was too ashamed to tell my parents at first, particularly because there were other issues monopolizing my family's attention. I knew if I told them, they'd do their best to be sympathetic. But I also felt that, in their distracted state, they would likely not have the magnitude of reaction that I required. I also did not want them to suffer, nor did I want any of their own rape myths to infiltrate my experience. I opted not to tell them, and later, the pain around that felt like nobody fought for me. So at the core of my early work is this desire to fight for other people, to make rape a big deal. I know what it's like to feel alone in this. Often, the community response—a downplaying of what happened, a questioning of the victim's perception, victim-blaming, judgment, even from the best-intentioned people—feels like a double assault, a second attack on your self-worth. That's why it's so important to examine the surrounding community and how they respond in the wake of assaults. It's essential to go back and see if those mindsets have changed at all, because the experience of past and future victims depends on the reactions of the people around them. We need to ask, what does justice look like, inside and outside a courtroom?

## CHAPTER 8

# THE TRIAL

**O**N THE MORNING OF March 12, 2013, only days before the trial, on *Good Morning America*, George Stephanopoulos teased an upcoming *20/20* segment about "the sexual assault trial tearing apart the Ohio town of Steubenville." Two boys were accused of rape last summer, he referenced, as fresh-faced images of Trent and Ma'lik appeared beside each other on a split screen, "and anchor Elizabeth Vargas sat down with *one* of them for an exclusive interview."

"High School Football Sex Scandal" read the ticker at the bottom of the screen as Vargas took the baton, offering background on the "divided" town. As footage of protestors with colorful signs at a rally outside the Jefferson County Courthouse played, she spoke in voice-over of "wild rumors," the arrival of activist groups, and the fact that "some were convinced the police were slowing down the investigation to protect the beloved team."

"The question," she said, "was whether the girl was too *drunk* to consent."

They cut to Ohio attorney general Mike DeWine: "My job is to focus on the evidence and not try this case in social media," he said, blinking behind wire-rimmed glasses, his stately silver hair projecting years of experience in politics. "The only thing we want to do is determine what the facts are, what the truth is."

What followed was a series of clips and sound bites, a who's who for the upcoming court proceedings: Ma'lik appeared next, as it was he and not Trent who had agreed to be interviewed on camera. He looked like a deer in headlights, as if confused about how he'd ended up face-to-face with a TV reporter, his thick football neck framed by a black zippered sweater. He claimed that Jane Doe was actually alert as she was photographed being carried out of Jake Howarth's house by her wrists and ankles. It was just "a joke picture," he said, looking doubtful.

"The boys' attorneys will try to make the case that the alleged victim was not incapacitated," the reporter explained. "That she was alert enough to remember the passcode on her phone later that night."

Next, Ma'lik's attorney, Walter Madison, popped up on screen with his pressed suit and slick bald head. "We don't care what it looked like," he asserted, referencing the seemingly damning photograph. "We know that afterward she exhibited the ability to make decisions."

This was not defense attorney Walter Madison's first time on a major network TV show defending Ma'lik and lobbying for public support. On January eighth, he had appeared on the *Today* show alongside Greg and Jennifer Agresta, Ma'lik's guardians, who were paying for his legal representation. They talked about how out of character this all was for Ma'lik, who was generally "laid back."

"Have you had the talk with him about what happened that evening?" a deeply concerned Matt Lauer had asked, leaning in.

"No, because it doesn't matter to us," said Jennifer, wincing beneath her Kate Gosselin hairdo. "We love him irregardless of what happened."

"The interview, to me, showed blatant disregard for what happened, trying to whitewash what occurred," said onetime Ohio football coach and sexual assault advocate Tyrone White. "And because this approach was presented to Ma'lik as a way to address this, I think he felt the pressure to go through with it. It's like they weren't looking out for [Ma'lik's] development as a young man." White saw long-term issues with this kind of "boys will be boys" attitude. "It actually promulgates toxic masculinity, a sense of entitlement, that you can abuse another human being, sow your wild oats, without regard for another person's humanity," he continued. "Because of the errant decisions of his guardians, Ma'lik is now put in a position to believe that he is a victim."

*Did the Agrestas think Ma'lik was guilty?* Lauer asked. After a heavy pause, Walter Madison broke in. "You know, Matt, that's a very difficult question for them." He went on to try to distance Ma'lik from Nodi's video, as if whatever else Ma'lik did, he would never have spoken about Jane Doe in such callous and disrespectful terms.

Lauer followed up, referencing the image of Jane Doe being carried by her limbs. "But was he one of the people involved in that photo?"

"Yes," Madison admitted. "The…problem becomes that the photo, [alongside] the video, draws this negative inference that's gone way out of proportion."

Even if *Today* was asking the right questions, they also framed the story as a "sex scandal" to draw viewers in, feeding on rape myths. What does it mean to interview an alleged perpetrator on a major TV show, but not have anyone speak for Jane Doe or even mention her absence? To not have the victim, or a representative, present in this discussion to describe the impact of this assault, the emotional consequences and humiliations? And what about the stark reality of having Matt Lauer, who was on the cusp of being accused as a sexual predator himself, conduct the interview?

————

On *GMA*, Brian Duncan, one of Trent Mays's lawyers, a slightly doughy guy who looked as if he might have once played Big Red football, seconded that argument: "We have witnesses…who will testify that that photograph was, in fact, staged." The boys' defense teams were working in alignment to discredit the glaring photograph that implicated their clients, testing the boundaries of interpretation. Of course, the tweets calling Jane Doe "dead" that night supported the original reading of the picture.

Back in the studio, George Stephanopoulos, now parked at a table with Vargas and a legal analyst, followed up with a furrowed brow. Apparently, Trent's attorneys had filed a Hail Mary motion to dismiss, arguing that, because they were unable to subpoena some of Jane Doe's friends to testify, as they were out of state in West Virginia, the case was unfair.

But this was to be a juvenile proceeding, the minor equivalent of an adult criminal case, so the rules were different, and the deciding judge was not inclined to pressure minors to cross state lines and appear in court. Some argued that the defendants had already won when the judge decided at the October probable cause hearing that they would be tried as minors and therefore the punishments would be less severe. It was not possible to have it both ways. Per the rules of juvenile court, the arguments would be heard and decided by a lone juvenile justice brought in from outside the area, Judge Thomas Lipps. There would be no jury.

———

On Wednesday, March 13, 2013, the trial began. In Steubenville, it was a classic March day, not yet true spring. Light snow flurries fell from the sky, the ground a flattened concoction of mud and ice with the beginnings of green poking through. There was a sharpness in the morning air, exhaust visibly expressed from tailpipes as cars sputtered on and temperatures rose throughout the day. The wind was blowing. A forecast you couldn't quite trust.

Instead of being held at the grander courthouse across the street, the combined trial—the *State of Ohio v. Trenton W. Mays* and the *State of Ohio v. Ma'lik Richmond*—was convened in a squat industrial red brick annex across the street called the Jefferson County Justice Center. But it was still daunting for Trent and Ma'lik, perhaps to varying degrees. After all, the journey to this day looked different for each, the weight of walking through those courthouse doors not equally intimidating. Trent was a white middle-class kid who seemed to feel invulnerable, although he faced child pornography charges on top of the rape. Ma'lik's life experience had been more fractured. "It's the story we've all heard before," said Walter Madison to me during our interview after the fact, in his offices in Akron. He had filed a request for separate trials for Trent and Ma'lik in January and had been denied. "A young African American child growing up in a poor city. His father was away at times. And he…did not have that influence in his life for a number of years in different stints. That would have an effect on anyone. [He] witnessed, because of his environment, violence. But through it all, he survived, and that's one resilient thing about him that makes him special." Madison also pointed to factors outside of Ma'lik Richmond's immediate family. "My client's an African American. My client came from, or is part of, a low socioeconomic class. And he's in a town that's depressed. He's in a town that has its values, and what they value for their morale." At that time, Madison told me proudly that he is always a defender of the underdog. He would later represent the family of Tamir Rice, a young boy who was shot and killed in Cleveland, Ohio, by police.

The Black community in Steubenville, which makes up around 17 percent of the population, has been even more marginalized than the white unemployed former mill workers. There is even less opportunity for elevation or escape, with football as a notable exception.

The town itself, built around the steel mills, was literally constructed to the Black community's detriment. "The steel industry…

is why the neighborhoods were laid out in the way that they were," said assistant professor of history Gabriel Winant. "Steel mills hired certain ethnic groups into certain kinds of jobs and that meant that they had certain levels of income and status, which meant that [communities] would be laid out on the hill above the mill in a particular order, because lower is cheaper because it's closer to the pollution. And that meant that the Black neighborhood and church would be at the bottom of the hill." That remains the case to this day.

According to Winant, African Americans worked in the steel industry as strike-breakers until the unions integrated in the 1940s—considered one of the major achievements in organizing at that time. "The big industrial unions became politically committed to the project of civil rights nationally," Winant explained. "In fact, the UAW [United Auto Workers] funded the March on Washington in 1963. However, there were persistent structures of inequality inside the workplace which the union was typically not that interested in trying to root out because the majority-white members wanted to be able to place their sons in the same kinds of jobs that they had. So, in steel mills, Black workers were typically found in the least desirable jobs, which meant hottest, most dangerous (like in a coke oven or blast furnace), and most replaceable."

Black workers were also typically the first let go and the last hired back in cyclical layoffs. That meant that the loss of employment that many white workers experienced in the 1980s began earlier, in the 1960s and '70s, for Black workers as jobs began to dwindle. Ultimately, the pool of Black workers turned to the as-yet-unregulated healthcare industry, which was the remaining industry in town. Eventually, some white men and many women, forced to take on jobs as the men lost their mill work, joined that workforce as well. But, as Winant says, "Because this is how racism in America works, there were built-in advantages that allowed white people to enter that industry on better terms" too. After all, if one person's father or grandfather had a better position at the mills, they might have saved money, for example, which would allow them to afford to complete a more extensive training program before entering the healthcare field at a higher level. Once again, Steubenville's Black population was at a disadvantage, which impacted all elements of life.

Gun violence in Steubenville also disproportionately affected those living downtown and in public housing. At city council meetings, disgruntled residents blamed law enforcement for not doing enough, and the police often blamed drugs and invoked "gangs" for what was wrong with the town, claiming that they exercised influence over Steubenville from bigger cities like Youngstown or even Chicago.

According to Jeno Atkins, who is biracial and grew up with "very present" divorced parents, football actually felt like it equalized race relations, at least at Steubenville High School. "It was a pretty diverse school, and sports alone forced us to get [rid of] any racial tension there was," he recalled. "'Cause nothing mattered but the name on [the] front of the jersey." Once football ended, though, so did opportunities for many of the students. It wasn't just adulation and a sense of direction that got lost, but also that built-in support from coaches, who had been invested in the kids' success during their time as players.

"Football is a way out [for kids from low-income households], but a lot of the players chosen to play in college usually don't make it 'cause they get sucked back into the gritty parts of Steubenville," said Atkins.

Though Steubenville's high school football team offered a period of distinction for some teenage boys post-graduation, if the players didn't matriculate to higher education or if they returned after college, they were left to fend for themselves, often unsuccessfully. "If you're good on the field and you're a Black boy, they love you," said one former player in his late twenties whom I interviewed. "You're a hero. You're included. You get a false sense of power and position. Maybe you make it out of town? But once you get back, there's nothing for you."

Delores Wiggins, founder of the Ohio Black Caucus and president of the local NAACP chapter, seconded this sentiment about scarce opportunities, particular for Black youth, when I talked to her at her local church. "I tell the kids when they graduate to get out of Steubenville and don't come back."

"Even if we were once a part of [the structure] through athletics or entertainment, then suddenly we realize at the end of the day, that's all we were: the entertainment," said Tyrone White, speaking to the shared experience of being a Black athlete. "Is that the case for white people? No, but the system is still the same. Unless we've accepted the myth that things have truly changed, we go in with an expectation that there's going to be a difference [for men of color]…in such a way to try to protect ourselves, as much as possible."

Given the historical context of this American steel town, would Ma'lik and Trent be afforded the same treatment and tried the same way?

————

Outside and across the way from the Jefferson County Justice Center, a smattering of protesters and supporters milled about holding "Justice for Jane Doe" signs, alongside TV reporters and photographers hoping to get a shot of the defendants' arrival. The world was waiting to see what would happen.

Large and small media outlets had converged from around the country to cover this case, more high-profile than the area had seen before. A small town, Steubenville was not equipped to handle such a massive influx of people, so proper hotel rooms and food options were scarce.

Rachel Dissell of the *Plain Dealer* came in from Cleveland. She remembers a general sense that a lot of locals, at restaurants like Naples Spaghetti House, weren't thrilled to have the news media there. "I'd been to the courthouse already and I'd covered so many trials, even ones in juvenile court," she said. "But this one was different because Steubenville wasn't used to…lots of attention. On the day the trials started, there were deputies directing traffic, checking IDs, and protesters and Jane Doe supporters posted up near the courthouse. There was a lot of tension, kind of a charged atmosphere. Fred Abdalla, Jr., the current sheriff's son and also the court's chief probation officer, was handling news inquiries—yet another reminder of the tangle of connections. Juvenile Judge Sam Kerr had already recused himself from the case because of ties to the football team."

Inside, the wood-paneled courtroom was small and cramped. Each of the boys sat beside his lawyer in a formal button-down shirt and tie, facing the judge. Behind them, the families of the defendants and other involved parties sat in rows on benches. Most of the other townspeople were not present, as there was limited space. Members of the press were wedged awkwardly beside the families on rickety folding chairs. Stripped of their cell phones, computers, and all technology for the duration, the journalists were armed, as if in a time warp, with legal pads, reporter's notebooks, and pens. Some leaned over and attempted introductions to the families, meeting with varying degrees of reticence. There was barely enough air to go around.

A satellite room had been set up in another area of the courthouse for additional press, with a live feed of the proceedings. Though there were occasional opportunities to rotate into the primary courtroom when someone else left, the court had prioritized local press over national, aside from CNN, much to the chagrin of some of the other larger outlets. "Trials themselves are normally tense, but when you have a really small town and it is just invaded by people who are trying to gather information, it raises the tension," Dissell noted. She exhausted more than a few pens while covering the trial from inside the courtroom. "There was a real feeling that they wanted to get this over with as quickly as possible because it was a stress for the people in the courthouse and the town."

From the beginning, Judge Lipps, cloaked in his requisite black robes with white hair parted neatly to one side, stressed the vast differences between juvenile and adult court. As the gallery quieted down, he reminded all present that this was a civil, not criminal, case, which meant, for one thing, that the teenagers were not on trial with a possible guilty verdict. If found responsible, they would be "adjudicated delinquent," which meant they would be remanded to a juvenile facility and registered on the sex offender registry.

With that, the proceedings began.

Before the trial, Walter Madison had filed many motions on behalf of Ma'lik, including a petition to refer to Jane Doe as "the accuser" rather than "the victim," arguing that the term was inherently prejudicial. Prosecutor Marianne Hemmeter shot that down, asserting that the prosecutor's office was the accuser, not Jane Doe. His petition was denied.

For now, Jane Doe was not present in the courtroom.

Hemmeter stood to begin her opening statement, making an impression with her ordered bob, dark suit, and striking red pumps that Dissell dubbed "ruby slippers." Right away, Hemmeter accused Trent and Ma'lik of having treated Jane Doe "like a toy," exploiting her while she was intoxicated and unable to consent. Hemmeter punctuated each argument by repeating, "The degradation continues." Stressing that, when intoxicated, Jane Doe could not have agreed to participate in any act, the prosecutor argued, "This has nothing to do with consent or force, it has to do with substantial impairment. Holding these two responsible for what they did, holding these two responsible for the degradation of [Jane Doe]," she said at the end of her statement, "will be perhaps the easiest decision you have to make."

Both defendants were charged with rape, which in this case meant digital penetration without consent while Jane Doe was incapacitated. Trent also faced charges for "illegal use of a minor in nudity-oriented material" because of the image of Jane Doe on his cell phone. The photographs on Trent's phone also suggested the possibility of other nonconsensual sex acts, but they were more difficult to prove beyond a reasonable doubt. Ohio rape law was clear:

—No person shall engage in sexual conduct with another who is not the spouse of the offender or who is the spouse of the offender but is living separate and apart from the offender, when any of the following applies:

—The other person's ability to resist or consent is substantially impaired because of a mental or physical condition or because of advanced age, and the offender knows or has reasonable cause to believe that the other person's ability to resist or consent is substantially impaired because of a mental or physical condition or because of advanced age.

Though it wasn't specifically relevant here, the fact that, in the state of Ohio, a husband and wife don't have the same protections under the statute pointed to a whole mess of systemic issues.

There was murmuring in the courtroom as Fred Abdalla, Jr.—the bailiff, the sheriff's son, and a mentor to many of the Big Red football players—walked the first witness to the stand from a door behind the judge's bench: Julia Lefever, Jane Doe's friend, petite, soft-spoken, with brown hair that fell past her shoulders, took her oath. At Hemmeter's coaxing, she recounted the events of the night: how Jane Doe was meant to sleep at her house, how they drank vodka at the Belardine home, how she tried to convince Jane Doe to stay, but Trent dragged her away.

To poke holes in Julia's credibility, the defense attorneys questioned how much she'd drank—about half a fifth of vodka between the two girls. She had seen Jane Doe drunk before, Julia said, but never like this: "This time, she went downhill extremely fast." How reliable, the defense wondered, was Julia's memory of the night? Their argument that Julia was too drunk to accurately remember seemed only to underline how inebriated Jane Doe must also have been and how far from being able to make cogent decisions. Multiple times throughout the trial, Walter Madison, inclined to theatrics, pulled out a classic red Solo cup, a staple of keg parties the country over, to demonstrate how much Jane Doe and others drank as the night went on. The defense attorneys' goal was to make the victim seem reckless enough to drink heavily, but not quite reckless enough to be beyond the point of consent.

"So you are her true friend and you're still on her side, right?" Walter asked Julia, attempting to demonstrate Julia's bias.

"Yes," she said.

As each underage witness came up, he or she was accompanied by a guardian, usually a parent, who sat on a reserved bench directly to the left of the jury box. Knowing how uncomfortable it might be for the teens to discuss their questionable behavior in front of their families, Hemmeter approached each young witness with a kind of schoolteacher's patient firmness, underlined by her faint Southern lilt: *Here's what's going to happen now.* It was only when she met with resistance, the teens asking, "Do I really have to read this out loud?" as she presented them with their own text messages, that her tone grew more stern.

After Lefever exited, Jake Howarth's girlfriend, Elayna Andres, took the stand. She was white and blond and wore a gray shirt, as she confirmed through tears that Jane Doe "was conscious, but couldn't lift her head" when the boys carried her out of Party B. Though the defense attorneys couldn't subpoena Jane Doe's West Virginia friends, some of whom had supposedly given the police "incriminating" accounts of her reputation and might have conveniently called her integrity into question, they did have Elayna. When prodded, she revealed that she stopped being friends with Jane Doe because she was posting "inappropriate" things on the internet after the incident happened. This represented a common occurrence. Victims of rape often lose friends in the wake of the assault, loyalty diminishing in the face of larger social pressures. For other girls, distancing themselves can seem like the path of least resistance and a way to protect themselves from the taint of being raped or being seen as a slut.

Next, his face flushed with nerves, Jake Howarth took the stand. Once on the wrestling team with Trent and now nineteen and a college freshman, he confirmed that the victim had been swaying while sitting on the couch at his home and had thrown up both in his bathroom and outside. On cross-examination, Madison referenced threatening calls Jake and his family had received since the incident from people who believed the Howarths "had facilitated the rape." When asked whether the incident felt significant in his life, Jake shrugged. "Not at the time."

The next witness, Pat Pizzoferrato, another Steubenville High School buddy, apologized for his "bad joke," since he'd been the one to offer other boys money to urinate on Jane Doe outside. According to the *Weirton Daily Times*, he described the photo Anthony Craig had shared of "a female on her hands and knees, with a shirt on but no pants." Mays was standing behind her and Richmond was in the background. As the gallery shifted in their seats, he said, "I thought they just had sex with her."

When the trial reconvened the next morning, Thursday at nine a.m., the reporters knew to bring more pens. This promised to be a long day, especially as the judge took very few breaks. For many of the journalists, this would have been a tricky case to cover even if they had been afforded the luxury of recording devices and time. Some publications were uncomfortable with the blunt descriptions required to do the case justice. Dissell recalled challenging disagreements with her male direct supervisor at the time, as she argued that the paper needed to describe the sexual acts that comprised the assault in clear layman's terms so that the public understood exactly what happened. "It was difficult trying to navigate the language around rape with grown men who refused to discuss anatomy with a female reporter," she said.

That day, things started technically: a forensic analyst from the Bureau of Criminal Investigation talked about the confiscated cell phones and resulting trove of 362,972 text messages. She recounted a text chain (thanks to the binder Hemmeter kept handy) in which Trent said that, initially, Coach Reno was keeping him in the football rotation, but would suspend him for three games if anything additional happened.

That evening when court was in recess, adult film star and actress Traci Lords appeared on *Piers Morgan Live* on CNN to comment on the case. "I was born and raised in Steubenville, Ohio, and I was also raped in Ohio, as was my mother," she shared. "There is a sickness in that city. There is a lot of alcohol, a lack of regard for women. That was my experience, and definitely my mother's, and the whole thing has brought it all back to me." Lords was raped by a fourteen-year-old boy when she was ten and later went on to appear in adult films while she was underage, too young to legally consent.

On Friday, March 15, the early morning buzz in the courtroom had an elevated tenor. All eyes were on Mark Cole, his close-cropped hair and wrestler's build aligned with his dreams of joining the Marines, as he cleared his throat and read from a paper, "On the advice of my counsel, I invoke my Fifth Amendment right not to incriminate myself."

Back in September 2012, before the probable cause hearing, the district attorney's office had given the three main teenage bystanders and eyewitnesses letters pledging unofficial immunity in exchange for testimony: Mark (who had hosted Party C and filmed Jane Doe in the car), Evan Westlake (who had filmed Nodianos's rant and attended Party C), and Anthony Craig (who had snapped and shared photos and information between the Cole and Howarth homes). None were implicated in the rape, but they risked opening themselves up to culpability for having taken and exchanged photographs and videos and for enabling the crimes. Now as each teenager approached to testify, he demanded *official* immunity in exchange for not pleading the Fifth. In response, Brian Deckert, Hemmeter's prosecutorial counterpart, argued that Mark Cole should be compelled to testify as an eyewitness in furtherance of justice. The various attorneys argued back and forth over the terms of the transactional immunity.

More rustling in the gallery. Eventually, Judge Lipps denied the teenager's request to stay silent but agreed to immunity from criminal penalty "except for perjury, falsification, failure to produce evidence or contempt [of court]." The bystanders would be required to incriminate their friends face-to-face.

As Trent, in a yellow sweater vest, and Ma'lik, in his basic buttondown shirt and dark tie, watched from their seats, their buddy Mark Cole admitted to recording Trent "digitally penetrating" Jane Doe on the way to his house. He said his phone had a bright light and that Trent "pulled her shorts to the side." The prosecutors started using anatomical terms like "labia" to get specific about the penetration because in the state of Ohio the finger must be inserted into the vagina to prove rape. Mark got flustered trying to answer. This scientific terminology was less comfortable to the boys than their usual slang.

Mark swore he didn't share the video with the other guys. "It was one of those moments when you realize you did something wrong and stupid," he admitted, "so I deleted it."

But that wasn't all he had witnessed.

After the group had arrived at his house, as the victim lay on her side on the rec room floor, having just vomited again, Mark admitted to seeing Trent try to force her to give him oral sex—a further invasion.

"Trent tried to receive a blow job from her," Mark said.

In court, Mark confirmed that he saw Ma'lik lying behind Jane Doe too, touching her while she was passed out. Deckert asked if he was shocked by what he saw; he said no.

"Is that an everyday occurrence?" the prosecutor asked.

"I was drunk at the time," Mark answered. "So I didn't think it was that bad." He also didn't view a finger in the vagina or a penis in the mouth as "sex."

When Evan Westlake, who had been the sober driver to Mark's house, was escorted to the stand, he also pleaded the Fifth and was granted transactional immunity. He had snatched Mark's car keys away, though he was nervous driving a bunch of drunk kids in an unfamiliar car. Rap blasted from the speakers.

Once they arrived at Mark's Party C, he had witnessed similar acts:

He saw Ma'lik's two fingers halfway inside of Jane Doe and Trent behind her smacking her bare hip with his penis. "It wasn't what I expected to see," he commented.

"Was she moving?" special prosecutor Marianne Hemmeter asked.

"Not at this time," Westlake said.

"Was she talking?" Hemmeter asked.

"I didn't hear anything," Westlake said.

Why hadn't he intervened? "It wasn't violent," he said. "I didn't know what rape was. I always pictured it as forcing someone." The boys, coached by defense attorneys, were intentionally minimizing the incident and claiming they didn't understand the definition of rape. Yet several of them used the term "rape" on social media and in texts. They knew that what was happening to Jane Doe as she lay unconscious was wrong. They didn't need to know the official Ohio State rape law, and the microdifferences between rape and sexual assault, to know that it wasn't right. Evan claimed to be "stunned" by what he saw at Mark's house. "You were stunned," challenged one of Trent's attorneys, "and then went to the next house [back to Party B] and filmed what you say was a funny joke and then you promulgated it to the world?"

Many of the teenagers faced down the same moment of dread as Hemmeter approached with her binder, asking them to read their own tweets and texts from that night aloud—in front of their families, community, reporters, and the world. There were gasps from the gallery; mothers' and fathers' mouths dropped open in horror. Intermittently, Ma'lik's biological mother, in attendance along with his guardians, the Agrestas, burst into tears.

"There was one mom in particular whose reaction stayed with me," Rachel Dissell recalled, as a mother of a toddler herself at the time. "Her kid was reading a text message that talked about a girl's body, and you could just see the color drain from her face. I can't imagine being that parent. You know your kid is a problem, but you feel like you're supposed to protect them too."

Before she'd left home, Dissell had explained to her young son that she was going to cover a trial and that, at the trial, a judge would decide if someone did something wrong and should be punished. Her son responded, "What if it was a mistake?"

After that, Dissell made a conscious choice to introduce some of these concepts early. "It isn't easy to have conversations about consent with children, but it has to start at a young age," she said. "We can't expect them just to know. So I made an intentional space to talk to him about getting permission. Asking, do you want a hug? When he started jiu-jitsu, I remember the instructor explaining again and again that if you were grappling with someone and they tapped your shoulder, that was the sign to stop because they were no longer okay. It was an ironclad rule in the class. They practiced that response again and again. We talked about that during a car ride home, why that same thing that was important in class was also important with friends or people we liked."

———

Others took the stand: Anthony Craig, Farrah Marcino, J. P. Rigaud, who walked the court through the investigation, some witnesses for the defense, a BCI specialist who matched the DNA found in the sperm on the Steelers blanket to a control sample swabbed from Trent Mays's mouth. When Madison asked, the specialist noted that Evan Westlake had refused to give a DNA sample, possibly to avoid incrimination.

The defense attorneys continued to argue that the victim was a willing participant. They argued that she insisted on leaving the party with the boys despite advice from other girls, that she was interested in Trent, that she was awake enough to cuddle and kiss.

But the following day of trial, Saturday, would be the moment of truth: Jane Doe would be in the courtroom to take the stand.

"Jane Doe is a tough kid," said Marianne Hemmeter, "but when the state of Ohio stepped in, the case was out of her hands."

By the time the trial rolled around, Jane Doe's testimony seemed key to winning the case. According to her attorney, her parents encouraged her to speak, but she wasn't forced. Ultimately, the decision to put her on the stand, the notion that she could handle it, was based on her innate strength and bravery. She agreed to testify.

According to renowned women's rights attorney Gloria Allred, a victim's testimony is almost always essential for a case to have any chance. "The reality is that most prosecutors are not going to prosecute unless the victim will testify," she explained. "And even then, sometimes they won't…because nobody wants to lose a high-profile case."

Rape cases are rarely simple convictions, especially with teenagers involved. As Allred said, the fact that Jane Doe was courageous enough to testify was important because there was so much media focus on the trial. "[The] attention…might encourage some victims to say, 'I want to have the same courage to testify if necessary in a criminal case,'" Allred said. "It's empowering to others to know that a victim would do that and did do that."

As Jane Doe settled into the witness stand, avoiding the eyes of Trent and Ma'lik, the courtroom was respectfully somber and quiet. Marianne Hemmeter approached with extra softness and care. The questioning began: Jane Doe testified that the Smirnoff drink she had at the party seemed to have a different effect on her than normal; she said that she'd been interested in Trent and trusted him. She spoke calmly and clearly about waves of realizations—about waking up scared, surrounded by the boys, in a place she didn't recognize, about feeling "freaked out and embarrassed," about trying to piece together what happened to her, about the boys frantically texting her not to tell the police, about having been betrayed by people she trusted. She spoke about having to navigate the aftermath in which people who she thought cared spoke about her in damning and shameful terms, about the resulting threats and bullying.

Hemmeter read texts aloud that Trent had sent to the victim in the days that followed the assault, including one that read, "Reno just called my house and said I raped you."

But when Hemmeter showed Jane Doe the photo of herself naked, lying on the floor of Mark Cole's rec room—a picture the victim had never seen before—the girl broke down and burst into tears, as did her mother at her side. According to an article in the *Atlantic*, at least two other women in the courtroom began to cry too. "I don't think there was anyone in there who couldn't feel how hard that was," recalled Dissell.

"How do you feel about seeing this photo of yourself?" asked Hemmeter.

"Not good," Jane Doe answered.

All told, Jane Doe testified for two and a half hours.

Afterward came closing arguments in which both defense teams argued that the burden of proof had not been met, Madison stating that his client's DNA was not found on the scene.

Hemmeter had a different story to tell: "The things that made Jane Doe an imperfect witness…made her the perfect victim," she explained. In other words, the very fact that Jane Doe had no recollection of the assault spoke to how incapacitated she was at the time, how unlikely it was that she could reasonably have consented. "This case isn't about a YouTube video," the prosecutor continued. "This case isn't about Big Red football. This case is about a sixteen-year-old girl who was taken advantage of, toyed with, and humiliated, and it's time that the people who did that to her are held responsible."

At ten a.m. the next morning, the attorneys, defendants, reporters, and gallery crowd gathered one more time at the Jefferson County Justice Center. News vans clustered in the narrow parking lot outside the entrance alongside a larger crowd of voyeurs and activists.

Inside, the nervous energy was palpable as Judge Lipps took his seat on the bench and called the courtroom to order. Jane Doe and her family watched remotely from another room.

Ma'lik and Trent sat at attention in their respective blue and yellow button-downs, fear all over their faces. As they watched, the judge read his decision, reminding them of how serious these charges might have been had they been tried as adults. "Many of the things that we learned during this trial that our children were saying and doing were profane, were ugly, with alcohol consumption shown as a particular danger to our teenage youth," he said calmly, as the gallery held its collective breath. "It is the court's decision that both of the defendants are hereby adjudicated delinquent beyond a reasonable doubt on all three counts as charged."

Trent Mays's defense attorney rubbed his client's back to comfort him as he bowed his head.

"My life is over," Ma'lik whimpered. His mother cried out as if in pain.

Marianne Hemmeter rose, arguing that considering the lack of remorse shown on the part of the boys, particularly Trent Mays, there should be substantial punishment. Trent began to cry into a crumpled tissue as his lawyers argued for leniency. As Walter Madison appeared to wipe tears from his own eyes, he made a statement in which he reported hearing Ma'lik's father apologize moments before for having been absent during his son's childhood. He argued that Ma'lik had endured a difficult life, growing up without advantages or present parents, with a father in jail. He said, "I don't believe a commitment is necessary to rehabilitate this young man. Everything he was working to get away from would suggest he was heading in that direction…No matter what the commitment is, he'll have to deal with this for the rest of his life." Sending Ma'lik to the Department of Youth Services (DYS) would just "continue the cycle," he argued, for a boy who already felt cursed to repeat what he'd witnessed his whole life.

"These are serious charges. Rape is a felony of the first degree in the state of Ohio," said Judge Lipps, after various parents and guardians made their statements. That included Jane Doe's mother, who pronounced in a recorded statement, "This does not define my daughter."

The judge closed his eyes for a beat before delivering the sentence: Ma'lik would serve a minimum of one year in a juvenile detention center, while Trent would serve two years for both the rape and possession of the naked photos on his phone.

"There is a disparity in terms of the criminal justice system," said Coach Ty, who pointed to the very short sentences sometimes doled out to wealthy white offenders (including, later, Stanford swimmer Brock Turner, who was released after three months) versus Black defendants. "We don't always look at it through the same lens based on who the perpetrators are. [In Steubenville], I think the court got it right based on how the facts came out. That doesn't always happen."

Both defendants rose to give statements of apology, which would forever color the perception of them each in the public eye: "I would truly like to apologize to [Jane Doe], her family, my family, and the community," said Trent flatly, his slight Ohio accent coming through. "No pictures should have been sent around, let alone taken. And that's all, sir." Trent's apology was curt and perfunctory, focused primarily on the fact that he got caught taking pictures. He notably ignored the assault.

Ma'lik stood up next. He crossed the courtroom to stand in front of what would have been the jury box, where the victim's mother had entered in person. "I'm sorry to put you guys through this," he said, as he broke down weeping. Through sobs, as the bailiff embraced him, he repeated almost unintelligible apologies. *I'm sorry, I'm sorry, I'm sorry.*

The teenagers would be committed that same day, but the story was far from over. Within minutes of the decision, before the defendants had left the courthouse, CNN's Candy Crowley, in the studio, and Poppy Harlow, who was outside on the scene, exchanged on-air comments about the emotional tenor in the courtroom. Harlow described Ma'lik's outburst as "hard to watch," inspiring Candy Crowley to lament, "What's the lasting effect though on two young men being found guilty in juvenile court of—rape, essentially?" Immediately viewers were in an uproar. Why, in the face of this decision and a stirring statement by the victim's mother, was the first response to pity the rapists?

From a broadcast perspective, Ma'lik's breakdown felt surprising, authentic, and dramatic. I later chose to highlight it in my film, especially in contrast to Trent Mays's non-apology. I felt strongly that it was important to show Ma'lik's humanity and what felt and looked like legitimate remorse. It is possible to commit an act of violence and regret it. But at the culmination of a rape trial, to wonder aloud on national news first about the potential impact to the perpetrators rather than the victim is an example of how much ingrained bias is inherent to our analysis.

Victim-blaming and raising concern for the boys and men who have been accused of rape is a standard tactic in courtrooms across the country and in the court of public opinion. Later, when I traveled to Akron, Ohio—the birthplace of LeBron James and Alcoholics Anonymous—to interview Walter Madison about the case, he continued to project that attitude. He sat behind a big desk, the sun gleaming off his bald head, and shot me a smile. This would not be an easy interview, but at least he had agreed to speak to me. During the course of production on my film and later this book, I reached out to the families and guardians of all the implicated teens and their peers, but none, except a few on the periphery, were willing to talk. Still, I could tell Madison was going to try to haze me, the pesky filmmaker wanting the interview after he had lost the trial. And once the camera started rolling, I was supposed to melt into the background. This gets to the core of what can be unnatural about making a documentary: it was my job to let the people on camera speak their minds, but not my job to interrupt or object. "In the state of Ohio, the law is that if one is substantially impaired then they cannot properly give consent," Madison argued, pausing dramatically, an eyebrow arched. "Even if they do give consent, the impairment negates the consent that was given. If both parties, as it was in this case, were intoxicated, and that's the basis for rape…the question becomes who raped who?"

The way the legal system handles victims is another huge issue when it comes to prosecuting rape and letting it slide. When we allow courts and media outlets to become centers for victim-blaming and shaming, we're failing our victims once again. When Aya Gruber, a professor of law at the University of Colorado, Boulder, and author of *The Feminist War on Crime: The Unexpected Role of Women's Liberation in Mass Incarceration*, was in law school, she was sexually assaulted by the roommate of a person she was dating. "It never crossed my mind to report him because—as a person involved in law—I knew that would be so damaging to me, personally, to go through the system. There's a huge pressure on victims to be the solution. It makes so many assumptions about what these systems can do for you as a victim…and undercounts how exhausting and traumatic the adversarial process is."

This is a primary reason why so many people don't report their assaults, because sometimes there's more a sense of punishment than closure—a sense of judgment, of dragging through the mud. And it seemed like the adults in this case, especially, should know better and be better.

Perhaps, in Steubenville, they'd get the message. That same day, Attorney General Mike DeWine announced he would be convening a grand jury in mid-April to further investigate complicity in the case, which might include additional arrests for "obstruction of justice, failure to report a felony, and failure to report child abuse." Now, the entangled adults would not escape scrutiny.

That evening, Traci Lords appeared on *Piers Morgan* again, this time alongside Walter Madison. (Trent Mays and his attorneys opted not to participate in media appearances as frequently, representing a different strategy.) Gloria Allred was on the show as a legal analyst and pulled no punches: "Why don't you just say it?" she confronted Madison. "He raped her. He put two fingers inside the vagina of a child when she did not have the opportunity to resist, and that was clear." Lords, who appeared rattled, her voice pitched high, referred to Steubenville as "Stupidville," a derisive local nickname. When Madison argued that it was unfair that Ma'lik should have to register as a sex offender in perpetuity because he shouldn't be judged for his teenage behavior for his whole life—both boys would be required to register—Lords was incensed. "I was a rape victim," she said. "I have been judged my whole life because of what happened to me when I was a young girl!"

In the Ohio Valley, the reaction to the verdict was intense. Two days later, on March 19, two local fifteen- and sixteen-year-old girls were arrested for threatening Jane Doe's life, an act that Mike DeWine made clear law enforcement would not tolerate.

After a rape, there are rippling repercussions, issues that creep from beneath rocks to give clues to where the problems lie—for example, the threats Jane Doe endured. The bullying that happens in the aftermath is indicative of another underlying problem, a level of tolerance for hostility, anger bubbling below the surface, a sense of entitlement to express that anger at another human being without empathy, no matter what they might have suffered. It supports the notion that a real man (or a loyal woman) protects what they know at all costs without asking questions or considering the possibility of nuance. Loving Big Red and the football program and feeling pride in your school shouldn't then elicit rage toward a victim because the crime perpetrated against her exposed fractures and sicknesses in the community. Why shoot the involuntary messenger? Being willing to listen, being open to new perspectives, and even exploring one's own complicity shouldn't be signs of weakness. But, in Steubenville, you were either a team player or not.

————

On March 22, Elizabeth Vargas's *20/20* segment aired. The verdict cast a whole new light on the viewing experience, as Trent Mays's father described his son as a "role model" and Ma'lik's guardian, Greg Agresta, implored, "People need to step up and learn from this!"

Even DJ Bloomdaddy seemed to have new insight about the case. "This is one of the preeminent programs in the state of Ohio," he said. "This is how we identify and that's what gave it the air of, 'Okay, we don't have to answer to anybody.' But that's the mentality that's gotta go. Then the truth does get out and then let the chips fall where they may."

Some were touched by Ma'lik's emotional outburst in the courtroom, even as he denied culpability in the national TV interview. Others were less impressed. "The way we viewed the emotion—you would have liked to see that on the night of August twelfth," said special prosecutor Brian Deckert. "A little bit of compassion for another human being."

That lack of compassion the teenage boys demonstrated during the actual assault, especially on social media, and the reaction after the trial spoke to a larger systematic issue in the country. As Mike DeWine told Elizabeth Vargas in his interview, "This is not just a Steubenville problem. It's a nationwide problem."

## CHAPTER 9

# HURRY UP AND HEAL

I N THE WAKE OF THE TRIAL, that April, a relative quiet settled over Steubenville as the townspeople worked to resume a sense of normalcy. Football season had ended, along with its cocktail of excitement and tension. Even with all the upheaval, the team had made it to the Ohio High School Athletic Association semifinals and the third round of the playoffs, so the town had that to celebrate.

As president of the Historic Fort Steuben board of directors, whose mission was to revitalize the town and attract tourists, Jerry Barilla—wearer of many hats—began to share his vision for a newly restored mural to add to the roster. It depicted Abraham Lincoln (who, according to lore, visited Steubenville en route to his inauguration on February 14, 1861) alongside two local natives: Edwin Stanton, secretary of war during the Civil War, and David Homer Bates, chief chronicler of Lincoln's telegraph operations. It seemed especially important now to honor the positive elements of Steubenville's past.

The Ohio Valley Opera Club opened its 2013 season in the Steubenville High School auditorium. City council approved the annual budget, saving the Pleasant Heights Fire Station for one more year and sparking a heated debate over using surplus safety funds to open the Belleview Pool for the summer. Small-town business continued as usual—or tried.

For many, this moment was a beat to process: could things go back to how they were before? Should they? This desire to forget and move forward without introspection or change was at the root of the problem. Rape culture flourishes if no one is willing to take a look at the why and how. The rush toward patched-up normalcy hurts everyone, including both those guilty of assault and of looking the other way.

"The idea that you can acknowledge that what you did was wrong—that's a long, cultural process," said Aya Gruber, who argues that thinking of all sex offenders as monsters, while we tolerate other kinds of physical abuses and aggressions, doesn't allow for self-reflection or reform. "I don't think these high school boys, parents, and coaches are likely to engage in that because the first step is them being willing to see themselves and people they love as rapists. There's a natural disgust with sex offenses that rests at the intersection of old norms of male privilege. So, the only way of thinking about sexual wrongdoing is to put the offender in the realm of monster, in which case there's no alternative: they have to be in total denial and blame the victim."

Had locals learned about rape in this new social media context, and rape culture from the circumstances surrounding Jane Doe's assault? Or was the truth too ugly to digest? Was change afoot, or even a sense of how to untangle the intersecting catalysts? Or was the town mostly focused on trying to forgive, forget, and prepare for the next football season? Of course, forgetting is not a privilege afforded to victims.

At that same city council meeting where folks voted on repairs to the public swimming pool, one resident stood and proclaimed without apparent context, "I don't think Ma'lik Richmond received a fair trial! He was convicted in the court of public opinion before the trial. There has been talk about healing, but that healing can't begin until this wrong is righted." That seemed to begin and end that particular discussion, but the case was clearly still on people's minds.

Some of the students at Steubenville High had taken note of social media's risks, at least. "It was a learning experience, it honestly was," said Jeno Atkins at the time, "[about] what to post and what not to post online."

Regardless, the town's quiet pause wouldn't last long. After all, Ohio DA Mike DeWine had promised to convene a grand jury with the Jefferson County Common Pleas Court to investigate further crimes related to Jane Doe's assault—and the start date, April 15, 2013, was drawing near. DeWine, a born-and-bred Ohioan who also earned his bachelor's degree and graduate degree in law in Ohio, was a former lieutenant governor. A Republican and Catholic, his political stance was against abortion, same-sex marriage, and marijuana legalization, but pro–gun control and making drinking-and-driving laws stricter in the state. One of his eight children, Becky, died at twenty-two years old in a car accident in 1993. That August would mark the twentieth anniversary of her death, which the family honored through charitable work in Haiti. Sensitive to the experience of grieving parents, DeWine attended the funeral of every Ohio soldier who died in the Iraq War.

He was a man who believed in showing up. Now he convened a grand jury to question the culpability of the surrounding adults in Jane Doe's case, particularly those community members who had not cooperated with investigators the first time around. The adults would need to take responsibility for their actions. "A lot is incubated in middle school, elementary, and definitely in high school classrooms," said Tyrone White, speaking to the impact adults can have on young people in those formative years and the importance of reinforcing respect for boundaries and consent. "And there still is not a concerted effort within education to teach this notion of healthy relationships. And then we have a lot of adults [who] themselves are broken and, in their roles as coaches and teachers and mentors, they reinforce some of these [negative] things from their brokenness."

During DeWine's March 17 press conference following the delinquent verdict against Trent Mays and Ma'lik Richmond, he stood somberly in a basic gray suit and striped tie at an official wooden podium, American and Ohio flags draped behind him. He explained that at least sixteen potential witnesses had previously "refused" to meet with special agents from BCI. Those who had stonewalled the investigation would no longer be permitted to shirk their civic responsibility. They would be compelled to show up and testify. The DA's office was determined to get to the bottom of how the adults, positioned to offer guidance and support, were negatively impacted by this incident.

"This community needs assurance that no stone has been left unturned in our search for the truth," said DeWine, who argued that clearing the air through a grand jury probe would ultimately help the town of "good people" who had "been through a lot" move forward. Adjusting his glasses on his lined face, he shuffled his papers and continued, "I'd like to take this opportunity to talk not as the attorney general of this state, but as a parent of eight and now grandparent of nineteen...Any rape is...horrible for the victim. I think it's even more difficult when the victim is continually re-victimized in the social media and that is what has happened here. This is a societal problem. Crimes of sexual assault are occurring every Friday night and every Saturday night in big and small communities all across this country. And there comes a point where we must say, 'Enough is enough!'...We shouldn't tolerate it anymore as a...country. We, as a society, have an obligation to do more to educate our young people about rape."

On Prinnified, weeks later, Alex Goddard issued a kind of challenge: "The Grand Jury begins selection tomorrow and will convene next week. Rather than pointing fingers and accusing others of creating a path of destruction through Steubenville, it is time to let go of the hate and move forward. This can only happen when that one person has the audacity and courage to be the one person standing to create change. The ball is in your court. Healing begins with change."

Just as the rallies tested the definition of "unity" in this town, the word "healing" became a trigger, signifying a move toward marked change on one side and a desire to go back to "normal" on the other.

As promised, the grand jury was convened on April 15, 2013, also coincidentally the day that the FBI raided KYAnonymous's house because of his alleged hacking and took him into custody. His court case would be two years down the road. The reverberations of Jane Doe's assault were still being felt, far and wide.

DeWine, fired up during his press conference, had said he anticipated that many witnesses would be called during the hearings. He said the grand jury probe could last days. It lasted months.

Throughout the rest of spring, summer, and into fall, the grand jury called in more than one hundred witnesses as they assessed possible criminal activity. No one was outside the scope of inquiry, and everyone was on edge.

Many speculated that an indictment for Coach Reno Saccoccia might be on the horizon. After all, during the trial, there were texts read from Trent Mays and others that documented phone calls from Coach to the players and their families, warning them that Jane Doe was "saying rape." A petition circulated on Change.org demanding that he be fired. It received 136,405 signatures. A dueling petition in support of him garnered 734.

But the town wasn't interested in what some strangers on the internet thought should happen. On April 23, the Steubenville Board of Education extended Coach Reno's contract for two more years as director of administrative services, separate from his football contract. This sparked outrage online from columnists at publications like *Yahoo! Sports*, the *Washington Post*, and the *Nation*—where an article by David Zirin was titled, "What the Hell?"

By this point, the conversation online was going strong and showed no signs of letting up. The town might not have changed its ways, but the outside world was still knocking, demanding answers. Alex's blog was getting as many as 50,000 hits a day as a source for inside information on the case and happenings in Steubenville. As the months went by, she continued to use her platform to spotlight other stories she felt were unjust. With the hashtag #JusticeForJake, she rallied on behalf of Jacob Limberios, a nineteen-year-old Ohio man whose death was ruled a suicide after what some deemed minimal investigation, though the family believed he was murdered. She called out adults in Steubenville—or "Roll Red Roll Models," as she named them—for hateful rants on Twitter, sometimes directed at her. She drew parallels between their behavior and the teenagers in town, who she felt didn't know right from wrong. Where, she wondered, could they have learned those values?

But she had also become a kind of media darling beyond Prinnified's highly trafficked posts, a reliable local expert, someone who could don a blouse and lipstick and offer articulate insight into, and social media analysis of, the Steubenville rape case. She was a guest on programs including multiple CNN shows, *20/20*, *Democracy Now*, and *Dr. Phil*, as well as acting as a source for countless print interviews. She was earning respect for the investigative work she had done and for speaking out, however unpopular her views were with certain locals.

Then, on August 5, the *New Yorker* published a piece by staff writer
Ariel Levy called, "Trial by Twitter." The in-depth article, typical for
the publication, had an unexpected tenor: in it, the writer described
Alex Goddard as "a big woman" and her home as "ramshackle" with
"bits of the ceiling missing." Most of the quotations Levy chose to
represent Alex were colorful, but painted her as a beer-swilling,
vengeful parody. "[Goddard's] brand of women's liberation is one in
which individual scores are settled with habañero sauce or Internet
sleuthing—and, if necessary, by demeaning another woman," Levy
wrote, apparently extrapolating from a story Alex had shared.

The article positioned Jane Hanlin as more of a rational voice,
though the prosecutor repeatedly downplayed the seriousness of the
assault and hadn't been deemed impartial enough to try the case. In
the piece, Hanlin accused Goddard of doing damage from a "feminist point of view" by helping spread Jane Doe's story to national
media, thereby exposing the victim to more derisive attention. Alex's
actions undoubtedly had complex consequences, but her intention—
to ensure justice for the victim and the many other local women who
were victims before her—went unmentioned. Instead, Levy quoted
the prosecutor, who—like many in Steubenville—followed up admissions that the teenage boys had behaved badly with a firm "but."
That "but" rendered any condemnation of their behavior meaning-
less. Yes, what happened to Jane Doe was bad, *but*—what about the
boys' futures? What about the town's reputation? What about how
much she drank? What about the interruption to our lives? What
about the team? Was that even *really* rape? Levy gave air and space
to the town's grievances seemingly at the expense of Jane Doe and
rape victims everywhere. "'What happened to the girl is atrocious,'
Jane Hanlin told me," Levy wrote. "'But what they're putting out
there about her is worse—and false.'"

Levy also included her own perspective, writing: "Nobody

urinated on the victim. She was not 'brutally gang-raped.' At the trial in March, Mays and Richmond were accused of putting their fingers in her vagina while she was too intoxicated to give consent."

Despite what Levy seemed to minimize, according to national anti–sexual assault organizations like the Rape, Abuse & Incest National Network (RAINN), what Jane Doe experienced *is* by definition a gang rape. As to whether it was "brutal"—that was not for Levy, or anyone but Jane Doe, to determine. The idea that a "real" or "bad" rape involves punches or bruises is also an outdated rape myth. Coach Reno clung to similar beliefs early on, explaining his initial confusion to me by remarking, "But they didn't beat her up or nothing." Like Hanlin, Levy downplayed the severity of the incident, as if the collective response was an overreaction because there wasn't proven intercourse involved.

As reported in Levy's article, witnesses like Mark Cole admitted during the trial and in police interviews to seeing Trent Mays attempt other graphic sex acts with the victim. So the discussion of what *didn't* happen to Jane Doe was an oversimplification of her experience. Surely, more happened in that basement than could be proven in court. The article cast Alex as, at best, a drama queen and, at worst, an opportunist who knowingly spread misinformation. Alex struggled with fears about exploiting Jane Doe, but ultimately decided that raising awareness so that the case was duly prosecuted, setting an example for future cases, and shining a light on Steubenville's systematic issues were important.

"There is a better explanation than that everybody here is evil," Jane Hanlin was quoted as saying in defense of Steubenville, her words hanging on the page without comment from Levy, "intoxicated teen-agers are the world's worst thinkers." The statement seemed to absolve the local adults and perpetrators, suggesting that run-of-the-mill, poor adolescent decision-making led the football players to publicly humiliate and assault an underage drunk girl. Further, Hanlin posited, "'…if you were to interview a thousand teen-agers before this case started and said, "Is it illegal to take a video of another teenager naked?" I would be astonished if you could find even one who said yes.'" Her argument, which normalized the incident with a teens-will-be-teens attitude, was in opposition to what Marianne Hemmeter argued in court and what Mike DeWine emphasized during his press conferences about rape being a rampant and serious problem.

Levy's story sparked a reaction from publications like *Slate*, where the writer remained unconvinced that Goddard had done any damage since the case's legal outcome turned out to be just. *Business Insider*'s headline read, "*New Yorker* Writer Slams 'Vigilantes.'" Either way, the article became more of an evaluation of Alex Goddard's behavior than of the rapists, the bystanders, or the enabling adults.

Blindsided and upset, Alex went into a kind of hiding, already contending with threats and raging Twitter battles with former friends online. Suddenly, she had fallen out of favor.

———

That's when my own story intersected with Steubenville's. Back in New York City, I had read the *New Yorker* article and been surprised by its tone. I decided to reach out to Alex.

For the months since the incident happened, after my father pointed the *New York Times* article out to me in December 2012, I had been researching and staying on top of the case, wondering with growing seriousness whether there was still a part of the story that needed to be told. From what I could tell based on the available documents and social media online, Steubenville offered a fascinating perspective on male pack and perpetrator behavior. If I was to make a film about such a sprawling and complex case, I would need contacts in the town who could help orient me. From that point on, Alex and I slowly began to build a rapport, though she was, reasonably, distrustful of outsiders and coastal women looking for a story.

A week after the *New Yorker* story came out, on August 12, 2013, I arrived in Steubenville for the first time. I wasn't sure that after all the media attention there was a film to make, but I planned to take the weekend to immerse myself and see what I'd find.

Since the incident, I had heard stories from print journalism contacts about Steubenville: tales of a closed community, open hostility, and the domineering football coach, Coach Reno, who threatened a *New York Times* reporter, growling, "You're going to get yours. And if you don't get yours, somebody close to you will." So, when I arrived, on top of being compelled by the beautiful bones of a former steel town, I was nervous. Entering a community already shaken by the presence of unwanted press, could I differentiate myself from "breaking news" reporters or journalists and convince people to talk to me? Could I establish a different relationship as a documentarian, someone who would stick around to take a closer look and tell a longer story? I never expected this town, and the legacy of this crime, to still be with me ten years later.

Wanting some physical distance and a little privacy, my cinematographer and I were staying across the river in neighboring Weirton, West Virginia. This was partially inspired by Sandra too, the onetime rape crisis counselor and Jane Doe's victim advocate, whom we were meeting to interview and who was afraid to cross over into Steubenville. She felt like a walking target after attending the rallies against her employer's wishes.

And she looked terrified. That was my first thought as we approached her booth at the Eat'n Park in Weirton with the big salad bar. She looked as benign as a favorite aunt with her short, permed hair and glasses. But she kept glancing over her shoulder like she was being followed.

She had agreed to meet because she knew me a bit from the internet and my first film. An excerpt from *The Line*, in which I had interviewed my rapist, had circulated widely on feminist outlets like Jezebel. Later, I would get to know Sandra, a quiet force, supporter of victims, and a different type of Valley local. Proud of her heritage, she foraged pawpaws or "hillbilly mangoes" and made salves and balms from local herbs. She knew the secrets of the land, what it would grow and how to sustain herself. She shared her own experience with sexual assault and how, eventually, inspired by what I did in my film, she had worked up the courage to ask the man, whom she was still forced to see around town, about that night. Like my perpetrator, he shrugged and said that he didn't think about the incident much once he realized he wouldn't get caught. He expressed no remorse.

"He gets to just forget," she told us, eyes downcast. Haunted, she didn't have the same luxury. She shared some basic details about her experience with Jane Doe's case and her own fear of repercussions with townspeople—how she drove miles out of her way to avoid that bridge to Ohio. Fueled by panic, was she exaggerating the tension in her mind or reacting to a real threat? Did anyone here care about this case anymore?

Later, I got my answer: I headed next door to a cheerful spot, Dee Jay's, a barbecue joint with an upbeat but random Hawaiian theme. As I perused the ribs menu, my ears pricked up as I started picking up snippets of people's conversations:

*"I heard Ma'lik is getting out of jail soon."*

*"That poor girl."*

*"You know, parents have to be careful these days."*

All around us, I realized customers were talking about the

case—in an adjoining booth, by the bar, at the ladies' room sink. If the incident was still drawing this much focus, even in the next town over, and people were expressing sympathy for Jane Doe here, then there was plenty left to learn. It wasn't possible to erase the impact of what happened, no matter what some people wanted. Sandra's personal history and the stories told at the rallies demonstrated that Jane Doe's rape didn't happen in a vacuum. And the conversation in Weirton suggested that the case was nuanced and still alive for locals.

Cautious at first, Alex agreed to guide me via text around Steubenville on my inaugural trip, offering snippets of advice and gossip as she saw fit. "Where will I find the cops hanging out?" I asked her. "The town powerhouses?"

"Up the hill," she texted back. She directed me to a local bar. As soon as I arrived, I wanted to leave.

The exterior of the place looked run down. A couple of Harley-Davidsons were parked outside in the gravel lot along with some trucks with assault rifle decals on the windows. Despite a faded breast cancer fundraiser banner, it didn't look like a friendly spot, especially for women. Maybe if this had been a gloomy dive in a bigger Ohio city, I wouldn't have felt so intimidated. I know big cities. But this was Steubenville and the bar conjured every negative story that had been reported about the town. I longed for the sticky plastic booths and neon palm trees at Dee Jay's. I steeled myself.

We ventured inside. Sure enough, the dark, smoke-filled space was as unwelcoming as I'd ever experienced. The hostility emanating from it felt quiet—and personal. As a documentary filmmaker, it's my job to try to blend in and strike up conversation. I've chatted people up at three a.m. in New Orleans dives; loosened lips talking about ghosts in Baltimore pubs; learned about secret gun-loving Libertarian meet-ups by the Grand Canyon. But here, the hostile looks left no pathway in. Hunched defensive shoulders, faces turned away from us spoke volumes. They knew we were outsiders, possibly with the loathed "mainstream media." My attempts at small talk about local football fell flat. Men around me made snide comments. One, seemingly in cahoots with the bartender, thought it would be funny to hit on me, knowing I'd arrived with another man.

We ordered drinks to buy us some time—a Budweiser (nothing foreign) and a Chivas Regal. I listened to any snippets of conversation I could catch. I expected grumbles about jobs or lack thereof, fracking, biking, or the weather. To my surprise, all around us, people were discussing the case: men grumbled with resentment about trumped-up charges and girls who deserved what they got.

As soon as I could, I got us out of there.

That was my first window into the culture of Steubenville in the aftermath of the trial and looking toward the grand jury indictments. The air was thick with resentment. There was no softness here. This didn't feel like a place that had learned from its mistakes. To be fair, I would later discover friendlier environments in town, but this bar spoke volumes about an undercurrent of entrenched local attitudes. And that was only the beginning.

"What's downtown?" I texted Alex.

People like Sandra and even the desk clerk at our hotel had warned me away from downtown, sketchy and unpolished, but we needed to get a clearer sense of the area and talk to some willing people. Once in the car, we took a leisurely route down the hill, rounding the corner to Mingo Junction, the next town over. There, we were confronted with the zombie steel mill from the opening scene of *The Deer Hunter*—looming and green, a rusted-out hulk of a structure. When the iconic Vietnam War movie was shot in 1977, the mill would have still been running, though the industry's downfall was soon to come. It was once the heart of a town; now it was a staggeringly beautiful

ruin. I felt a pang of nostalgia for a faded American story, but maybe
that wasn't even real, just a romantic fantasy. Mingo felt empty and
abandoned, the Midwest's version of a Wild West ghost town. A wake
of buzzards circled overhead. We rushed to capture them on camera.

But this wasn't Steubenville proper: this was Mingo, its ghost of
future past. So we got back in the car and drove the five miles to
town. What I saw on South 4th Street was the bones of a 200-year-old
historic town: once, there was architecture, there was history; this
was a gathering place. I saw tall columns on the bank, small busi-
nesses holding on for dear life. Fliers abounded for a fundraiser to
save an old theater, the Grand, where Dean Martin had performed.
The Ohio River, wide and storied, ran parallel to Main Street, once
the site of Steubenville's famous brothels. My dread gave way, for a
moment, to understanding. I thought, "This is a beautiful old American town, trying to survive." On all sides, we were surrounded by the
decaying remnants of a lost civilization—a lost America.

As we drove deeper, we passed weathered storefronts and a crisis
pregnancy center. Crisis pregnancy centers in general are unlicensed
facilities run by anti-abortionists falsely presenting themselves as
medical centers and disseminating misinformation to pregnant
women. There were billboards about curbing gambling addiction, a
former fast-food spot turned into a Cash n' Loans, Frank & Jerry's
Furniture & Appliance Store—owned by Jerry Barilla. Finally, I spotted a decrepit but intriguing antique shop, and we pulled to a stop.

Figurines clustered in the windows; a battered American flag
sulked outside. Inside, beyond a ravaged enclosed porch, the store
reeked of cigar smoke. The shelves were cluttered wall-to-wall with
memorabilia—framed portraits of the crooner and Cal Jones, the first
Black football player to make the *Sports Illustrated* cover, who was
also from Steubenville. There were Sambo figurines, an old Victrola,
and some X-rated Traci Lords collectibles. The adult film star grew

up here, I would be told repeatedly with a smirk. No one mentioned what she had talked about on CNN: that she was also raped in this same town.

The shop owner was a cigar-chomping former steel worker whose shirt proclaimed his name: *Vinny.* "It sounds sick," he said, as he cranked the moaning Victrola, coaxing out Dean Martin's "Ain't That a Kick in the Head?" I performed a fascination with ashtrays, bruised footballs, and kitschy tumblers until I could strike up a conversation with him about the town and its unfortunate negative publicity. He warmed to the topic quickly, so I asked if he would let us interview him. He agreed.

Vinny offered us a tour of his three-story shop, including his "clubhouse" gun room—a surveillance state take on a "man cave." The walls were covered in signs and CCTVs. There were La-Z-Boys from which you could admire his stuff and keep tabs on the neighbors through the windows. When we got inside, he pulled out a shotgun, cocked it, and said, "I call this my street sweeper."

The *bing* of a follow-up text from Alex startled me. "Did you find downtown?"

To me, an outsider, Vinny seemed like a man suspended in amber, living in the past. He'd surrounded himself with what for him were nostalgic treasures from bygone glory days. He too was like a relic, and his views on the case reflected that. When I finally asked him for his thoughts on the rape, he looked confused and sad. He couldn't understand why Jane Doe's assault had torn his town apart. "Back in my day, you were a bad boy," he lamented during one interview, shaking his head. "Now they want to lock you up."

Vinny's shop felt miles away from the leafy, trim streets up the hill. A block away, sex workers walked the long, wide alleys behind the police station, and many of those on the street appeared to be struggling with addiction. I tried to picture Steubenville as my home, imagining the ghosts of the teenage boys who grew up avoiding these streets, the teenage girls tucked away in their suburban homes, but feeling the darker reverberations.

To this day, I see those initial warnings about the dilapidated downtown as a metaphor for how the Steubenville locals felt about their home. They warned me away because it represented the community's underbelly, the part they didn't want the outside world to see: crime, signs of neglect, poverty, survival sex, the boarded-up gentlemen's club, the beautiful but nearly deserted Carnegie library. But it was their history and their town—the shameful parts hidden safely until the internet collided with their reality and broadcast their decline. It was *our* history, as a country, the wound of the heartland, the boarded-up windows on Main Street.

As we drove back to the hotel, I thought about how, on the hill at Harding Stadium, Big Red football had already started training for their upcoming season. Some of the teenage boys embroiled in the case would be suited up in pristine uniforms and ready to play as a stadium full of fans cheered for them. Was all of Steubenville consumed with resuming business as usual?

Over the coming months, I traveled back and forth documenting the changing seasons, the holidays and rituals. I observed firsthand that tug-of-war between the impossibility of ignoring what had happened and the desire to restore the town's dignity. It wasn't necessarily that everyone either supported the football team or Jane Doe; Alex Goddard or Coach Reno. For some, it was more complicated.

Many members of the older set, who remembered Steubenville in its heyday, yearned for "simpler times," but didn't understand that those days hadn't been simpler for everyone—particularly people of color and women. At least on the surface, for men like Jerry Barilla, those had been happier times. And it's true that then the economy had been thriving.

"In the fifties, Steubenville…was a very vibrant town. The streets were filled with people pretty much every day," he told me, recalling five separate packed movie houses, as TV had only just emerged. There were lively Friday and Saturday nights downtown, and Christmas windows "like Macy's does in New York." "It was a family event and most people dressed up when you came downtown. Women would wear white gloves, hats. It was that way. You never went out without being proper. And everybody seemed to be positive." He referenced the Grand, the theater that he, as president of Steubenville Revitalization, and some members of the community were working to revive. This was one of his seemingly countless roles in the community. "The steel mills were working at full capacity," he continued. "And so it was a cool town to be in—Steubenville, Ohio. But then, as time evolved and the steel industry started to move south in the United States… and also offshore, the steel production in the valley here started to dwindle. And as of today, both mills that functioned, well, one is out of business; the other one is very minimal. They both employed something like fourteen thousand per mill, so it's a big drop."

In many ways, for people like Jerry, downtown Steubenville was like a ghost town haunted by its thriving past—the former bank buildings, department stores. But there was a disconnect between what it felt like for them and what was happening behind the scenes, which allowed rape culture to develop and flourish here: the women toiling away at home, trying to make ends meet on an inconsistent steel mill salary, hoping their husbands would return from work in one piece and in decent moods. And if the men didn't return in a kind mood or someone else hurt these women, what recourse did they have? It's not that rape culture hadn't existed in the old days; it was that people had the good sense to keep it behind closed doors—and there was no social media or cell phone cameras to document it.

When I met Jerry, he felt emblematic of a large sector of the community. He was an important reminder that coalition building around complex issues is a struggle. People are dimensional, and many have their hearts in the right place, but still unconsciously normalize inequality and gender biases. At that point, Jerry's desire to preserve a romantic snapshot of his beloved hometown was also blocking him from confronting the gravity of what had actually happened to Jane Doe, and from seeing the behavior the boys were absorbing from the men in town.

Each day, in the years before, during, and after Jane Doe's assault and the resulting trial, Jerry gathered with a group of older men in town to eat cookies, drink coffee, and read through the local paper together. For decades, they had spent their mornings debating high school football, basketball, and baseball. But for this past year, they had been talking about rape instead.

Jerry, who was slight and always immaculately dressed with a thick head of gray hair and a kind face, called what happened to Jane Doe "tragic" and did not defend the boys, though he preached forgiveness and referenced his Catholic faith. Dusting off an antique oven with his palm as he passed, he welcomed me into his shop and delighted in talking up the finer points and history of town. He wanted to make sure I knew Steubenville had nuance and goodness and deserved to be remembered as a historic American place. But in fall of 2013, with the players serving time in juvenile detention, he didn't see Big Red football as anything but wholesome. As we ate cookies together, the old timers at the table still wore their Big Red letter jackets as badges of honor. Jerry's frustration with Trent Mays and Ma'lik Richmond seemed largely to be about "hurting people" by dragging the entire town down. His greatest ire was reserved for Michael Nodianos and his viral YouTube video. More than anything, his allegiance was not to high school football or to the victimized women—it was to Steubenville itself. It was to a better day.

"Nobody is hidden from the problems that society has today," he said. "It's how you deal with them and address them. We're faith-based, strong, and we are going to survive. We've been hit hard with…unemployment and [the] mills. But we have to handle it and turn it around." As for downtown, "I don't think it'll ever come back to what it was in the fifties," he admitted, "but we can certainly bring it back to being a viable community." He shook his head. "You just can't let it die, at least that's my feeling on it."

He and most of the other residents just wanted the drama to end so they could return to a time before all of this.

Then the indictments came down.

# CHAPTER 10

# THE GROWN-UPS

THE GRAND JURY MET on eighteen different occasions, called 123 witnesses (some of whom testified twice), and reviewed copious evidence submitted by BCI investigators. The proceedings were closed to the public and press, as was standard per Ohio State law.

On October 7, 2013, as the first whispers of autumn blew in on the breeze, unsettling the leaves in their trees, the initial indictments were handed down. Many people anticipated the singling out of recurring characters in the drama: Coach Reno, the Howarths, parents of the convicted teens, and more. Instead, Attorney General Mike DeWine surprised everyone by releasing less expected names, adjacent supporting characters instead of protagonists: first came William Rhinaman, the fifty-three-year-old gray-haired director of technology for Steubenville City Schools, who looked more likely to tend a garden than cover up a crime. He was indicted on three felony counts—tampering with evidence, obstructing justice, and perjury— as well as one misdemeanor charge for obstructing official business. He was arrested that afternoon, with his first appearance in court scheduled for two days later on Wednesday, October 9.

"This is the first indictment in an *ongoing* grand jury investigation," Mike DeWine stressed in a statement. "Our goal remains to uncover the truth, and our investigation continues." The implication was clear: there were more to come. The town held its breath.

Rhinaman, known as "Bill" to friends, was also a former adjunct professor at the local Catholic university, Franciscan. He had erased potential evidence about the rape off the school superintendent's computer days before the crime was reported to the police. Yet news of his attempt to cover up Jane Doe's assault to protect the football players and coaches, which some believed was a directive from a higher-up, did not inspire outrage from his peers. Instead, it further cemented many town members' sympathy for the perpetrators. Once again, their instinct to protect their own trumped their moral compass.

Two weeks later on October 24, on Prinniefied, Alex Goddard reposted a leaked group email chain in which a Steubenville High School basketball coach, Mark Masloski, expressed despair over Rhinaman's situation:

Fellow Staff,

Kim and I are feeling completely upset for Bill and we are thinking many of your [*sic*] are probably feeling the same way. It seems outrageous that he is in jail without bond. I believe we should show some support for him but not quite sure how?.... Let me know what you [think] about how are [*sic*] voices can be heard.

Mark and Kim

Also using his official school email account, a Steubenville City Schools guidance counselor, Timothy Daugherty, responded in kind, offering to "pick up a card" and leave it on the "Guidance Office Table" for people to sign, as one might do for a coworker's birthday. "Letting him know his friends are behind him may go a long way," he added.

When the email exchange went public, it instigated a further rupture in the town's foundation, offering a window into the clear divide that still existed, though Ma'lik and Trent's trial was long over. Townspeople began posting and debating on online forums again.

One woman—the president of Tree-Climbers.org—shared a letter she had sent directly to both school staff members, saying:

> Where is the compassion for the young lady who was raped and, according to the Grand Jury, it appears the knowledge of which was covered up by your co-worker(s)? (assuming more indictments to come) Yes, Mr. Rhimaman [*sic*] deserves his day in court. But for a moment think about this. What if it's true—that ADULTS knew about the social media recordings of the RAPE of a young girl—and then conspired to cover it up by deleting evidence? Do you have daughters, Mr. Masloski, Mr. Daugherty? Wives? Sisters? Mothers? What if this happened to someone you knew? Honestly, I am astounded by your apparently misplaced 'loyalty.' If Mr. Rhimaman shouldn't be where he is because "others" told him what to do—then step forward. Do the right thing. A little girl was RAPED and the adults who were entrusted with her safety knew and tried to cover it up (allegedly).

That thread also included a comment plucked from William Rhimaman's daughter's Facebook page, apparently by a former classmate: "…they want to do this to people that don't deserve it. If anyone deserves [to be] indicted it's Reno and the ones that provided the alcohol to the teens. Our town is so corrupt it isn't funny anymore."

Once again, the townspeople saw the investigation as an assault on their home, school, and team, as opposed to an attempt to root out and discourage dangerous behavior. They didn't see how refusing to look at these patterns, and thus allowing them to repeat, would perpetuate a less safe environment for all of their children, and the women in the community too.

During this same time, I remember noting with surprise that the local domestic violence shelter was quietly handing out teal ribbons in support of rape survivors at Harding Stadium during football games, to recognize awareness of and opposition to sexual violence. I watched as most who took them shoved them deep into their pockets.

In the course of the grand jury investigation, BCI had searched Steubenville High School and the local school board offices, as well as combed through emails and digital files. During that process, the state investigators had stumbled upon another crime, tangential to Jane Doe's rape: on October 23, 2013, William Rhinaman's twenty-year-old daughter Hannah, a sprightly redhead who at times sported heavy black eyeliner and a lip ring, was also indicted and charged with felonies, two counts of receiving stolen property (including a school iPad) and one count of grand theft. She faced up to three years in prison. According to DeWine, the younger Rhinaman, who had been arrested the month before for driving under the influence and possession of drug paraphernalia, stole equipment from Steubenville High School while working there part-time and sold it. Though the crime was unrelated, the state felt obligated to prosecute any illegal activity discovered during the course of the investigation. After all, while Hannah's theft was not directly connected to Jane Doe's rape, the fact that her father had handed her a school district job, and she stole while employed there, spoke to the exchange of favors. Hannah Rhinaman got caught in the net.

"It's not fair that her face is all over CNN," her girlfriend at the time told *Newsweek* in a phone interview as she defended Hannah's innocence and accused lawmakers of trying to pit the family members against each other.

Days later, on October 25, 2013, father and daughter appeared in a spare local courtroom together to plead not guilty, the senior pressing his lips together in a perpetual, consternated frown. While Hannah was arraigned on charges of theft, her father's hearing was postponed. He had requested a public defender days before, but now informed the judge that his new lawyer, who was unable to be present, was associated with a large Beverly Hills law firm. According to CBS Pittsburgh, his fancy new counsel raised eyebrows. It was never revealed who was footing the bill.

As the locals went about their business, visiting pumpkin patches and planning for Halloween, they were distracted, waiting for the next grand jury indictment to drop. In the meantime, under pressure, the Steubenville School District contacted the Ohio Alliance to End Sexual Violence and the Cleveland Rape Crisis Center for help. It had been over a year since the assault. They hoped the organizations could provide some guidance and tools to teachers, coaches, and parents—and they were eager for it to happen quickly.

In an effort to address rape culture at its source and stop an incident like Jane Doe's assault from happening again, the organizations planned to equip coaches and staff with "tools to help their players learn respect, nonviolence, and the laws related to sexual assault," according to Rachel Dissell. But the reception was lukewarm at best, recalled Dan Clark, a former suburban police chief who made the trek more than two hours from Cleveland to run the workshops. The first session was mandatory for staff, held in the school's auditorium, and included the basics on the dynamics of sexual assault and reporting responsibilities. There was little engagement, said Clark, who recalled that no one asked a single question.

"They came, they listened, they left," he said.

The district invited 600 parents and community members to a second, public session, Clark said, recalling row after row of folding chairs and tables to the side, topped with coffee and cookies.

About twenty people showed up.

"It was unbelievably disappointing that there weren't more parents interested in what we had to say," Clark said.

At that session, most of the questions from the adults who did show up were about drinking. Parents figured kids were going to drink anyway, and they wanted to provide "safe" ways for that to happen. The fact that their permissiveness was part of the problem didn't register.

For Clark, a father, grandfather, and former member of law enforcement, it was upsetting that the parents didn't see that they could just tell their teenagers not to drink and hold unsupervised parties. And in the wake of an internationally publicized teen rape case, why weren't more parents interested in learning about violence prevention and their role in the solution?

In his mind, the power dynamic was clear: the teens had all the control.

———

Days before Thanksgiving, on Monday, November 25, the other shoe dropped—again: four more indictments were handed down, landing with a thud. This time, some of the names were recognizable to those following the case closely: Matthew Belardine—the volunteer assistant football coach who had witnessed and allowed Party A, where the victim got drunk to the point of stumbling—was indicted on four counts. He was charged with allowing underage drinking, obstructing official business (for colluding with his sister to keep their false stories straight), falsification for lying to police about what time he arrived at the party (initially he said midnight, then changed his story to ten p.m. during the grand jury investigation), and contributing to the unruliness or delinquency of a child.

This also spoke to the direct ties—echoed by Mike DeWine, the rape crisis leaders, and so many more—between binge-drinking and these types of incidents. According to *Campus Safety Magazine*, approximately 90 percent of rapes perpetrated by an acquaintance of the victim involve alcohol. "The Steubenville High School case...was yet another circumstance of a minor, a high school girl [in this case], incapacitated by alcohol and/or drugs," said women's rights attorney Gloria Allred. "That continues to be a major issue because there is so much alcohol and drug use by minors and young adults and so much gender bias against the victims who are incapacitated. There are a lot of rape myths out there, such as, 'It's her fault, she got drunk. What did she expect would happen?' No woman should have to expect that, if she's under the influence, someone feels as if they have the right to rape her. But...then, of course, a lot of young women blame themselves."

Big Red's assistant wrestling coach and a special education teacher, Seth Fluharty, was indicted for failure to report child abuse or neglect. "On or about August 13, 2012, at Jefferson County, Ohio, Seth Fluharty...to wit a school teacher; school employee; school authority, who was acting in an official or professional capacity and knew, or had reasonable cause to suspect based on facts that would cause a reasonable person in a similar position to suspect, that a child under eighteen years of age had suffered or faced a threat of suffering any physical or mental wound, injury, disability, or condition of a nature that reasonably indicated abuse or neglect of the child, failed to immediately report that knowledge." Fluharty had learned about the rape by word of mouth from his cousin and texted Anthony Craig, "hey, who's the smart one who put the video of that Nodi kid talking about Trent raping that girl on YouTube." Despite being a teacher with a direct line to the students, he appeared to text a joke instead of reporting to law enforcement or the school administration. This was one of several circumstances that called

Steubenville High School's digital protocols around teacher–student relationships and teachers text messaging children on their private phones into question. According to the License Code of Professional Conduct for Ohio Educators, educators must use technology "responsibly" with students and "maintain appropriate boundaries." "Appropriate" is not fleshed out or defined, but what is clear is that the adults in this situation failed to satisfy the requirements of their jobs as mandated reporters.

Steubenville superintendent Michael McVey faced the most serious charges. McVey had come under fire for giving Coach Reno authority over disciplining the football players instead of calling the police or taking the helm himself. He had compounded the issue in January 2013 during a CBS News interview, when, sweating, he insisted over and over again that, "Protocol was followed, sir, protocol was followed," but failed to give any explanation for abdicating control.

Now the repercussions extended beyond public opinion. The superintendent was indicted on felony charges for tampering with evidence, two counts of obstructing justice, and misdemeanor charges for falsification and obstructing official business. He was charged with concealing the timeline and records of the school's investigation—and also their knowledge of a separate but related incident. He allegedly discouraged other district employees from cooperating with the investigation too. Media outlets across the country reported on the story, including the same CBS News team who had interviewed him previously, calling this new development "an unexpected twist."

"While this started out being about the kids, it is also just as much about the parents—about the grown-ups, the adults," said Attorney General Mike DeWine in his statement. "How do you hold the kids accountable if you don't hold the adults accountable? What happened here can—and does sadly—happen anywhere in this nation.

Teenagers and alcohol-fueled parties. Absent adults. Bad decisions. Acts of violence. And cell phones to capture and record all of it. It is up to the adults to intervene. It is up to the adults to set boundaries. It is up to the adults to teach the kids right from wrong." In direct opposition to the parents' apathy at the rape crisis workshop, DeWine was asking adults to take responsibility and set solid examples and rules for their teens. At the same time, DeWine defended the other residents of Steubenville. "This community has been torn apart by the actions and the bad decisions not of the many—but of the few," he added.

The fourth and final person indicted was Lynnette Gorman, a neighboring elementary school principal. The charges against her underlined an insidious pattern of behavior that tolerated violence against girls, a policy of looking the other way. Her indictment related to her failure to report a prior rape of a fourteen-year-old by Steubenville high schoolers that predated Jane Doe's assault. In this case, Gorman also texted Anthony Craig instead of going to authorities. This was the *other* incident that McVey was charged with covering up and that inspired the "rape crew" rumors that Alex had heard.

Like Fluharty, Gorman was officially charged with failure to report child abuse or neglect, but her alleged crime dated back to four months *before* Jane Doe's assault—and the complainant was a different teenage girl. The bystander effect was rampant among the adults too. Had they acted in April, could Jane Doe's assault in August have been prevented?

––––––––––

According to police reports, just days after Jane Doe and her parents reported her assault, on September 3, 2012, another family of a young teenage girl appeared at the Steubenville police station. Their familiar story involved athletes including Trent Mays, Anthony Craig, and

Evan Westlake, a house party, and a teenage girl who was new to the crowd. Over the course of the next months, another investigator, Special Agent Charlie Snyder of BCI, and J. P. Rigaud interviewed many of the parents and teenagers connected to the incident, in which a recent transfer student to Steubenville High School was allegedly raped at a house party for Big Red's baseball team. Though accounts differed, the narrative remained consistent: a group of sophomore girls had gathered for a sleepover at their friend Isabella's house, where Trent Mays, Mark Cole, and some others were also hanging out. April Jane Doe was new to this group. One girl had grabbed a bottle of Malibu rum from her mother's liquor cabinet, and the group was sneaking swigs off it as the boys cajoled them into coming along to a gathering at the home of a senior, Jo-Jo Pierro, and his brother Brian—the baseball coach's sons. (The coach was out of town.) The girls were on strict orders from their parents to stay home. But two, April Jane Doe and her good friend Taylor Young, hopped in the car with Trent Mays and another friend.

The group entered the house through the front doors, walking past the kitchen where a few people were gathered, before heading down to the basement where the majority of the kids were hanging out. They were met with rowdy games of beer pong, a radio blaring, people dancing and talking—a classic suburban adolescent party. Beer was on offer, along with coolers (the kind that might hold bug juice at camp or Gatorade on the football field) of spiked jungle juice that the victim described as "tasting like fruit punch." There was no food around.

"[When] I'm giving talks to college football teams about how they can be active participants against rape culture, what always comes up is binge drinking," said Dave Zirin. "There's no conception of affirmative consent. There is only the aura of what they perceive as consent, which is, 'You're in the path, you're having a drink, you're celebrating, you know why you're here.' So even if that ends in violence, there's an expectation that it will be covered up. They don't refer to it as 'violence,' they call it a 'one-night stand.' And we know this isn't just athletes; it's also 'the nice guy.'"

At this party, the initial group of fifteen or so teenagers eventually swelled to about thirty. (This exact number was repeated by so many sources in police interviews that the stories almost sounded coordinated.) People remember Trent, Anthony, and Evan being among the group, as well as Charlie Keenan, prosecutor Jane Hanlin's son.

April Jane Doe had a drink or two. Later, she remembered feeling so tired that she almost fell asleep, so she headed upstairs to be alone. Soon, a boy from school, whom some say she had a crush on, Matt Petrella, arrived and, according to her, carried her "like a baby" to Brian Pierro's bedroom, where he stripped off her tank top, yoga pants, bra, and underwear, put on a condom, and began having intercourse with her. The girl didn't remember anyone else being in the room, but that was when she lost consciousness. The next thing she recalled was a blinding flash of light, like a camera going off, and an awareness that other people were present. She felt ill, like she was going to be sick, and someone carried her to the closet and instructed her to throw up there. Many of the attendees claimed they didn't think she was that drunk, although most of them did confirm that she vomited in the closet and once more back in the basement bathroom. In this case, one young woman did bring her bread and water to try to help her. Others, like Jake Howarth, for example, told police he remembered how "intoxicated and goofy" she was being. He said he'd heard from other friends that she had a reputation for being "easy" at her old school.

Her friend Taylor noticed she was missing from the basement and went looking for her on the second floor (which was supposed to be off-limits). Eventually, she came to Brian's door and found it locked. She knocked repeatedly, and no one answered until about fifteen minutes later, when someone opened the door to reveal Trent Mays and Anthony Craig standing there, both wearing pants and no shirts. Her friend was on the bed, naked except for a bra with a missing strap. Matt Petrella was also there, according to many eyewitnesses, though Taylor claimed not to be able to recall his presence. Like Farrah did in the August case, Taylor helped April Jane Doe get dressed. Her clothing was strewn everywhere, and she ultimately never found the bra strap or her top. The back panel of her phone was also gone, though the phone was functioning. Eventually, the girls gave up looking for the missing items and headed back downstairs.

By that time, everyone at the party was whispering about how April Jane Doe had had sex with two guys, though she herself seemed unclear about what had happened. Some reported her having admitted to being a willing participant; others said that she couldn't piece together what had happened even in the immediate aftermath.

By midnight, the other girls from the sleepover had snuck out and gotten a ride over to the party too. One of them, whom a mutual friend said had been "text dating" Matt Petrella, was angry at April Jane Doe for "hooking up" with the guy she liked and told her off.

Soon after, Isabella's mother discovered that the girls had snuck out and called her daughter, instructing them to walk to Taylor's house, where she would pick them up before dropping them off at their respective homes, where their parents could dole out punishments. April Jane Doe, who lived farther away, again out of her element and on someone else's turf, stayed over at Isabella's until her mother picked her up the morning after.

Once again there was a trail of Twitter posts about how "that one girls [sic] life might be ruined" and in Nodianos's infamous video about the August rape, he says, "You thought it was bad when that girl got raped at Palooza. This is worse. This is a dead body." "Palooza" was the kids' slang for the party at Coach Anthony Pierro's house.

The next week at school, according to multiple classmates and April Jane Doe herself, rumors swirled about how she'd possibly been "trained" by Matt Petrella, Anthony Craig, and Trent Mays. The victim said she had previously had a crush on Trent Mays in addition to Matt Petrella, but she described him as "mean."

According to the victim and fellow students, other teens openly called April Jane Doe a "slut" and a "whore" as she walked down the halls and taunted, "Choo, choo!" to signify that she'd been trained. Anthony Craig texted her to ask if she was okay, a familiar move, which led her to believe he'd been in the room. He also asked her directly to tell Coach Pierro that he hadn't raped her. Matt Petrella texted to see if she was okay too. She heard rumors that Trent hit her head while she was in the bedroom; she heard that many others were in the room during her attack, including Charlie Keenan, prosecutor Jane Hanlin's son.

Once home from his trip, Pierro, the baseball coach, got wind of the party that had occurred at his house and was angry. With Anthony's request in mind, April Jane Doe approached him in the Steubenville High School hallway to say she was "sorry about everything." He concluded, according to his police interview months later, that she was probably just crying rape because the August Jane Doe had. He said he thought she was a bit "strange" when she apologized. That week, Anthony Craig, Matt Petrella, and one other boy, whom the coach said he couldn't recall, also apologized to him for breaching the second floor of his home when they knew it wasn't allowed.

After she made her complaint to the police, the victim began to experience severe emotional stress and her schoolwork suffered. According to the *Washington Post*, though no national statistical studies exist, anecdotal evidence suggests that sexual assault greatly impacts the victims' academic performance. April Jane Doe had never wanted to come forward, but when Jane Doe's rape had come to light in August, people started talking, and her parents caught wind of the rumors. They had encouraged her to file a report.

Once she went to the police, multiple people accused her of trying to get them in trouble and "ruin their lives." Her family hired Bob Fitzsimmons, the same lawyer as August's Jane Doe, to act as liaison between them and law enforcement. Soon after, Fitzsimmons's office reached out to Special Agent Charlie Snyder to let him know of a possible conflict of interest raised by some of the teens: Taylor Young, the victim's friend, was now dating Matt Petrella and could not be relied upon to give unbiased testimony.

There were anonymous tips about kids who knew or saw what had happened, but none of it was fruitful for police. Ultimately, because her memory was spotty and law enforcement couldn't convince eyewitnesses to testify, there wasn't enough evidence to prosecute. But it was around then that the Steubenville boys got dubbed "the rape crew." April Jane Doe never had her moment in court, but hopefully the impact of August Jane Doe's case made the high school halls a little bit safer for her.

———

Though April Jane Doe's alleged attackers would never be punished for their actions, perhaps some of the adults who failed to help would. Lynnette Gorman, a petite, forty-year-old woman with wavy dark hair and big eyes that made her appear always on alert, was charged with texting Anthony Craig about the April rape. She also apparently talked to multiple parents but never reported the possible assault to authorities of any kind, despite being a member of the school system and a mandatory reporter. Teachers in her orbit were instructed by higher ups not to talk. "We got warned and warned, then warned again," one teacher said. "You don't talk about it. Keep it quiet."

On December 6, 2013, like her indicted cohorts, Gorman was arraigned at the Common Pleas Court of Jefferson County. All of the indicted adults pled not guilty. She drew the first court date, January 7, 2014. Three days later, on December 9, the Steubenville School Board voted to reinstate her as principal of her elementary school, saying that she had a good record and was innocent until proven guilty. She got to return to work.

The town pressed on, as folks like Jerry Barilla and Catholic to the Max owner Mark Nelson tried to pull focus away from the negative publicity and rape investigations and instead to organizing the annual Christmas Parade. Because the parade fell on Pearl Harbor Day this year, they would honor veterans and active military. "In the past, the Steubenville Parade, the Christmas Parade, was the draw because most smaller communities around really didn't have their own parades; they were really fantastic," Barilla reminisced. "But, over the years, other, smaller communities started to have their own parades, so this…dwindled. But last year we were able to get it televised, and we wanted to try to bring it back! It was just glorious! So this year, we have something [like] ninety-four participants!"

The new year arrived without incident, last year's threat of a dox a distant memory. Ma'lik Richmond tiptoed quietly out of juvenile detention and back into school, but not extracurricular activities like sports, as those were considered a privilege. Walter Madison released a public statement on his behalf that did not acknowledge Jane Doe.

Meanwhile, the town and lawyers readied for Lynnette Gorman's day in court. Nine potential witnesses were lined up to testify in a trial that was expected to last just one day. But the proceedings never began. At the last minute, her attorney struck a deal with prosecutors. "Lynnette Gorman believes she committed no crime," said a statement released by both parties. "She also believes that if she had the ability to go back to April 2012, she would have acted differently.

School teachers and administrators should always err on the side of caution when the interests of children are at stake."

By January 9, 2014, the national media reported the story: the misdemeanor charge of negligence would be dropped by June 1 if Gorman agreed to complete forty hours of community service at a rape crisis or victim assistance center and also speak to educators about the importance of reporting child abuse at the Ohio Alliance to End Sexual Violence conference in April—Sexual Assault Awareness Month. Attorney General DeWine released a statement defending the decision, saying that Gorman otherwise would have gotten minimal jail time with "no ability to move forward. This is about the long-term healing of the community." No one acknowledged the potential problem of forcing inexperienced people, who had publicly disrespected victims' rights, to work with survivors of sexual assault, a sensitive undertaking. Neither victims nor survivors would benefit from this solution. It put the violators in a kind of public stockade, forcing them to live out their penalty with eyes on them. It put victims in the position of seeking help and healing from uneducated, potentially unsympathetic laypeople who were only there under court mandate.

The community was far from healed. Alex Goddard hadn't covered the case in a while, but felt under attack by a group of Steubenville locals she dubbed "The Shrew Crew," and posted about the complicity of adults. She felt they set poor examples by attacking each other online and continuing to victim-blame Jane Doe, even as their friends and colleagues were being indicted. "I have read tweets disputing rape vs. digital penetration where the author claims they do not believe Jane Doe was raped based on their very uneducated assumption—or statements such as, 'I would not let my hypothetical daughter or my actual sons be around the victim for even a moment in time,'" Goddard marveled. "THIS is exactly the attitude that perpetuates rape culture. With adults making these types of statements, in my very humble opinion, there is a reason those who participated in or were witness, cyber or otherwise, to a rape behaved the way they did. Learned behavior." The case was important, she insisted, because it gave the world "a bird's eye view of rape culture in action" and "revealed the insensitivity of a group of entitled kids who believed they were immune from accountability—an idea that the adults online reinforce regularly." Fired up, she continued, "It is also an important case because it empowered so many survivors of sexual violence who may never have been able to let the unspeakable pass their lips to do so and [showed] that there were people out there who were willing to stand up and do the right thing…regardless of the personal cost."

On February 26, 2014, Hannah Rhinaman pled guilty to theft charges. She was granted "intervention," instead of conviction, for the drug dependency that the court found had contributed to her impetus to steal, and had two years to complete a treatment plan or face a traditional sentence.

On April 11, wrestling coach Seth Fluharty was also granted a deal. In exchange for the charges being dismissed, he was required to perform twenty hours of community service at the A.L.I.V.E. shelter or another approved domestic violence organization in the Steubenville area, attend a sexual assault prevention training session with OAESV (the same group who had led the largely unattended workshops at the high school) and, having learned how, facilitate their "Stand Up!" program with high school and middle school students. Again, an educator who texted Anthony Craig instead of supporting Jane Doe was put in a position to lead the conversation about sexual assault prevention.

"This resolution acknowledges how very important it is to report child abuse and neglect," said Attorney General DeWine. "Mr.

Fluharty will be part of the work that is being done in Steubenville to educate students and school officials about the seriousness of sexual assault and the need to report these incidents." While, in the abstract, the resolution had a tidy, full-circle feel, it didn't practically consider the potential downside of forcing someone who was not a willing advocate to speak on a topic about which he had only nominal information.

Murmurs began about the lack of substantial punishments for the indicted administrators and teachers. Community service didn't seem like enough.

Next up, on April 22, Matthew Belardine's sentencing came down—this time as a no contest plea agreement. He sat in the courtroom, his dark hair close-cropped above a blank face and a thick neck, as the consequences crystalized before his eyes: for allowing underage drinking and lying to authorities, he was given ten days in jail, plus a year of probation, forty hours of community service, and a $1,000 fine. It was more punishment than the others had received, likely because he had lied to police, but still a slap on the wrist.

The cases involving School Superintendent McVey and the Steubenville High School IT director, William Rhinaman, continued to drag on.

Alex was not impressed by the outcomes. In June 2014, following a story about recent illegal gambling raids in Steubenville and what that suggested about the seedy culture in general, she posted about the latest in Superintendent McVey's ongoing proceedings. In her update, she expressed outrage and disbelief about the behavior of school officials who were meant to be advocates for children. "There was a reason that locals were worried about a cover-up from the beginning," she explained, referencing the charges against McVey that suggested he had destroyed evidence.

Alex was not alone in her concern, as Rachel Dissell had received a tip with a similar message back in August 2012. "Because that's just how it is in Steubenville. Cronyism, nepotism…It has been that way for a very long time…Lots of hate for 'outsiders,' but honestly without the outrage of outsiders, would we even know about Steubenville? This is a systemic problem that goes far deeper than one man's desire to protect an institution or a football program. It goes way deeper than Mike McVey, and nothing is going to change in Steubenville until the trash is taken out and a clean-up is done from the top down."

Attorney General Mike DeWine, in the midst of an election year, remained invested in the idea of Steubenville having endured enough. At least, that was his refrain. When the indictments came down, after lamenting the role of devices and technology in making people feel less accountable to one another, he said, "We must treat rape and sexual assault as the serious crime of violence that it is. And when it is investigated, everyone has an obligation to help find the truth—not hide the truth, not tamper with the truth, not obstruct the truth, and not destroy the truth." But, he added, "It's time to let Steubenville move on."

But what did that even mean?

## CHAPTER 11

# THE PRODIGAL SON

TWO YEARS TO THE day of the rape, Ma'lik Richmond rejoined Big Red football's roster.

On Tuesday, August 12, 2014, the players suited up for a preseason scrimmage against Cambridge, a local rival. The Ohio High School Athletic Association left the question of Richmond's eligibility up to the school, who in turn left the decision up to Coach Reno Saccoccia—again.

In a rare NBC News interview with local affiliate WTOV-9, Reno—seated in front of a blackboard and an American flag, in a black polo with "Big Red" embroidered in white block letters over his heart—thanked the interviewer for giving him a chance to explain his decision to let Ma'lik back on the team. "It was a horrible crime," he repeated twice. "Everything that the judicial system of Ohio asked him to do, he completed. Everything that the school system asked him to do upon his release, he completed, both academically and socially. He was back in school since January and was suspended from all extracurricular activities for the remainder of the year…I feel he's earned a second chance. We don't deal in death sentences for juvenile activity. I've thought about it hard and I'm going with that decision." For Coach Reno, exclusion from football was tantamount to capital punishment. In many ways, Reno's assertion represented the early echoes of defiance against "cancel culture" and the idea that a "mistake" should not render someone a lifetime pariah.

In a restorative justice framework, which some states use for youth offenders, there is an idea that the offender must take responsibility and then work carefully toward reform with the victim's wishes in mind. The offender and the victim would determine together, with members of the community who were involved, like teachers and parents, when and if the offender was welcomed back and in what capacity. Should other people have been included in the decision to put Ma'lik back on the team to make it feel more victim-centered and holistic?

Still, this was a more media-savvy version of Coach Reno, in stark contrast to the hothead met by journalists covering the case, and even deputies collecting evidence, early on. Instead of fighting the press, he was attempting to head them off at the pass, killing them with kindness and hitting talking points with a calm, earnest demeanor. He didn't apologize for the choice he'd made, but he didn't come across as angry either. Steubenville might have been unwilling to explore the root causes and their own complicity in what happened to Jane Doe, but they had learned something about anticipating pushback against controversial decisions.

Afterward, most major media outlets ran articles about Ma'lik Richmond's return with headlines like, "Steubenville Rapist Back on School Football Team." However, *Slate* ran a story titled, "It's Time to Stop Shaming the Steubenville Rapists" in which writer Amanda Hess argued, "What is he supposed to do? Drop out of school and live under a bridge for the rest of his life?" In her opinion piece, she argued the importance of re-entry for rehabilitation, arguing, based on another article that ran on *Slate* the same day entitled, "Sex Offender

Laws Have Gone Too Far," that recidivism rates are "much lower than commonly believed." Her assertions sparked an important debate: what is rehabilitation and when is it relevant?

Aya Gruber, an advocate for restorative justice, has argued that prison itself isn't the answer, one school of thought: "Part of what makes the criminal legal system such a bad model is that we want the offender to learn something and improve as a person, but the entire way the sex offense system is set up is designed to make that not happen." How, she asked, can offenders re-enter society with a real chance to be re-educated if they're viewed as a group of homogeneous monsters instead of human beings on a spectrum?

To tackle this issue, Gruber felt we must unravel certain myths about rape, for instance, the idea that women are in constant danger of being raped, which dates back to the turn of the century. "The idea of being raped at any moment was in large part a creation of publications and warnings from male-dominated groups to keep women in cities afraid of the public sphere," she said. "In fact, the biggest risk of sexual violence is with friends and family. It's interesting how the imagination of rape is disconnected from the realities, which are very much structural: football, homosocial male bonding, hyper-masculine atmospheres, young kids, alcohol-soaked parties." We need to get clear on what actually spurs rape.

In her book *We Do This 'Til We Free Us: Abolitionist Organizing and Transforming Justice*, Mariame Kaba wrote, "Of course, a system that never addresses the why behind a harm never actually contains the harm itself. Cages confine people, not the conditions that facilitated their harms or the mentalities that perpetuate violence." In other words, all the prison terms in the world are useless if we never investigate the underlying causes of the problem and try to change them. Cycles continue.

"If you're concerned with racialized mass incarceration and

our baseline idea that telling people that the measure of their self-worth and healing and justice is jailing another person, in jails that are themselves places of rape and sexual violence, you have to seek restorative methods," Gruber said. "It makes you wonder: is there another way to try to change culture where conviction isn't the measure of progress?"

Gruber's solution includes reframing how young people are taught to approach sexuality. "It's so hard, because we're trying to shift how people think about sex. Especially young people and boys, [about] sexual conquests and how they bond as men, the massive insecurities and groupthink, it's so learned and social and cultural. I don't have any illusions that we can stop these towns from teaching abstinence, or [that we can immediately] get kids comfortable with sexuality so they don't have to drink themselves to oblivion to be comfortable in their bodies. But when the detective told Mark [Cole] to 'Man up'—if that's how cops talk, we're in trouble. We need to change our mindset about sexual violence from this [notion of] the individual monster." In other words, we need to shift the patriarchal systems so inherent to our culture and start thinking about the larger issues versus the individual crimes and assailants. What does it mean to "act like a man"?

In Gruber's model, Ma'lik may have rightly rejoined the team, his community, but not everyone was convinced. After all, allowing someone back into school and society doesn't necessarily extend to rejoining the lauded football team and being celebrated in a town that considers their players role models. Was football a right or a reward? Was it constructive to put Ma'lik back into an athletic program that didn't address gender-based violence among players, even after a highly publicized rape? Or was it just good for the team? With juveniles, these decisions must be made on a case-by-case basis, taking many factors into consideration including, for example, if someone has shown remorse and a willingness to take responsibility for their actions, or if he has reoffended. Some saw Ma'lik's return to the field as proof that nothing had changed, despite what the town had experienced. In an email interview with BuzzFeed, Alex argued, "I wanted to be shocked, but I think we all knew it was bound to happen. Steubenville City Schools hasn't really done a lot in the past two years to prove to the world that they don't tolerate rape culture and allowing a Tier II registered sex offender on the team pretty much solidifies the assumption that they are concerned about wins rather than the safety of young girls or the destruction of rape culture in their area."

The divisive decision angered more than the usual suspects. When people search #Steubenville on Twitter, they discover two worlds—a loud community of football fans and a huge Catholic revival culture. When Ma'lik Richmond was allowed back on the Big Red team, the religious contingent was not pleased, and they didn't sit by quietly.

Mark Nelson, owner of Catholic to the Max, was sometimes called the unofficial "conscience of Steubenville" at that time. This father of ten and his wife spent their days stocking and shipping items from their warehouse, marked with a giant billboard. They sold branded tote bags, life-size cutouts of Pope John Paul II, anti-abortion t-shirts, anti-IVF paraphernalia, and John Kerry flip-flops as a nod to the candidate's stance on choice as a lapsed Catholic and "flip-flopper."

The Nelsons saw Coach Reno's decision as too permissive given the crimes perpetrated and thought it sent a negative message to the world about the town. Concerned, Mark Nelson wrote a letter to the city council saying, "School is a right; football is not." He argued that they were dropping Ma'lik back into the same atmosphere that bred this behavior in the first place. He said Steubenville would look terrible; he said the decision made it seem like the town prioritized football over their children. He and his cohorts staged a protest.

The morality of the town was complicated at best with Nelson at the helm. While I appreciated his empathy for Jane Doe, his political beliefs about women's roles and reproductive choice were at direct odds with my own. In September 1990, Mark Nelson had been sentenced to four to twelve months in Allegheny County Jail for participating in anti-choice "operation rescue" actions by blocking access to abortion clinics in 1989. Going limp upon being sentenced, Nelson was taken to the mental health unit, where he refused a psychiatric evaluation. After four months, he was up for parole, but the judge decided he should remain.

Years later, when I met him, I had trouble reconciling his actions and beliefs with his feelings about Steubenville in the wake of Jane Doe's rape. Unlike many in town, he had respect for Jane Doe's bodily autonomy when it came to her right to be safe from violence. However, our conversations about why this happened to her always veered to a sexualized culture and alcohol, not patriarchal norms of male violence against women. He respected her right to live free from harm and was clear that a football program shouldn't protect perpetrators. But how did these views align with stripping away the rights of women and girls to make their own reproductive choices? In this ultraconservative sphere, the solution was never sexual education (unless it was religious). Instead, it was highly supervised children, separate-sphere ideology, and procreation-forward marriages. There was no acknowledgment of homosexuality, the gender spectrum, or even the widely documented and condemned sexual abuses within the Catholic church.

Mark Nelson's two teenage daughters had their own take on the situation. When I met them, and Mark encouraged them to sit down for a filmed interview in a classroom adjacent to the Catholic to the Max warehouse, they were open and forthright. They talked about girls with parent-friendly Instagrams, wholesome and basic, and then their secondary "slut accounts." With a harsh judgment unfortunately not atypical among girls, they expressed a sense that Jane Doe played her own role in what happened. "She put herself in that situation by deciding to go to that party…at a certain point, she needs to take some responsibility for what happened to her," one commented. They seemed to be parroting the surrounding culture's view on girls' behavior. Perhaps they felt that if Jane Doe's rape was the result of her own poor behavior, they could consider themselves, as girls who followed the rules set out by the patriarchy, protected.

Part of what contributes to rape culture is the oppression of women's rights, inflicted not just by men but by other women. This was a big contributing factor to the rape culture in Steubenville, almost as much as the football-or-death mentality. The moral center of this town was one that cast biblical shame and judgment. If you didn't have control over choices for your own body—whether or not to have a baby, for example—why should you be able to choose who touches it in another scenario? If men could tell you that you didn't know what was best for yourself, why should anyone believe you when you asserted your own opinions? And if you were going to hell if you made a mistake like having premarital sex or "hooking up," then you'd have nowhere to turn if you were raped.

"What we teach women in America—from cradle to grave—is that they, and by extension, their bodies, are dispensable," said feminist writer and TEDxWomen speaker Aditi Khorana. "We teach women to mistrust, judge, and even hate their own bodies. We teach women to mistrust, judge, and even hate one another. Women endure physical, emotional, and sexual violence at the hands of men, as well as the state, but this can only happen when and because we've been simmering in the stew of a misogynistic culture our whole lives. Dismantling the culture is a critical piece of preventing rape and sexual assault." But in order to dismantle what isn't working, a community has to be willing to admit to its failings.

In the end, football won out over religion. Mark Nelson did not get his way. I was in Steubenville on the day of Ma'lik's first scrimmage. Big Red football fans did not seem overly concerned about his return—or Trent Mays, still in juvenile hall. Those who weren't tailgating by the stadium pregamed at Scaffidi's, the Italian restaurant owned by Anthony Craig's family, filling up on lasagna and calzones. Eventually, the fans and I filed into Death Valley to find our seats.

As we waited for kickoff, the crowd roared like one giant beast. Coach paced the sidelines—the stadium's kingpin. I was surprised to see a young Franciscan Catholic priest in full robes mingling with the coaching staff and players on the field, the only non–team member allowed on sanctified ground. The first bars of "The Star-Spangled Banner" began to play, and everyone rose. As the American flag flapped in the wind, in the distance plumes rose from the smokestacks, a fantasy of Main Street Americana. But the steel mills were closed; and a convicted rapist was playing on the field. This American dream seemed like something that died long ago.

The players rushed in under a large banner to thunderous hoots and cheers.

The scrimmage began, boys pouring onto the field in their red jerseys. The fans were immediately sucked in. Mothers, with their teenage daughters slouching beside them, shouted unabashed cheers of "Go, Ma'lik!"

Long before this game and the moment Ma'lik Richmond strutted back onto the field, in an interview with me, Rachel Dissell had posed perhaps the most salient question of all. It kept haunting me: "Is this football town putting its daughters at risk by protecting its sons?"

If the town wouldn't stand behind one victim, wouldn't stop normalizing the objectification of underage girls, what made them believe that their own daughters, and even sons, wouldn't be next? To weed out rape culture, the town had to protect every victim, not pick and choose at their convenience. Otherwise, they put their own children and loved ones at risk, even if they believed they were protecting them.

In some ways, Coach Reno, and the role he had the potential to play for these boys, seemed at the root of the answer. He represented the old guard, the epicenter of the boys' club, the town's patriarch. He was the perfect example of someone who seemed to perpetuate this problem without realizing his apparent complicity. Though he might have initially been portrayed by the press as a villain, by this point, when I actually knew him, he had been humbled enough to approach the situation more carefully.

When I approached Coach for the first time on the football field, as he walked past us, he gave my director of photography a playful—or was it a warning?—soft punch in the arm. Still, with teenage boys huddling in and around his office area, he seemed more like a salt-of-the-earth grandfather, there to offer sage advice and a pat on the back, than a bad guy. He was likable and charismatic, telling me stories about his love of Brooklyn and Little Italy, about how he once accidentally got stuck on the subway during the Mermaid Parade, about taking his wife to see *Beautiful: The Carole King Musical* on Broadway. At his house was a figurine that proclaimed, "Behind every big man is an even better woman!" He joked about he and his wife having a "mixed marriage"—he was Italian, she was Irish Catholic. His wife was moved to tears talking about how dedicated he was to his students, how he cared so much that he took them in and bought the girls prom dresses.

As I stood over him, as he sat on a workout bench during one of our conversations, he seemed down.

"People have made me seem like a monster. As if I don't have granddaughters, as if I don't care about what happened to that little girl."

He didn't understand why kids did everything on their phones and felt he did his best to keep them out of trouble. He seemed genuinely confused about the changing landscape of youth culture, sex, social media, and the role of someone in his position, and it was hard not to feel empathy for him. While he represented an older patriarchal generation, he was unsure of how to adapt. As a football coach, and not a social worker, he wasn't trained to support the needs of modern teenagers navigating a sexually charged culture.

But when, much later, I watched the tapes of the police interviews from before the trial, I was shocked to see a very different man before being humbled. Those videos and transcripts told another story, and it was clear why many in the community had expected him to be indicted along with the others.

*"I said, 'Did you rape her?' They said, 'No.' I said, 'Did you fuck her?' They said, 'No.'"* he'd told Rigaud. *"Can't they use another word from, from 'rape'?"*

Coach Reno was the embodiment of the way rape culture hides. It was about entrenched patterns of behavior in which people might not even realize they were complicit. It was about the male-dominated culture, the patriarchy, the way girls were excluded except as cheerleaders in tight, skimpy outfits. It was about a desire to keep things the same, despite the fact that not everyone was getting their share. Coach was in a position to effect positive change in a deeper sense, beyond the football field, but he wasn't equipped for that role, and maybe out of willful ignorance didn't understand that he would have to adapt to a new way of seeing.

"Most players really respect their coaches," said Coach V, founder of Open Door Abuse Awareness & Prevention. "They're there to carry out whatever his plan is and they've committed to that. So if a coach is the person who is promoting...respect toward women and girls, their players are gonna fall right in line. More than likely, those guys are going to look to live up to that standard because that's the norm on the team now. Most young men on the team are trying to do just that—fall in line with what the play is, if you will." Coach Reno promoted values that many in his position stress—loyalty, commitment, hard work. But at the end of the day, the emphasis was, and often is, on what those terms meant within a brotherhood, not how they impacted women in the community.

Ultimately, in order to model better behavior, Coach Reno and others like him would have to understand that respect can't develop in a vacuum. It's not about opening car doors and being chivalrous; it's about creating an environment in which women and girls are viewed as and treated as actual equals, with as much to offer as the men and boys. It's about an understanding that women are not just mothers or sexual objects. I experienced this lens firsthand while filming in town. Men we met in Steubenville seemed uncomfortable or unfamiliar with the idea of my role as director or boss to my crew, made up of men. Some even asked if they were my "boys," casting me in the role of their mother, though many of us were the same age!

"Athletics in its best form builds teamwork, accountability, and community responsibility," said Dave Zirin. "It's thrilling and fun, but humbling because you're subordinating yourself to a higher purpose, which could combat rape culture. But far too often sports is left to its own devices, is part of [rape culture] instead."

———

That November 2014, *Salon* ran an article with the headline, "Steubenville hasn't changed at all: 'You trying to write about that whole rape thing?'" The writer Emma Goldberg, who traveled to the town to get a sense of its status, described students at Steubenville High School and their relatives laughing out loud at the thought of change. "If anything, things have gotten worse," one woman told the journalist. "These guys still do the same disgusting things." A student who was dating a boy involved in Jane Doe's case back in 2012 agreed that the incident had "no effect at all" on "attitudes towards sex and consent." Goldberg added, "…the community's religious conservatism makes it difficult for adults to engage the youth in conversations on sex and other sensitive subjects." And yet the local movie theater that fall and winter was hawking a stew of confusion with the hyper-masculine *American Sniper* and the BDSM-infused *50 Shades of Grey*. What was and wasn't appropriate? The conservatism, picked and chosen, was feeding into this culture of nondisclosure and shame.

It was unseasonably warm at the Christmas parade in 2014. Everyone remarked on the beautiful weather, not acknowledging what I saw as the likely effects of climate change. Coach and the current players shook hands and tossed candy canes into waiting palms.

In December, assistant coach Matthew Belardine was arrested again for disorderly conduct. In Scottsdale, Arizona, he instigated a drunken fight in front of a bar, shouting obscenities at people protesting the killing of Michael Brown by police in Ferguson, Missouri, three months before. Back in Ohio, he was charged and ultimately pled guilty to four counts of violating probation for leaving the state without permission, going to a bar, drinking alcohol, and for the disorderly conduct itself.

Alex Goddard, as usual, kept herself informed about what had happened. On Prinnified, she reposted some tweets by a woman whom Belardine had allegedly attacked during the incident, who said that he not only punched her, but had also told her that where he was from, "we rape whores like you." Commenters on WTOV-9's Facebook page took umbrage not only with Belardine himself, but also with Mike DeWine for letting the indicted adults off the hook with a "slap on the wrist." If anything, the former assistant coach seemed angrier for the experience with Jane Doe's case, not more evolved.

On December 17, a week before Christmas, Belardine sat in an orange jumpsuit facing the judge again. "By no means do I take this lightly," he said. "I am ashamed and I am embarrassed, but one thing that I am not is a criminal."

"The bottom line is you don't get it," the judge responded. She sentenced him to sixty days in jail, plus six more months of probation, regular drug and alcohol testing, and possible rehab, to be determined.

On January 8, 2015, Trent Mays was released from juvenile detention and enrolled in a different local high school. He would not play for Big Red again. The lawyer for Jane Doe's family, Bob Fitzsimmons, released a statement saying, "We hope the guilty parties hold a higher standard of morals and values as their rehabilitation continues. We also hope they realize the magnitude of lifelong pain that they have caused the victim, and pray that the memory of their crime lives in their souls as a constant reminder to treat women with dignity and respect."

Trent's family also released a statement: "The Mays family is elated to be reunited with their son after this trying ordeal. Trenton has excelled during his rehabilitative process, and has earned the right to be released. He is an extremely promising young man, eager to prove himself on behalf of his family and his community. The family would appreciate their privacy during this time together, which they have so longed for." There was no mention of Jane Doe.

Back in town, Trent kept a low profile. At one point, I saw him in the Steubenville High School gym, attending a basketball game. He was bigger and thicker by then; the air seemed charged around him. A registered sex offender mingling with his former peers.

Again, the WTOV-9 article about Trent's release incited comments, some of which blamed Jane Doe: "She's been around the block more than 5 times…was it rape?" Another woman blamed Alex for the media attention.

"THIS is what is wrong with the lunatic fringe of Steubenville," Alex wrote on her blog. "They still don't get it and the good people of Steubenville are tired of their bullshit."

On Monday, January 12, 2015, in another Jefferson County courtroom, jury selection in the trial against former school superintendent Mike McVey was finally scheduled to begin. Subpoenas had been issued for many of the townspeople, including Coach Reno, Jerry Barilla, Ma'lik's guardian Greg Agresta, Anthony Craig, the baseball coach Anthony Pierro, William Rhinaman, and more. But, before the case could begin, all charges were dropped in exchange for his official resignation. McVey was barred from contact with any victims or defendants in the case, as well as school administration.

"I think a lot of people are just glad to see this case finally put to rest," wrote Alex in a measured response, though she also said she was confused about the nature of the punishment. "Sure, there are questions, but we are not the judicial system and they did what they saw fit to do. The good part of all of this is: this case has spawned an international discussion about rape culture and bystander intervention that has continued to grow over the past two years. That, in itself, is more important than the outcome of judicial proceedings against some of the players in this case."

McVey's lawyer made a statement claiming that the state was unable to prove his client's guilt. Attorney General Mike DeWine put out a press release:

"I am satisfied that he has been held accountable for his actions with this agreement and consider this a just result," it read. Though McVey had been on paid leave for over a year, in a WTOV-9 interview DeWine said, "Losing a job…has economic consequences. It also sends a very strong signal. So we felt it was a just resolution." Only seven months later, in August 2015, McVey was hired as principal of an elementary school just an hour from Steubenville in Hannibal, Ohio. When contacted by journalists, the school board there refused to comment. Again, the cards seemed to be shuffled around instead of exchanged for a new hand. The adults involved in these two crimes continued to work in positions of leadership around youth.

On Friday, February 27, 2015, the final case against the indicted adults was resolved. William Rhinaman, the IT director accused of wiping items from Mike McVey's computer and hard drive, pled guilty to obstructing official business and was sentenced to ninety days in jail, eighty of which were suspended in exchange for one year of community control (a version of house arrest), forty hours of community service, and responsibility for court fees.

The cases were all settled. The repercussions, or lack thereof, had been doled out.

Trent Mays had his eye on college, and with Ma'lik back on the team, Steubenville made the state semifinals.

In what would be her last post on the topic of Jane Doe's case for the next three years, Alex seemed depleted. "What has changed?" she wrote. "Not really anything."

# CHAPTER 12

# THE REVERBERATIONS

**W**E'RE THE BENCHMARK NOW of all of this," a frustrated Jerry Barilla said of the town's association with rape in the aftermath. "Anything that happens anywhere, they refer back to Steubenville."

On this, he and Alex Goddard agreed.

"Google Steubenville, you're not gonna get 'Dean Martin' anymore," she quipped.

———

After Trent Mays and Ma'lik Richmond were released from juvenile detention and the indictment cases were wrapped up without fanfare, the people of Steubenville again set their sights on moving past what had happened. For some, that might have meant taking a hard look at the culture of the place; for most, it meant trying to forget—even if the rest of the country wouldn't. The owner of Steubenville's quaint and stately Bayberry Inn, Scott Dressel, who had visions of transforming the town into a charming bedroom community, probably spoke for many when he said, "Everybody who lives here would like to see this story stop being in the media, so we can get past it and heal and move on." He turned his attention to rehabbing the Grand Theater.

Mark Nelson had mentioned honoring victims and their families with a quilt or a ceremony in town to break the silence and spark healing, but no ritual materialized. He mused about opening a coffee shop downtown that also sold popcorn, to provide a wholesome hangout for teens.

The case continued to have an impact. Outside the confines of the town itself, people at neighboring educational institutions seized the teachable moment. In March 2015, a Carnegie Mellon graduate directing student and Fulbright Scholar, Eleanor Bishop, staged her play *Steubenville*, which responded to "rape culture in the United States" through the blending of interviews with female students at CMU, Jane Doe's story, and an adaptation of *Sleeping Beauty*. The theater departments at the Big Ten universities commissioned another play, *Good Kids* by Naomi Iizuka, based loosely on the events of Jane Doe's 2012 assault. In October 2015, the play ran at Ohio State University. Each performance finished with a discussion led by the Sexual Assault Response Network of Central Ohio. Detective J. P. Rigaud was invited to attend. "To even be in the play you had to go through their victim advocacy training," he recalled. "That play was powerful and the auditorium was set up as bleachers. When it ended, they opened the discussion and there was a meeting that we stayed for. It was powerful to witness."

Later, in 2016, Rigaud, who had taken a job with BCI, was also invited to speak to a criminal justice class at Youngstown State, where the professor showed him that the case was profiled in their textbook, *Violence: The Enduring Problem*. Alex Goddard was cited in several graduate theses.

And, while the country's gaze regularly wandered back to Steubenville, the focus was also on other high-profile sexual assault stories coming up in the news. In January 2015, a nineteen-year-old white Stanford swimmer from Ohio, Brock Turner, was arrested for assaulting an unconscious young woman behind a dumpster. In this case, bystanders observed the assault and intervened, stopping something even worse from happening. The case resulted in a widely criticized sentence of only six months, which became three. Initially, Brock Turner, an elite swimmer, was pictured in the papers in a jacket and tie instead of the standard mugshot. After people protested, the press went from referring to him as "the Stanford swimmer" to "the alleged rapist," and the photo was replaced. Increased scrutiny on the case led to the judge being recalled. It also led to stricter prison terms in California for raping unconscious victims and the inclusion of digital penetration in the state's definition of rape—issues that came up again and again during the Steubenville trial as well. Turner's case became even more of a lightning rod when his father wrote an open letter that journalists for outlets like *Huffington Post* said "epitomizes rape culture." The letter "referenced the 'steep price' his son was paying for '20 minutes of action.'" The word "action" was a trigger. Again, the country was reminded of the power of language to reveal the truth about ingrained attitudes and the failure of male role models to take entitlement and violence out of the definition of masculinity. These are the words of Brock Turner's role model. From then on, the Steubenville and Turner cases were often discussed in tandem.

People, especially student activists on campuses across the country, were outraged by Turner's lenient sentence and said so openly, rumblings of a movement to come. Relatively new organizations like End Rape on Campus and Know Your IX (in reference to Title IX, a law that prohibits gender-based discrimination) were forcing the Department of Education and Department of Justice to pay attention. Brock Turner's victim—known as "Emily Doe" and then as Chanel Miller when she released her memoir, *Know My Name*—gave a victim statement at the time of the trial, which went viral. It began, "You don't know me, but you've been inside me, and that's why we're here today."

In March 2015, Vice President Joe Biden and Maryland senator

Barbara Mikulski announced $41 million in new funding to accelerate testing of hundreds of thousands of backlogged sexual assault kits, the story that Dissell had been working to break locally in Cleveland years before. Biden and President Barack Obama's "It's on Us" campaign against campus sexual assault was picking up steam with 300 schools coming on board, PSAs garnering more than 10 million views, and celebrity participants like Zoe Saldana and John Cho. The campaign raised awareness about sexual violence prevention and strongly highlighted bystander intervention.

In April 2015, Jon Krakauer's bestseller *Missoula: Rape and the Justice System in a College Town* was published, shining a light on systematic sexual assault at the University of Montana in a town that some dubbed the "rape capital." A movement was beginning to take shape as frustration with the same old outcomes mounted.

In July, after court records from a 2005 civil suit were unsealed and the media released them, allegations against beloved actor and comedian Bill Cosby hit the front page, shattering his idealized paternal image. By November, one criminal case was brought against him, as well as at least eight civil cases. Gloria Allred, who had appeared on CNN to discuss the Steubenville case two years before, represented thirty-three of the alleged victims. Sexual assault was at the forefront of a national conversation. The country was more educated on these issues than ever before. The internet was fueling a bigger, more inclusive surge of activism organized around hashtags, not just for internet-savvy hackers. Steubenville had demonstrated the power of social media to incriminate, but also to communicate and heal. Now that power was in everyone's hands. The tools were democratic and accessible, and their use had skyrocketed.

Bill Cosby's case was just one of many that inspired Allred to work to get statutes of limitations changed for sexual assault cases. This was a huge step in bringing justice as more women began to come forward thanks to increased public conversations since Steubenville. "[Even if] the statute of limitations, the arbitrary time period set by law, has passed, it's never too late to speak out in the court of public opinion," Allred said, referencing the fact that, for many of the women in the Bill Cosby case, it was too late to press charges. "Many victims live in fear. They decide they want to do something and find out it's too late. I've worked…in California, Colorado, Nevada, to change the statute of limitations both in civil lawsuits and criminal cases, so that more victims would have an opportunity to seek justice. It's a really important effort."

———

As Jerry Barilla noted, the Steubenville High School rape case was a flash point in a growing conversation about rape culture in America, especially in high schools and colleges. It had become a symbol for rape culture festering in small-town America, and the problematic hyper-emphasis on high school sports.

"An eighteen-thousand-person town and a ten-thousand-seat stadium, for fourteen- to eighteen-year-olds, is such a weight on their shoulders," said Dave Zirin. "It creates a culture where young boys are exalted and put on a pedestal and, in a healthy society, they wouldn't be. Same for college athletes, treated like half gods, half chattel. They've historically had no collective bargaining rights, no contracts renewed once a year, no long-term healthcare. And, really, the only form of payment is idolatry. I would argue that, culturally and psychologically, it opens the door to seeing women as the spoils of what they do. It's the gutter economy of college athletics. It's naïve to think that it wouldn't have a ripple effect at the high school level, as well. The assumption of protection…another word for that is entitlement."

In June 2021, an antitrust Supreme Court ruling against the NCAA changed these rules, creating avenues for college athletes to earn from their name and personal brand while students at university. This posed a new set of challenges, however, as well as possible solutions. Would athletes feel even more untouchable, or would having something to lose curb their behavior? Would survivors who pressed charges be seen as "gold diggers" now, as they often were in professional sports, or would there be a concrete recourse in the form of fair financial settlements for the victims of college athletes?

In 2015, Tyrone White, joined by Ohio State linebacker Jerome Baker, visited Steubenville to try to recruit Trent and Ma'lik to speak out against rape culture and violence against women in football. Though White thought that supporting this cause could also help to improve Ma'lik's image, a win-win, he met with resistance from the player's guardians, Jennifer and Greg Agresta. "She's a schoolteacher and he worked at a…bank, so, the assumption is that you have two very well-educated parents," said White, recalling the conversation. "Her husband said this, which was quite striking: 'Well, you know, in West Virginia and in Pennsylvania, it's not considered sexual assault to digitally penetrate someone.' In other words, he was still minimizing the actions of the young men involved. And so, there you have adults reinforcing these ideas and these [boys] continue to live a life where, if they don't physically victimize women, they do it mentally through their mindset." Just like Brock Turner's father, Greg Agresta seemed to defend Ma'lik by downplaying the invasiveness of the act and underlining the negative repercussions it had on Ma'lik instead of Jane Doe.

Ma'lik did come to Cleveland to attend one of Coach Ty's events, but he decided against doing more, and the Agrestas didn't appear to encourage him, arguing that he was too shy to speak in public. Trent also declined. "Neither one of them wanted to step up and say, 'Hey, you know, we were wrong. Hey, this is what young men our age group should be thinking about doing. And when we are confronted with inappropriate sexualized jokes or conduct, we're going to be those guys who stand up and stand tall to stop these things,'" said White. "They were only concerned about whether they were going to be able to continue to play college ball. All they were concerned about was trying to get on with their lives as though this had never happened; no sense of…redemption and how could they make this right."

Ma'lik, who had been a first-team All-Ohio selection as a high school senior, started school at Potomac State College of West Virginia University. And, in fall 2015, Ohio's Hocking College (with a 100 percent acceptance rate) welcomed Trent Mays as a freshman and quarterback, hoping to boost enrollment by building a successful football program. According to investigative journalist Kenny Jacoby, who covered sexual assault, education, and sports for *USA Today*, this is not an unusual path for football players who miss out on opportunities after brushes with sexual assault. After losing a scholarship and place on the team due to their misconduct, it's become practically commonplace for young athletes to transfer to community or junior colleges before being scooped back up by stronger programs, often at Division I schools. Everyone deserves a second chance, said Hocking's new president, Dr. Betty Young, of Trent Mays.

According to an Associated Press story at the time, not everyone was equally thrilled. "'I believe most of us like the idea of a football team,' said student Isobel Hutchinson, 22. 'However, there are just so many other issues on campus that were kind of thrown to the side when this football team was created.' The inclusion of Mays on the team, she said, has led to 'nervousness' on campus. An avalanche of social media postings about Mays' participation have been more pointed and angry."

Mays himself was quoted as saying, "Especially because of my case, people weren't just going to open their arms and give me a scholarship, just because of who I was. But I have to prove myself, and that's what I'm ready to do. I have an added pressure, but it's nothing I can't handle. I'm prepared for it. If anything, it just motivates me more."

Jeno Atkins, who attended the same college, ran into his former teammate from time to time. "You would've thought Trent never went through all that," he said. "He still claims [Jane Doe] was awake and everyone was drunk. He regrets taking pics, but still to this day will claim that she was very coherent." Remorse was not in play.

Campus protests didn't move the needle. Trent remained on the team.

Back home, Jerry Barilla and Mark Nelson continued their crusade to restore a more wholesome reputation for Steubenville. In October 2015, the town unveiled their newly retouched Abraham Lincoln mural, depicting the former president seated, with a stern expression, his hands on his knees, with the two local legends from his cabinet in the background. "I think it's our history," Barilla was quoted as saying in an article for WTOV-9. "It's important to show our history on these walls."

The mural was dedicated during a ceremony at Historic Fort Steuben and, though the intentions were good and a lot of time and energy was put into the celebration of history, the language on the website indicated that perhaps Steubenville still wasn't quite aligned with a changing world. "This historic fort originally was built in 1786–1787 by the 1st American Regiment to protect government surveyors from hostile Indians," it read. Perhaps focusing on the past, instead of moving forward, was a step in the wrong direction.

Barilla and Nelson teamed up to go a step beyond the quieter Christmas parade and bring back a higher level of festivity to the town, to make Steubenville a destination again. Together they launched an annual Nutcracker Village packed with holiday spirit. "The Steubenville Nutcracker Village is an apolitical, non-controversial and a joyful intergenerational event and Historic Fort Steuben is proud to be a part of it," reads the website. "Be sure to include a visit this holiday season!" Couldn't everyone just get along?

The Nutcracker Village, complete with a live-action nativity, was truly a fantasy land, as the encroaching outside world seemed to be growing tenser by the day. By June of 2016, Donald Trump had secured the Republican nomination and red MAGA trucker hats could be spotted all over town. The state had widely supported former Ohio governor John Kasich in the primary, as he reflected a more traditional type of conservatism. But Steubenville was willing to settle for their second choice with Trump, someone who seemed to thrive on encouraging the very animosity and derision they were trying to keep out of their town's conversation.

Trump had plenty to say about his Democratic opponent, Hillary Rodham Clinton, the country's first female presidential candidate for a major party. As the *New York Times* reported, he constantly targeted her for being a woman. "'It seems like a real strategic misstep for him, considering he has unprecedented problems with women in his own party,' said Jess McIntosh, vice president of communications at Emily's List, which works to elect Democrats who support abortion rights and is backing Mrs. Clinton." Ultimately, it didn't seem to matter much.

At one presidential debate, then Fox News anchor Megyn Kelly introduced a question for Trump by saying, "You've called women you don't like fat pigs, dogs, slobs, and disgusting animals…your Twitter account has several disparaging comments about women's looks. You once told a contestant on *Celebrity Apprentice* that it would be a pretty picture to see her on her knees. Does that sound to you like the temperament of a man we should elect as president?"

After making a dig about Rosie O'Donnell, which was rewarded with whoops from the crowd, he said, "I don't, frankly, have time for total political correctness and, to be honest with you, this country doesn't have time either." Afterward, he told reporters that Megyn Kelly was acting up because she was "bleeding out of her wherever." He effectively changed the conversation from one about his own blatant misogyny to one about the oppressiveness of political correctness and the left's attempt to censor people. This was not a hopeful sign for the future of feminism under his regime. Women who were already progressively charged up about rape culture and inequality in the country bristled. If he wanted them angry and galvanized, he got it.

In Steubenville, however, many women and men seemed to embrace Trump. Even if he wasn't the ideal for everyone, he was, at least, not Hillary. "They loved Trump in Steubenville," recalled Alex, "which was shocking because it was a blue-collar Democratic city because of the very strong position of unionizing and maintaining unions in the steel industry. I think that they loved Trump because he embraced the generational racism, bigotry, and misogyny that is so prevalent in the rust belt. Look at the utter lack of female leadership in this valley."

Jeno Atkins concurred: "I've definitely lost respect for people through the election, but nobody is vocal about it in person."

As an "October surprise" just before the election, the *Washington Post* released video footage and an accompanying article featuring Donald Trump and onetime *Access Hollywood* co-host Billy Bush discussing the candidate's sense of sexual entitlement as a male celebrity back in 2005. "I don't even wait," he bragged, describing what is tantamount to sexual assault. "And when you're a star, they let you do it. You can do anything…Grab 'em by the pussy. You can do anything." Though powerful fellow Republicans from Mike Pence to Mitch McConnell criticized his remarks, they continued to support him.

I've never seen feminist ire like what "grab 'em by the pussy" inspired. Streets filled immediately with outraged women. In New York, the city rushed to Trump Tower to protest outside. Steubenville locals and lifelong Republicans like Michele, one of the women from the Anonymous rallies on the courthouse steps, were disturbed by this crude and foul language, and uneasy about it. Traditional folks, like DeWine or Kasich, would never speak this way about women, she felt. Mitt Romney mentioned binders of them, but that wasn't insulting. Trump's bluster and foul language worked for and against him, but his alignment with evangelical Pence and the entire religious movement was giving him an edge.

The country was suddenly in an uproar, in defense of Trump and against him. Multiple women came forward as past allegations surfaced as well, to tell their stories about being groped and sexually harassed by the candidate.

But when I canvassed for Get Out the Vote in only barely blue Columbus, Ohio, a week before the election, the director of the FBI, James Comey, had just dropped Clinton's supposedly damning emails. Instead of talking about Trump's assaults, people were ranting about YouTube conspiracies involving pedophilia, #pizzagate, and Huma Abedin, the vice chair of Hillary Clinton's campaign. Longtime anger toward the Clintons, plus a kind of smear campaign and the circulation of misinformation online, was too much to overcome. In Ohio, I remember one woman answering her door with wild eyes, screaming about Hillary, "She's evil! She's evil!" Another woman, a survivor from the courthouse steps, said, "I just don't trust her. And those emails. I don't like how Trump speaks, but I really just don't trust Hillary." The women of Steubenville, in large numbers, reluctantly cast their votes for Trump, as did the majority of white women in the country. Women's supposed solidarity around being potential victims of sexual violence was trumped by their allegiance to their own gender bias.

On November 8, 2016, Donald Trump was elected president of the United States. Ohio, a deciding factor, went red with 51.3 percent of the vote for Trump. Jefferson County, where Steubenville is nestled, voted 65.9 percent for Trump.

Progressive women across the country were deeply disheartened, not just because the election of the first-ever female president had slipped through their fingers despite polls predicting the opposite, but also because Trump's bullying behavior toward women wasn't alarming enough to dissuade voters. In his first week in office, he declined to form a new White House Council of Gender Issues or Sexual Assault, which effectively dissolved it. He didn't fill positions in the Office of Violence Against Women, making his priorities clear.

To make matters more dire, Betsy DeVos was soon to be confirmed as Secretary of Education, a terrible blow to all things Title IX thanks to her regressive sexual assault policies. Multiple organizations wrote "Dear Betsy" letters asking her to reconsider her stance. But she was soon joined by Candice Jackson as Deputy Assistant Secretary in the Office of Civil Rights for the Department of Education, and together they would set out to prioritize the concerns of men who were "falsely" accused of rape over rape victims themselves. They took steps like no longer requiring regional offices to report complaints of campus assaults. In reality, statistics say that as few as 2–8 percent of assault claims are false—and that doesn't include the 63 percent of cases that go unreported.

———

For many, 2017 started with a sense of deep foreboding. On January 21, 2017, the day after the inauguration, close to 500,000 people, many in pink "pussy hats," descended on the United States capital to protest Trump's stance on women's reproductive, civil, and human rights, as well as his historic mistreatment of women. Three million others gathered in various cities around the globe in solidarity. The inaugural Women's March was further evidence that, after years of tolerating abuse, women had had enough. The all-seeing internet, including the coverage of the Steubenville case, Daisy Coleman's rape (depicted in the widely viewed 2016 Netflix documentary about two parallel assaults, *Audrie & Daisy*), and Brock Turner's light conviction, had made it impossible to look the other way. By dismissing women, Trump had empowered a large portion of them. The march would become more than a massive onetime rally; it would become an activist machine.

Meanwhile, in April 2017, Trent Mays was being recruited to play quarterback for a more high-profile team at Central State University in Wilberforce, Ohio. Although his crime against Jane Doe was widely publicized, the athletic department recruited him enthusiastically.

In March, KYAnonymous received a sentence of two years in prison, harsher than anyone else involved in the Steubenville rape case. "At the time, the government was coming down so hard on hackers," said author and journalist David Kushner by way of explanation. But the prominent hackers and collectives had already made their mark. "They had figured out how to spread this idea of [online] 'activism.' They invented the memes, lexicon, and strategy of using the internet as a tool for protest, whether or not you agree with it." Steubenville was one of the cases that allowed the collective to hone these strategies. The tools that Anonymous specifically pioneered, said Kushner, spread into mainstream forms of activism, which would spearhead and propel movements in gun control (Parkland, for example) and #MeToo. "Now, hacking, mobilizing, and protesting on the internet is ubiquitous," he added.

In August, Coach Bo Pelini at Ohio's Youngstown State, where Ma'lik had transferred, recruited him to join the football team as a walk-on, though the coach claimed that Ma'lik himself hadn't sought out a chance to play. According to the *New York Post*, the team had enjoyed success under the guidance of Pelini and "university president Jim Tressel, the former Ohio State coach who resigned in 2011 amid an improper-benefits scandal." (Tressel had allegedly failed to disclose emails he received about players who received improper benefits, an apparent NCAA violation.) Once again, colleges were willing to look the other way, for both former coaches and players, if it meant benefiting their football programs. They could obviously see the plus of having a player like Ma'lik on the team.

A petition was immediately launched on Change.org to keep Ma'lik from YSU's team, which garnered almost 12,000 signatures. The university swiftly responded by disallowing him to play, sending a school-wide email condemning sexual assault, saying he would lose a year of eligibility and would only be allowed to practice with the team. Initially, Ma'lik quit the team in response. In the midst of all of this, on August 21, his biological father was shot and killed by the police near the Jefferson County courthouse in Steubenville after he tried to shoot a judge. The incident had nothing to do with Ma'lik's case, but would, of course, have impacted him. In September, Ma'lik filed a lawsuit against the university, arguing that he should be allowed to play. By October, he had settled out of court for his place on the team.

In the meantime, Mike DeWine was making a run for governor of Ohio, something that had clearly been in the works for some time. According to a few publications, that was more challenging than it might have appeared in a "post-Trump world" for a candidate who was more old school than populist, still ascribing to traditional GOP values.

Local leadership was also changing hands in Steubenville. After the former mayor retired, Jerry Barilla beat out his opponents and was elected as the first new mayor, and Republican, in twenty-six years that November. At the ensuing victory party at Froehlich's Classic Corner Restaurant, Barilla said, "This is a very humble and emotional moment for me to become mayor of a city where I grew up and have lived in all my life... We have our challenges just like every other community. That is what life is about. But I am prepared to take on those challenges."

As mayor, he would deliver on his promise, making himself available to the community, always easy to track down at his beloved Fort Steuben, in a way that was in keeping with his earnest desire to foster harmony. "It's rewarding to be mayor and it's a challenge," he later noted near the end of his first term. "I'm limited in my authority over policy. I can't introduce legislation. I can't direct a department to make a big change. But I can listen with sincerity. I can listen with my heart. In most cases, people just want to have some official hear their plight. It's expanded my thinking and wisdom, I hope." Jerry's perspective was opening up.

Outside Steubenville, the country was having its own watershed moment, the culmination of years of pent-up frustration and sense of injustice on the part of assault survivors and allies. On October 6, 2017, the *New York Times* published a story by journalists Jodi Kantor and Megan Twohey titled, "Sexual Misconduct Claims Trail a Hollywood Mogul." In it, the duo reported multiple claims of sexual abuse against infamous movie producer Harvey Weinstein, shocking to outsiders but common knowledge to Hollywood insiders. Recognizing the far-reaching implications of what was being uncovered, actress Alyssa Milano tweeted, "If all the women who have been sexually harassed or assaulted wrote 'Me too' as a status, we might give people a sense of the magnitude of the problem." She was invoking a phrase first coined in this context by activist and survivor Tarana Burke. Now the hashtag caught on like wildfire, eliciting posts about personal sexual assault experiences from celebrities like Gwyneth Paltrow, Ashley Judd, Jennifer Lawrence, Gabrielle Union, and Uma Thurman. This inspired millions of other women in the US, and eventually all over the world, to follow suit, sharing their own personal stories of mistreatment and, more often than not, the end of prolonged silence.

Soon after, *Today* anchor Matt Lauer, who had so righteously interviewed the Agrestas about Ma'lik's upcoming rape trial in 2013, was accused of serially locking women in his office and sexually assaulting them. He was never charged, but by November his contract was terminated.

Titans were falling on both sides of the aisle. Women in all different industries started naming names—from Wall Street to professional sports to publishing to the music industry, even at elite high schools. Groups of victims and their allies quietly collected evidence and then dropped bombs. There was a sense that shame was being cast aside; this was the time to speak out. No one was above the law. The viral nature of the Steubenville rape had helped motivate women all over the country to speak up. Nodianos laughed in the face of the world and helped ignite #MeToo.

Obviously, there would be a backlash, and those who called #MeToo a "witch hunt." In July 2018, Trump nominated Brett Michael Kavanaugh to the Supreme Court of the United States. Soon after, professor and research physiologist from Stanford University Dr. Christine Blasey Ford publicly accused the nominee of sexually assaulting her during high school in Bethesda, Maryland. A four-day Senate hearing was convened. "I am here today not because I want to be," Blasey Ford said in her opening statement. "I am terrified. I am here because I believe it is my civic duty to tell you what happened to me while Brett Kavanaugh and I were in high school." Two other women came forward about having allegedly been sexually assaulted by Kavanaugh too. An investigation uncovered other stories as well, of Kavanaugh reportedly exposing himself and putting his penis in women's faces—a scenario that felt uncomfortably familiar to anyone who had followed Steubenville and Trent Mays's behavior.

Because she's a neuroscientist, what Dr. Ford brought to light and shifted for the entire movement was an understanding of how trauma works in the brain and the body. Kavanaugh and his buddy, Mark Judge, had locked her in a room, she said, turned up the music, and laughed uproariously as she tried to escape. That laughter, which the country had heard firsthand via Steubenville in Nodi's video, was especially impactful. "Indelible in the hippocampus is the laughter," she testified, referencing how, to this day, she is haunted by the sound. As an adult, she had a second door constructed in her living room because she still lives in fear of having only one method of escape.

As I wrote in an article for *Ms.* magazine at the time, "When Boys Become Men Like Brett Kavanaugh," "During Kavanaugh's confirmation hearings, community leaders called him 'an outstanding man,' while the president called Dr. Blasey Ford's allegations a 'con job.' 'What you want to do is destroy this guy's life!' Senator Lindsey Graham shouted after Dr. Blasey Ford's testimony, speaking to Democrats on the Judiciary Committee. 'You have got nothing to apologize for,' he told Kavanaugh minutes later."

In Steubenville, many locals had also defended the perpetrators, saying, "These are good kids, good football players" without acknowledging Jane Doe. And both Trent and Ma'lik went on to play college football, so their actions didn't deter them. Only recently have men like Weinstein, R. Kelly, and Jeffrey Epstein had to reckon with their abusive open secrets and suffer life-changing consequences. In the case of Kavanaugh, once again, men in power defended their male peer while denigrating a woman for sharing her story. Once again, loyalty to party, cohort, and brotherhood won out over empathy and the condemnation of documented, but ultimately unproven, violence.

On October 6, 2018, Brett Kavanaugh was confirmed in a 50 to 48 vote. A month later, Betsy DeVos filed her new Title IX rule, which, among other things, would eventually posit that cases must permit students to be cross-examined by their rapists. This incited victims' rights groups. Back in 2011, then Vice President Biden had announced new federal guidelines for how schools must handle reports of sexual violence and harassment. These progressive terms that supported Title IX were outlined in a twenty-page letter, known as the "Dear Colleague Letter," written by the US Department of Education's Office for Civil Rights. Betsy DeVos rescinded that letter along with its protections, one of many rollbacks of the Obama administration's policies. As of this writing, it has not been reactivated.

This moment represented a fundamental culture clash, one that had been foreshadowed years before when the Steubenville Big Red rape story first broke. The more small-town America hunkered down and looked toward the past, the more outraged voices from outside demanded answers and change. The internet created a global village of interconnected problems and possible solutions. By the end of 2018, more than half the world's population, at 51.2 percent, was online. On one hand, there was an administration that was hostile to women's issues; on the other was a segment of the population who was energized and angry, stirred in commitment to a new order.

While certain roles, rights, and privileges remained status quo—Coach Reno Saccoccia was named "Coach of the Year" by the Ohio Valley Athletic Conference for the fourth time—Steubenville was feeling the sting of #MeToo in its own particular way. In winter of 2018, the classic Christmas song "Baby, It's Cold Outside," sung by their favorite local legend, Dean Martin, fell under scrutiny. Many radio stations refused to play the song. In the current context, the lyrics, which tell the story of a man pressuring a woman to stay for a sexual encounter despite her protests, seemed to some to suggest date rape rather than wholesome holiday fun. "What's in this drink?" asks the woman in the song, who also argues that her mother will worry if she doesn't get home soon. Radio stations began refusing to play the old standard, raising complaints from the right about the left "canceling Christmas." Singer John Legend teamed up with former *Saturday Night Live* writer Natasha Rothwell to dream up a contemporary version of the song that he covered with Kelly Clarkson, including lyrics like, "Let me call you a ride!" and "It's your body and your choice." The battle between change and stagnancy raged on.

## CHAPTER 13

# THE PRESENT

O N APRIL 3, 2019, as the last vestiges of winter melted away and the sun fought its way from behind clouds, the Cleveland International Film Festival convened a panel to discuss rape culture and my documentary about Steubenville, *Roll Red Roll*. After a whirlwind tour around the globe, starting with a premiere at New York City's Tribeca Film Festival and Toronto's Hot Docs, I was finally returning to Ohio. I had traveled with the film to festivals in Canada, Mexico, and multiple countries in Asia and Europe, racking up seven best documentary awards and Peabody and Grierson award nominations. I had traveled throughout an America dominated by rabid support or hatred for Trump and all that implied, but somehow I was most nervous for this event. Poetically, Ohio was the last stop on the tour.

I was joined by several of the most prominent voices from the film, the women who helped bring this story to the forefront in their different ways—journalist Rachel Dissell, blogger Alex Goddard, and local survivor Michele Robinson. A teenage boy who headed the feminist alliance at his high school rounded out the panel. I had specifically requested that male allies join me along the way. It's so essential for men and boys to speak directly to other men and boys about these issues, so that women aren't constantly left to fight male behavior on their own.

Held across from the *Plain Dealer* offices, the setting seemed inauspicious—a mall Cineplex bookended by a food court and the Gap. I was unsure of what to expect. But soon the seats began to fill and the energy in the room heightened. Dad-types clad in jerseys and baseball caps studied me from their seats, but I couldn't read if it was with curiosity or hostility. In the front row, I noticed a collection of Steubenville locals, mostly women, in attendance—had they come with genuine interest or in confrontational protest to defend their sons?

On tour, often in coastal cities and liberal bubbles, audiences were devastated and angry about what happened in Steubenville and gave the film a warm reception. But I didn't know how it would play here. I steeled myself. Would Michele and Alex be disrespected, would the young man on the panel, brave enough to call himself a "feminist," be mocked?

Instead, the event, sponsored by local public radio, turned out to be surprising and cathartic. Apart from perhaps the Steubenville contingent, the audience wanted to hear from Alex and Michele, to honor their personal experiences as survivors. They asked Rachel about violence prevention, how to make sure this didn't happen in their communities. The women were vocal; the men were silent and shaken. I realized that, even more than I'd already suspected, this story could spark essential conversations about rape culture in small towns and beyond. Following the high-profile explosion of the #MeToo movement, the focus had been squarely on Hollywood, but Steubenville was a story that could have happened in everyone's backyards. In concert with the current moment, this brought the realities home, and a rapid and growing awareness that rape culture pervaded all communities. #MeToo was, urgently, for everyone. The outcome notwithstanding, the movement had succeeded in raising awareness.

We built a campaign with *Roll Red Roll*, and I traveled around the country to educate audiences from Harvard University to Capitol Hill. I talked to people of every kind about what Steubenville's story demonstrated about the state of rape culture in this country, about how we could work together to stop this from happening again and again through restorative justice, comprehensive sex education, bystander intervention training, early lessons of consent, male allyship (especially within football in hopes of changing the culture), and more. Organizations, conferences, and companies reached out about sharing the film with their staff and attendees. To date, hundreds of colleges and high schools have screened the documentary, which has streamed in 190 countries via Netflix after launching the thirty-second season of PBS's independent nonfiction film platform, *POV*. The Steubenville story continues to resonate and spark conversation.

My team and I, including the founder of MenChallenging, Joe Samalin, created comprehensive high school and college tool kits to help facilitate the ensuing, always charged, conversations. The guide was for educators and coaches, and addressed issues like rape myths, a culture of complicity in institutions like high schools, colleges, and companies, and the critical role of coaches, parents, and other potential role models in prevention. Or, in the case of Steubenville, how silence and inaction promoted rape culture. The guide names and deconstructs toxic masculinity and gender norms, the very definition of sexual assault. It names the prevailing myths, from the idea that the act must be explicitly violent to be considered rape to the concept that rape must include intercourse. As we saw firsthand in Steubenville, it is essential that these terms be defined for adolescents and even adults in order for there to be positive change. Misinformation is everywhere.

Another theme that the Steubenville story brought to light was the role of the bystander: how responsible are you for helping another person who is vulnerable or in distress? How does technology enable violence and harassment? We suggested that these institutions, especially schools, collaborate with their local rape crisis centers and anti–sexual violence organizations to round out these discussions with trained experts. Students pushed for this education in their classrooms, organizing screenings and events, but we could not get this mandated from the top down and met with resistance from many institutions.

We shouldn't have been surprised. This is the pushback educators get when it comes to sexual education of all kinds. "In the decade since Steubenville, not much has changed," said award-winning sexual health educator Twanna A. Hines, MS. "While more states require sexual health education instruction than they did in 2012, many still do not require teaching students about consent. Several states have laws on the books that limit discussion about sex to abstinence-only programs, even though evidence proves they're ineffective. What's more? Even in states that mandate sex education, parents and guardians can still opt their children out at any time."

The solution, according to Hines, is to treat sexual education like any other essential element of a child's learning. "We know the US is a compulsory education country and, by law, all children must attend school. If you can't opt out of learning about multiplication, you shouldn't be able to opt out of learning about consent," Hines said. "We need comprehensive, medically accurate sex education mandated for all school children in the United States. The Department of Education, at state and federal levels, should establish, administer, and enforce education policies pertaining to sexual health education. Further, these policies should not be exclusionary or discriminatory in either intent or outcomes." One way for health educators, teachers, parents, researchers, and others to help fight rape culture in this country is by putting pressure on officials to further this cause toward enacting national standards.

These standards must be uniform as, too often, the sexual education that does exist in schools is more like the pamphlets handed out at "crisis pregnancy centers," meant to advance an agenda rather than impart scientific facts. "As of June 2021, only eighteen states mandate that sex education in schools be medically accurate," said Anne Hodder-Shipp. "That means that in those other states, it's legal to lie, omit information, and promote misinformation and disinformation related to sexual health, pleasure, identities, and relationships to young people. And that's a form of child abuse. And if this is how things are in 2021, you can imagine how things were in Ohio in 2012!"

This version of sexual education that Hines and Hodder-Shipp espouse includes way more than just the standard nuts and bolts. It's a truly inclusive, enlightened view of sexuality based on the experience of kids in today's world, the kids who watch *Euphoria*, not *Leave It to Beaver*. It's a world that's dramatically different than the one their parents were raised in. It's a world in which identity has a different meaning. "Expansive sex education means there is no baseline norm that is taught from," explains Hodder-Shipp. "It recognizes that human sexuality is vast and varied and impacted by a variety of components that are entirely human—our feelings, our values and core beliefs, our actions and behaviors, and the bodies we experience the world in. It must also include pleasure education, bodily autonomy and personal rights, and critical thinking skills that can be learned and used throughout the young person's life, well into adulthood." Much of what expansive sexual education is comprised of "has nothing to do with sex and everything to do with being a human in connection with ourselves and others," the expert said. "Sex ed is so much more than teaching about orgasms, genitals, sexual activity, and STIs!" So, for our guide, education was where this all had to begin.

In addition to targeting coaches and male athletes, *Roll Red Roll* hit the home page of Reddit, generally an internet "bro zone" not known for welcoming feminist content. The intrigue and role of hacker collective Anonymous sparked much of the interest. Due to this push, the film went viral when it launched on Netflix. Urged on by commenters, I participated in a Reddit Ask Me Anything (AMA). Although warned by many friends that those sometimes devolve into hyper-offensive free-for-alls in which you might be harassed, I wound up facilitating a discussion for four hours, drawing 1,800 questions, genuine inquiries about rape culture, collusion, and what could be done in the viewers' own communities. Only one Joe Rogan–inspired troll told me to go make him a sandwich. While maybe things in Steubenville hadn't changed outwardly, people on Reddit were outraged, curious, and open enough to see themselves in the social ecology of rape culture.

In no way did this lead me to believe that our problems were solved, only that, thanks in part to the wide reach of the Steubenville story and the impact of the teenagers' own callous words, people were more open to having these conversations. While assaults are still happening all the time, the reality of the internet has changed the landscape. As Jeno Atkins said, "I haven't spoken to Trent in years, but it bugs me because I know there are thousands of dudes like him all over the country. But my generation is good at exposing shit, so, if something bad happens, it will end up on camera for the internet to judge."

This story and others like it did change the culture's relationship to evading responsibility. There's a sense now that any public actions might be documented. "I'm a Black woman who grew up in a small Midwestern town in Illinois," said Twanna A. Hines. "I totally get how insular they can be. The entire city can know something without anyone actually saying anything *directly* to anyone. Social media changed all of that. Anyone can capture the town's happenings and put them on public record. Once that happens, it's available for the whole world to see. Steubenville showed us that for sexual assault. Minnesota showed us that when Derek Chauvin murdered George Floyd."

The exposure of these stories has encouraged victims to come forward. As attorney Gloria Allred acknowledges, more women and girls are requesting her services now thanks to the fact that others are now speaking out. "I have young women, older women, wanting to know what their rights are because the issues of gender violence are more in the news," the attorney said, explaining that collectively raised voices can inspire bravery in others. "Fear, as I always say, is the weapon used to continue to victimize those who already have become victims."

The internet as a platform, where streaming content can be seen and responded to immediately, created a dialogue about *Roll Red Roll* in real time. At one point, it turned its ire on the Nelson daughters because their comments about Jane Doe's responsibility were seen by fellow young women as blatant victim-blaming. People were viscerally upset that the girl-on-girl harm, so rampant in middle and high schools, normally reserved for whispers and DMs, was now writ large on screen. This spoke to a desperate need for addressing healthy relationships and anti-bullying among teens in all contexts.

Looking at these issues directly would mean meeting the kids where they are and confronting the real, complicated world they live in instead of some fantasy among parents. That means teaching about relationship dynamics and dignity versus respect, ethics versus religion. It's about enlisting high social status peers to help in ways that feel socially acceptable, according to Rosalind Wiseman, so the kids actually listen. "All kinds of schools have a tendency to teach morals and ethics in sound bites instead of in meaningful terms," Wiseman explained. "We're not willing to understand the culture and language that the kids speak. Because we're uncomfortable having conversations about, for example, the intersection of sexuality, pornography, and media, there's very little context for kids. But it's the norm for them. Explaining these dynamics is helpful. Being able to have sex education that addresses the history and legacy of shame, having honest conversations about pornography with young people would be helpful. Really understanding sexual development (instead of offering rudimentary classes) with trained teachers who know how to lead helpful, uncomfortable conversations with kids. If we listened first before we started teaching them and created an environment where they could talk to us and feel like we might not be judgmental in the context of the world they're living in, then that would be helpful."

The Nelson sisters' comments sparked murmurs with live audiences, but Twitter kicked up outrage. The now-married daughters posted a statement to their Facebook page (written by their husbands) defending their younger selves and voicing support for Jane Doe and all sexual assault victims. Mark Nelson went on to publish a statement about how the film twisted his words out of context, though he came off as sympathetic.

Today, Mike DeWine, always difficult to pin down in the vein of Mark Nelson in terms of his simultaneous defense of and assault on women's rights, is now governor. He became the first Republican since 2002 to win in historically Democratic Monroe County, as well as throughout Ohio, signaling a statewide swing to the right. In this position, he has pushed through some of the most restrictive anti-abortion laws in modern history, including a six-week abortion ban known as the Heartbeat Bill and a requirement that fetal tissue must be cremated or buried. "That was certainly a bill that I wanted to sign," he said. "I'm proud I signed it." A court blocked it, but it set the stage for states like Texas to pass the same law, even in cases of rape, sexual abuse, and incest. Somehow, the disconnect between controlling women's bodies through legislation and the right to sexual consent remains unrecognized.

The increased assault on women's reproductive choice, inextricably linked to sexual violence, has fueled the fire of the current women's movement. "There's a lot going on now, bringing awareness to #MeToo," said Coach V, reflecting on what has changed over the years. "There's a lot more prevention work being done in the area of sexual assault awareness and people are more frankly talking about it now. It still has a long way to go." Coach V, like many who focus on combating violence against women, is a perfect reminder of how many small acts can ripple and create big change. When she talks to the boys she coaches, she focuses on discussing the notion of consent, how a yes can become a no and that has to be okay. "This is one of the things we're doing as far as prevention," she explained, "to make sure that young men understand the seriousness of not hearing young women when they say no. To combat rape in our schools and in our culture, we have to bring awareness to it. Make it a safe space for women to come forward and for men to talk about their experience and mindset. Trying to undo some of the unhealthy learned behavior is part of what we must do to change the culture." Male educators have formed organizations like Joe Samalin's Men-Challenging, which give men and young boys a space to speak honestly, unpack their rape myths, and own internalized experiences of toxic masculinity without fear of being judged. Young men need to be able to talk about their unfiltered attitudes freely with a trained facilitator in order to work through them. Calling them out or "canceling them," as is often a go-to reaction, creates a more entrenched position. However, calling them *in*, in the right environment, enables young men to unpack sexist tropes and then rebuild.

In August 2018, just after our festival premiere and nearly a year before our PBS and Netflix broadcasts, we were invited by educators to do a test screening in Oshkosh, Wisconsin, with one hundred high school football players, facilitated by Joe. The room was full of rural, white, Christian boys, all of them varsity-level athletes. Joe is an excellent facilitator and has worked in the field of violence prevention for over twenty years. He led this screening and talk-back to gather information to help us shape our educational toolkit. It was devastating. After they watched *Roll Red Roll*, when asked who was to blame for what happened, the majority of the boys said, "Jane Doe." A few murmured, "Jane Doe's parents." They were so steeped in rape myths, and surrounded by pressure to conform, that they could not see predation or culpability in the boys' behavior and only knew the myth that a woman is the cause of her own rape. This was eye-opening because it's easy to be lulled into a sense of hope or progress by pop culture or a supportive bubble, but what these young men expressed was so unfiltered, so conformist, the screening demonstrated the alarming scale of how much work needs to be done.

In contrast, another test group, the graduates of the Relationship Abuse Prevention Program (RAPP) in Harlem and the South Bronx, was ready to use the film as a teaching tool with incredible self-awareness. After a several-week curriculum, these teens had a deep understanding of consent, rape myths, and peer-to-peer accountability. So, while teens at schools with no sexuality education seemed poised to repeat the cycle, all signs pointed to positive outcomes with the right kind of focused and sustained education.

We reached out to athletic administrators, counselors, and coaches like Coach V with regard to the film. Not only do coaches act as role models for students, but student athletes tend to be role models for their fellow classmates. Encouraging athletic departments to take a hard internal look at their culture is essential: do they mandate sexual assault training for their students? Do they invite and encourage athletes to become positive bystanders? If we can have respected and trained coaches teaching their athletes about concepts like enthusiastic consent and being respectful members of their community, as evidenced by the work that Tyrone White has done, that can go a long way toward making a difference for the future. If the quarterback of the football team behaves with respect toward girls, and even other players, then maybe the other boys will too. It may seem simple, but it's true. It's that notion of a "groupthink" arising again, but harnessed in a positive way. "If we don't have these direct, blunt conversations about healthy relationships, respect, and treating people with dignity, my fear is this is just going to end up being a continuation of what it's always been," said White. "And we have to move the needle. We have not moved the needle in our athletic programs or in the sports world. And that's sad. When we look at Steubenville and other high schools across America, not [yet] at the collegiate or professional levels, that's the incubator phase. That's where this stuff starts."

That's why sexual education and lessons about gender equality must begin early and with consciousness. "We need to build a foundation during K–12 education that incorporates lessons in comprehensive sex ed, social emotional learning, and social justice," said Soraya Chemaly. "By the time you're in high school, you should already have a foundation. That foundation should be diffuse in the curriculum: it's not 'a sex ed class once a week.' It should be in literature classes and more."

Brenda Tracy, of #SetTheExpectation, has made talking to men and boys the fundamental tenet of her organization's mission, as one example. As the survivor of a gang rape by football players, she set out to change the conversation. As she said, "I don't believe we can talk about men as the problem unless we are also willing to talk about them as the solution." So she set out to work directly with college football programs to get the players engaged in setting positive examples for their classmates, as well as other boys and men. She engages athletes in upstander behavior, pushes the NCAA to enforce repercussions for violent college athletes, and works to convince athletic programs to adopt what has come to be known as "the Tracy Rule." As her site explained, "The Tracy Rule is the most comprehensive serious misconduct policy in collegiate athletics, and it meets compliance requirements of the NCAA Campus Sexual Violence Policy. In 2020, the NCAA policy was expanded, and member programs must begin attestation in the 2022–23 academic year." In 2019, the University of Texas at San Antonio was the first NCAA school to enact this policy.

One tactic for engaging men and boys as future upstanders is to create opportunities for eye-opening revelations. "I see a lot of the work as trying to create 'aha' moments of awareness and discovery about gender violence and masculinity, and all related issues," said Joe Samalin. "We fully recognize that the fact that men and boys need 'aha' moments to recognize these problems is the very definition of privilege and patriarchy, but we need them." As Samalin pointed out, most people are willing to speak up against something that they feel isn't right, even if it's just, for instance, someone insulting their favorite sports team. That bravado is just waiting to be harnessed for the right cause. "The question is how to translate that impulse to this issue of violence against women," continued Samalin. "There are lots of ways to do that, and some people are more ready than others. But once someone is at a place where they know that what they're seeing is wrong, potentially harmful, or dangerous—and most people know in their hearts and their gut when they're seeing something that's not okay—we need to give them practice, modeling the behavior, and make it safer for people to stand up."

Some of that can be instilled using the kind of mentorship and training bolstered by MenChallenging, which needs to be widespread as a part of regular school and even corporate curricula. That's where practicing intervention comes in, as well as breaking down myths about masculinity, as Tyrone White discussed. But it's also essential that men stand up and model that behavior for one another. Men in positions of power or esteem must enact these principles in order for the next crop of boys to grow up with these values in place. "When we retell the stories about these incidents, we cannot forget to highlight those who did upstand like…with Shawn McGhee," said Samalin. "There are specific things about violence against women that cause men and boys to be confused, unsure, and unconfident before, during, and after something happens. And it takes education and practice to change that."

That's why role models must demonstrate treating women not only with respect, but with dignity, a distinction that Rosalind Wiseman feels is essential—a sense not just of admiration but of inherent worthiness. In an animated video entitled, "What is Dignity?" the author explained, "Respect is earned through actions we admire, not just because of someone's position. While respect is earned, dignity… meaning 'to be worthy'…is a given. It is an absolute, whatever our age, social status, or accomplishments. When we remember this, there's no conflict in treating someone with their rightful human dignity, even when you don't agree with their actions. Young people are living in a storm of disrespect. By recognizing that everyone has inherent dignity, we can unlock the door to more positive communication and equitable relationships." If coaches, for example, could imprint the idea that part of being a successful player is embracing this notion of dignity for all, especially women and girls, along with developing a growing awareness around gender-based violence, that would create safe spaces for upstanders, whistleblowers, and students in general.

In the past, "rape prevention" education was framed as though rape is inevitable and that teaching girls to protect themselves from their lurking attackers by carrying a rape whistle or not wearing headphones at night is the solution. The burden was on the potential victim to avoid her own attack. Of course, it's important to protect oneself and use general street smarts in any potential conflict situation, but this is a triage response, more suitable for combat or abandoned back alleys. Essentially, these tactics fail, as they are designed to protect potential victims from stranger danger, while the statistics clearly state that more than 85 percent of today's sexual assaults are perpetrated by people we know, our acquaintances, classmates, or families. Another failure of the "don't be a victim!" education and campaigns is that they do nothing to address the root cause of the violence, the behavior and attitudes that enable rape culture, and their framing centers blame on the victim if she fails to protect herself *enough*. Other red herrings in the discussion of sexual violence get lost in the dialogue about "hookup culture," as if the confusing modern way that kids today hook up without dating somehow causes rape, which it doesn't. In fact, from 2007 to 2017, the number of eighteen- to twenty-three-year-old men and women having casual sex declined from 38 percent to 24 percent and 31 percent to 22 percent respectively. Lastly, while alcohol remains a tool for predators to use in order to create more pliant victims, it certainly does not cause rape, as many people drink alcohol and do not commit sexual violence. Plus, it's actually a decline in drinking that researchers hypothesize has led to the decline in casual hookups.

The focus must fall squarely on how we educate young people and those who teach and mentor them to deconstruct rape myths, define consent, make clear that without affirmative consent there is no consent, unpack their own shame around sexual pleasure and intimacy, and practice and role-play intervention. Young people must also be encouraged to question norms instead of blindly accepting them. And of course, none of this sticks without accountability and repercussions when boundaries are violated.

"Teaching women to insist on their personhood above all else—something that we're seeing a lot of Black athletes doing—from Naomi Osaka choosing her own mental health over participating in the French Open to Simone Biles walking away from an Olympic gold medal because she didn't want to push herself to injury—is exactly the kind of resistance to social norms and pressures we need to see all around us at every turn," said writer Aditi Khorana. "There's always a reactionary wave that follows courageous acts like these—mediocre men telling us these acts of resistance set a bad precedent—what if we all walked away from foreign summits and board meetings and critical speaking events? But what if we, as women, *did* walk away from the things that simply don't serve us?

"I'm not surprised these public refusals on the part of women to participate for the pleasure and comfort of others are coming from athletes," she continued. "Athletes know their bodies far better than the rest of us, and perhaps the most sinister [undercover] marketing campaign we've run against women, certainly my entire life, is to distance women from the pleasures and pains of their own bodies. Of course, a 'no' in the bedroom isn't the same as a 'no' in the public sphere, but teaching women refusal, allowing them to see what refusal looks like in every possible circumstance, builds collective momentum for a movement. What we need now is a culture of unlearning, and the acknowledgment that unlearning is just as difficult, if not more so than learning itself. This decolonization of the mind should ideally take us to a place where we understand in our bones that all humans are relational regardless of gender, despite what we've been taught, but we need to remove the burden on women of being the sole carriers of a relationship that isn't reciprocal and that doesn't serve them, whether it's with a man, the state, or the culture itself."

Sexual assault, gender bias, and inequity remain difficult to talk about because they implicate all of us and impact us all with trauma. We are survivors, we know survivors, or we know perpetrators, who are also sometimes survivors. It's upsetting and complex, and is shrouded in shame.

In June 2021, in Jefferson County, Ohio, a man named Paul Voltz was found guilty on seven counts of rape, two counts of pandering obscenities (taking and distributing photographs and videos), and two counts of gross sexual imposition (by force). He was a one-time Steubenville teacher, though the rapes were not committed in that setting. His assaults were perpetrated between 1998 and 2007 against three individuals who were children during the course of the victimization. Two of them, a boy and a girl, were closely involved in Jane Doe's 2012 assault. So these teens, acting in abhorrent ways to victimize another, unbeknownst to everyone else, were processing their own traumas and violations, enacting the cycle of violence and/or judgment taught to them by an adult. An article on WTOV-9 quoted county prosecutor Jane Hanlin as saying before jury deliberation, "Imagine being these young people holding this secret all of this time. Imagine living with this for all this time and then having to walk into a room, look at him in front of everybody out there and describe what happened to you." One cannot help but see how Jane Hanlin's description mirrors the experience of Jane Doe in the Jefferson County Courthouse, having to stare down her attackers and absorb the assault of photos and evidence. Sexual assault prevention must become part of a real, open conversation, without victim-blaming and defensiveness, if parents are to protect their children. *All* of their children. Even from each other.

While we do not want to vilify one group, the reality is that sexual violence is most often (but not only) committed by men. The victims of men's violence are often (but certainly not only) women and girls. Boys are victimized, but their reporting numbers are even lower. In a college setting, for example, we know that a sexual assault can happen anywhere, by any student or professor. We also know that the majority of reported sexual assaults happen in fraternity or athletic contexts. Recent findings from a multi-campus study found that more than 87 percent of alcohol-involved sexual assaults were committed by serial perpetrators, and that men in fraternities and on sports teams were significantly more likely to be those perpetrators. As Tyrone White said, "One out of four women experience physical or sexual assault in their lifetime and almost 50 percent of them before they're eighteen years old." While this doesn't mean that most athletes commit rape or that most students who commit rape are athletes, it does suggest that college athletics, like everyone, can do more to challenge sexual violence at their schools, and that the status athletes carry increases what they can achieve. The same, of course, goes for high schools and life after graduation.

Despite the undeniable impact of #MeToo, which taught us to think again before doubting or ignoring victims, we still have a ways to go. It took sixty victims' testimonies against Bill Cosby to get a conviction, which was eventually reversed on a technicality. Harvey Weinstein raped and pillaged women as a widely open secret for years before anyone tried to stop him. Larry Nasser, a doctor who swore a Hippocratic Oath, is now in jail for 40–175 years for violating and raping girls under the nose of USA Gymnastics. R. Kelly, after thirty years of abusing girls, was finally convicted, thanks in large part to the efforts of Black women to bring attention to the atrocity. The larger questions are not only why did it take so long, but why did so many people enable the perpetration?

These situations were tacitly accepted by all as part of an unmovable, unchangeable reality. We all thought we had to live with it; this is "how it was," until survivors swelled up with enough momentum and journalists didn't give up. No one thought these men would fall, until they did.

America's smaller towns and cities, less glittery and in the spotlight than Hollywood, continue to be riddled with these issues, as does the sports world in particular. *USA Today*, in their investigative series "The Predator Pipeline," talks about how "college athletes can lose their NCAA eligibility in numerous ways, but sexual assault is not one of them. Even when facing or convicted of criminal charges, even when suspended or expelled from school, NCAA rules allow them to transfer elsewhere and keep playing. An investigation by the *USA Today* Network identified at least 28 current and former athletes since 2014 who transferred to NCAA schools despite being administratively disciplined for a sexual offense at another college. It found an additional five who continued playing after being convicted or disciplined for such offenses through the courts."

While "Big Ben" Roethlisberger has been quiet since attending rehab and finding faith, other NFL players continue to draw accusations of sexual assault. In 2021, Houston Texans quarterback Deshaun Watson, who has the highest career completion record of all time, was accused of sexual misconduct by twenty-two massage therapists. While civil suits have been filed and a grand jury was eventually convened, as of February 2022, no criminal charges had been filed. And yet NFL teams continued to pursue him. The list goes on and on. It recently came to light that coaches and administrators at numerous colleges joked with their players about the threat of sexual violence to motivate them to play harder, and sent their players to known abusers such as Dr. Robert Anderson at the University of Michigan and Dr. Richard Strauss at Ohio State. The lack of protection for these players and the open secret and minimizing of the sexual abuses by these doctors continues. In some cases, this extends to their families, as well. Courtney Smith, the ex-wife of one-time Ohio State wide receiver coach Zach Smith, hoped that head coach Urban Meyer would tell the truth publicly when her ex-husband was fired amidst domestic violence allegations, but instead she was ostracized by people she once considered friends. (In late 2019, now-Judge Marianne Hemmeter found Zach Smith guilty of violating a protection order and reminded him that he wasn't "above the law.") The culture of tolerating violence against women in the football boys' club continued.

So, with all of these seismic cultural shifts and backlashes, where is Steubenville now? Where is small-town America? Where is the whole country? Are we all just in echo chambers, hearing only our own voices reverberate and mistaking that for progress? Or are there small changes creating a ripple effect?

In Steubenville, and for those involved in this case, not much is different. Scaffidi's planned the opening of a gnocchi-themed offshoot. Under the umbrella of Nelson Fine Art & Gifts, the Nelson family now not only runs Catholic to the Max, but also companies such as Steubenville Popcorn Factory, Freedom to the Max, and Pro Life to the Max. However, a deeply conservative, absolutist Catholic faction in town spearheaded by the higher-ups at Franciscan University and joined by the Nelsons has begun dipping its toes in local Steubenville politics via the city council. This is alienating some previous allies, including more moderate Catholics, and potentially puts the city's day-to-day affairs into the hands of a powerful, rigid minority.

In March 2019, from her new home in Columbus, Ohio, Alex

Goddard posted a fresh story on Prinnified: "Trent Mays Accused of Sexual Assault...AGAIN." According to the blogger, there was chatter on Twitter about another alleged assault, this time at his new college, Central State University.

After many attempts, Ma'lik Richmond finally got himself removed from the sex offender registry. "He has demonstrated that he can live amongst society and no longer needs the supervision and restrictions necessary for Juvenile Sex Offender Registrants," said Judge Thomas R. Lipps, the same judge who presided over the rape trial.

The trajectories of Trent and Ma'lik in the decade since the incident suggest fundamental differences in their attitudes. Although Trent was not convicted of rape again, "We could file Trent as one of the dangerous few," said Aya Gruber, who supports the restorative justice–based idea that sex offenders exist on a spectrum. "His tendencies seem deviant even within the confines of the hypermasculine culture he's a part of. Judging by his texts and the pictures he circulated, he wanted the trophies. But not every young man who engages in social misconduct is a Trent." Even in Trent's case, Gruber felt that the community failed him in whatever ways he could be positively impacted. "He was young...and at a dangerous intersection of Christianity and sexual education," she said. "At the very least, he could have used some treatment and a lot of training about sex."

Ma'lik, she felt, was a different story, as he didn't seem to possess the same predatory patterns. He was an example, she felt, of someone who could have benefited from a more restorative resolution. "We have an adversarial and not an inquisitorial system," she said, referencing the process in Europe where, instead of legal "gamesmanship," there's an impartial fact finder in court. "As long as we're mired in these simplistic criminal logic notions of sexual misconduct and sexual offending, we can't move forward. I think we can get to a place where a conviction isn't the measure of progress and gender justice. It's about changing the cultural norms around sex and masculinity and how to heal from victimization."

The "three musketeers," as Marianne Hemmeter called them, and the other high school students moved on with their lives in somewhat predictable ways: Mark Cole joined the Marine Corps and then returned to Steubenville and started cage fighting, doing amateur MMA bouts, and coaching wrestling. He became a corrections officer. Prosecutor Jane Hanlin's son Charlie Keenan also participated in MMA and cage fighting. Anthony Craig earned his degree in physical therapy. Evan Westlake became a pharmacist. Shawn McGhee, the lone upstander in the crowd, became a wrestling coach. As for the others, Michael Nodianos moved to the south end of Columbus with his girlfriend and as of this writing was working at an arena, where the NHL team, the Columbus Blue Jackets, plays. Farrah Marcino, who sensed that Jane Doe was in potential danger and expressed the most regret among the bystanders, is studying early childhood development at Franciscan University and is a mother to a little girl and baby boy in Steubenville. Her Twitter profile picture, as of summer 2021, was an image of her and her baby outfitted in Big Red gear. Her children will likely someday walk the halls of Steubenville High School.

The legacy of high school football lives on in town. "People have the idea that we are just bred menaces," said Jeno Atkins. "That isn't the case. For the most part, we are raised to be kind and humble. But Steubenville has had a dark cloud over it for many years prior to the rape case. And the town is so small and run-down that the only light we have is Friday nights watching Big Red football. It's the only thing that we can proudly claim. So, that's why I think the community went crazy about this case. It almost felt like it put the school's legacy on the line and people overlooked the more important facts, such as these young men…did terrible things."

Atkins, who is now a union carpenter, was at home the night of the assault, exhausted from the scrimmage. But he also had the benefit of a strict mother who set clear boundaries and would not have let him out anyway. Still, Jeno didn't have a totally clear perspective when everything first happened, when he was seventeen years old. "Once I had the community out [of] my ear, I truly was able to understand. And it was hard to deal with 'cause the city treated us honestly like celebrities. But, as bad as the situation was, it definitely raised awareness and hopefully [next time] a situation like that will be prevented by someone simply speaking up. Parents needed to be more strict. Nothing good comes out of a party where underage kids are drinking."

Jeno remains loyal to his coaches, who he says did their best to teach the players to be decent people. "The coaches woulda sacrificed everything for any player. These coaches practically raised us for four years. And they only preached being a good human. Shit, Coach [Reno] always had us doing some community service work or holding mini camps for the little ones…With that being said, I still feel terrible for the victim and wish everyone could share that same compassion. But nobody wants to think if it was their sister or mom or aunt."

A young man like Jeno offers a sense of hope. At Rosalind Wiseman's son's high school in Boulder, Colorado, there was a similar assault incident to what happened with Jane Doe—with multiple accusations. In that case, when the alleged teenage rapist was found not guilty, the students staged a walkout in protest. They were not afraid to speak up. What would a world be like in which social currency among teens included standing up for what they believed in?

Alex Goddard has continued to commit herself to causes that matter to her. In fall of 2021, she was working on two federal cases against police departments for civil rights abuses against Black Lives Matter protesters and multiple cases against QAnon sovereign citizen fringe groups. She recently dipped her toe into environmental issues in the Ohio Valley too, pressuring the city to monitor a fracking wastewater plant that processes high-level radiated materials from wells so it doesn't contaminate the aquifer.

When it comes to interacting with sexual assault victims, especially teenagers, Detective Rigaud amassed a lot of invaluable knowledge from the Steuvenville case. In fact, after the case was resolved, he and Marianne Hemmeter compiled a list of lessons learned as a presentation for fellow members of law enforcement. In it, they addressed the fickle role of social media and how misinformed kids often are about rape myths. They stressed the importance of investigators asking the "blush-worthy" questions because the answers are important. Demonstrating comfort as the adult in the room is key, they said. Attorneys and police officers should always come from a place of compassion in these situations, according to Rigaud, especially when the victim is a child. Interviews should be "trauma-informed" and should consciously avoid any victim-blaming language. For the reason behind this, we can look at the deadly example of the police officer's report in the domestic violence incident with twenty-two-year-old Gabby Petito in 2021. Law enforcement officers on the scene of an altercation between the couple laughed with her then-fiancé Brian Laundrie and called her "crazy." Clearly, these officers had little to no effective training in the dynamics of violence against women or intimate partner violence. They misread the scene and sided with her abuser. Her remains were found weeks later.

In the midst of the Steubenville case, Jane Doe's mother specifically asked Detective Rigaud to be direct and honest with her and her daughter about everything along the way. "We hang on your every word," she reminded him, a message that would forever stick in his brain. Though some of the lessons might now seem obvious, they were a revelation for many individuals in these departments and continue to remain important. For Detective Rigaud, the experience was life-changing. "It still is a scarred memory," he said.

While Rigaud led a charge for trauma-informed policing, he's in the minority. Steubenville once again became a microcosm for American culture when one-time Anonymous rallies and counterprotests in defense of the town gave way to new cultural flashpoints: there were small fifty-person protests calling for justice for George Floyd, and there were protests against COVID-19 restrictions like mask-wearing, vaccines, and lockdowns. That June, in response to George Floyd's murder, confederate statues were torn down throughout the country, sparking heated debate. Mayor Jerry Barilla sided with the progressive movement. "Lee fought to keep Black people enslaved. Why are we preserving his statues?" he asked. "Why are we calling him a hero? I suggest that white people up here talking about tearing down statues look at it from a Black person's perspective."

The months leading up to the 2020 election were challenging in the US, rife with unrest, political division, anger, and, of course, a life-threatening pandemic, the protection from which made people dependent on each other's compliance. As it turned out, even on this front, people could not agree. During lockdowns and this period of increased anxiety, sexual violence moved home. According to a *Time* article, domestic violence rates skyrocketed all around the world from China to the UK to the US, where major cities saw spikes from 10 percent to 22 percent early on. In North America, one in three white women experienced domestic violence during the pandemic and, in more marginalized communities based on race, gender identity, citizenship, and cognitive and physical ability, that number increased to about 50 percent.

Suicide rates also soared. Daisy Coleman, sexual assault survivor, activist, and the subject of the documentary *Audrie & Daisy*, took her own life on August 4, 2020, at only twenty-three years old. On December 6, her mother, Melinda, also committed suicide. Their tragic story underlined the enduring trauma associated with sexual assault, as well as the ripple effect on family, loved ones, and other members of the community. There's no moving forward without resolution.

On October 23, 2020, right before one of the most highly charged elections in the history of the United States, Donald Trump's campaign felt Steubenville, representative of a certain belief system, was important enough to have Don Jr. show up in person with Congressman Bill Johnson to hold a rally. According to local paper the *Herald-Star*, approximately 500 people gathered outside of manufacturer Bully Tools to hear the incumbent's son fan the flames of their existing fears—about being "left behind," "the internet," the "radical agenda" of people like then-Senator Kamala Harris, who is widely considered a centrist. "This Democrat party has left you," he said. "They like Joe Biden because they can use him as the camouflage to bring in Kamala Harris and the radical agenda." He blamed Facebook, Twitter, Instagram, and "probably Google" for hiding the truth about Biden, an argument that might have appealed to the residents of Steubenville, who had once experienced the internet as a bogeyman. "We can make liberals cry again," he finished, "and make America great again, again. Let's make it happen, Ohio!"

Ohio did make it happen—in their state. The state and Jefferson County went for Trump by a slightly larger margin than in 2016 (53 percent and 68.5 percent, respectively), a perplexing development considering that Trump had promised to bring manufacturing back to Appalachia along with bolstering coal mining, but instead forty-one mines shuttered during his presidency. In the end, Joe Biden won the election, despite the incumbent president's attempts to contest the results and spread a false narrative about voter fraud. And on November 15, 2020, Mike DeWine, always a complicated figure, was one of the first Republicans to concede that Joe Biden had won, incurring Trump's wrath in the form of a vaguely threatening tweet referencing the upcoming 2022 elections that read, "Who will be running for governor in the great state of Ohio? Will be hotly contested!"

On January 6, 2021, when MAGA protestors violently stormed the Capitol to try to stop the official count of the electoral votes to formalize Biden's victory, an elected member of the Ohio School Board, Kirsten Hill, was not only in attendance but helped plan a bus ride to the "Stop the Steal" rally. In a statement after the fact, she denied wrongdoing by saying, "My participation at the event consisted of listening to President Trump's speech, walking to the Capitol, praying at a street corner along the National Mall, and waving my American flag in support of our great country."

Mike DeWine came out strongly against Trump, saying in a briefing, "The president's continued refusal to accept the election results, without producing any credible evidence of a rigged election, has started a fire that has threatened to burn down our democracy. This incendiary speech yesterday, the one he gave preceding the march that he gave to the protesters, served only to fan those flames, encouraging the mob behavior that ensued." The next day, as members of Trump's former administration scurried to distance themselves from him, education secretary Betsy DeVos stepped down.

Though he ran on a Republican ticket, Jerry Barilla, both a literal and figurative representative of a whole faction of Steubenville, also had negative feelings about Donald Trump. "In Jefferson County, we were heavily Democratic," he described. "In the last ten years, we moved Republican. Obama started to turn the tide to a more 'white' way of thinking. Trump really emphasized it. When I look at Trump, I see an evil person. Simple as that…National politics have really influenced us. If you're a Republican, Trump really enhanced this non-inclusive movement by mocking and degrading people."

For all of his enlightened thinking, Jerry was still not quite able to make the leap in terms of women's issues, pointing to outside influences, like the way girls are permitted to dress, for issues around consent and sexual assault. Boys will be boys. "You have to understand boys: things are flashed in front of them, they react to that," he said. "I'm not blaming the girls, but it's part of the culture." Still, on a fundamental level, he was and is trying to evolve in the face of a changing world and new challenges that arise, as, one hopes, is much of his community. "You don't stop at the conflict or the rupture," he said. "You're supposed to learn from the adversity, adjust to it, move on, and adapt."

Today, with Joe Biden and Kamala Harris in the White House, the federal attitude toward sexual assault is different, though we know we can't be wholly reliant on their power. In their early days in office, they formed a White House advisory committee on sexual assault and a gender violence council. Biden signed a proclamation demanding that the Department of Education review Title IX. The Defense Department announced that Lynn Rosenthal (under Obama and Biden, a key advisor in the Office of Violence Against Women) would head an independent review commission on sexual assault in the military. We are in more sympathetic hands for now, but still have circuit court judges and legislators who seem adamant about minimizing a victim's recourse against an offender.

As the GOP fights to overturn *Roe v. Wade* and turn the tide against women's rights, the Supreme Court is in the hands of conservative Trump-appointed justices like Brett Kavanaugh and devoutly

Catholic Amy Coney Barrett. According to NPR, in 2006, she told graduates of Notre Dame Law School, where she was an alumna and teacher, to view their ensuing legal careers "as but a means to an end...and that end is building the Kingdom of God." Municipal abortion bans doubled in 2021. In Steubenville, there have been multiple sexual assault charges centered around the local Catholic institution Franciscan University. In 2018, the school made a public statement in response. Franciscan Friar Sean Sheridan said, "I also apologize for any way that we have failed to protect you or have not taken seriously any concerns you have voiced, and I again ask your forgiveness."

The #MeToo movement has inspired certain lasting changes, but it can only make a real impact if we have a generational shift. If our schools teach prevention from grade school, our coaches, teachers, and clergy prioritize gender equity and safety for all. If our culture steps willingly into the present and near future to tackle evidence-based and consent-based sexuality education with a firm separation of church and state, so that girls learn bodily autonomy, personal boundaries, and that pleasure is their right; and boys and all folks on the gender spectrum can learn about affirmative consent. If LGBTQ+ rights, civil rights, and reproductive choice are solidified, we can teach our children respect, community building, and empathic behavior, without shame, guilt, or punishment.

In July 2021, a high school football standout from Ohio was charged with raping a girl as she slept. He will not be the last. Now, ten years since Jane Doe's assault, there's no neat bow to tie on the Steubenville story. The Big Red case inspired reaction and activism, but the entrenched violence against women, especially within the athletic community, persists. Hopefully, we can continue to draw on what it has taught us and continue moving toward a better solution.

As Mariame Kaba wrote, "The inability to offer a neatly packaged and easily digestible solution does not preclude offering critique or analysis of our current system. We live in a society that has been locked into a false sense of inevitability." We have to believe that change is possible.

On my last trip to Steubenville, I bid farewell to Detective Rigaud and headed to Fort Steuben to say goodbye to Jerry Barilla. Another of the town regulars was there, an old-timer and wise guy who I sometimes ran into at football practice. I hugged Jerry goodbye, knowing that my time embedded in this town, its hopes, dreams, and secrets, was coming to a close. The wise guy looked at me.

"You flying home?" he asked.

I nodded, yes.

"Oh, yeah?" he said. "Where's your broom?"

# NOTES

ALL RECORDS related to the trial of Trent Mays and Ma'lik Richmond and the grand jury indictments of school officials were obtained from publicly available court records and testimony. Materials include video and written eyewitness accounts, police records, cell phone data, social media evidence, and other items that were entered into evidence during the various trials. These events were widely reported in national and international news outlets.

Sources and subjects are interviewed in the documentary films *Roll Red Roll* (PBS) and *Anonymous Comes to Town* (Guardian) and cited throughout the book.

## AUTHOR'S NOTE

*one in six women:* RAINN, "Scope of the Problem: Statistics," accessed January 25, 2022. https://www.rainn.org/statistics/scope-problem.

*The risk for young women ages eighteen to twenty-four is three times higher:* "Campus Sexual Violence: Statistics," accessed January 25, 2022. https://www.rainn.org/statistics/campus-sexual-violence.

## PROLOGUE

*"She is so dead!":* Mark Bacchus, 2013, "Michael Nodianos Confession," Uploaded January 2, 2013, YouTube video, 12:28, https://www.youtube.com/watch?v=A0drRrNWpNE.

## CHAPTER 1

*an illegal gambling operation, forfeiting $1,526,104:* United States Department of Justice, "Steubenville man forfeits $1.5 million, sentenced to house arrest

for operating gambling business," June 21, 2016, https://www.justice.gov
/usao-ndoh/pr/steubenville-man-forfeits-15-million-sentenced-house
-arrest-operating-gambling-business.

*Originally completed in 1930:* Roll Red Roll, "Death Valley," accessed December
8, 2021, https://www.rollredroll.com/DeathValley.htm.

*Wheeling-Pittsburgh Steel first filed for bankruptcy in 1985:* Warren Brown,
"Steel Firm to File for Bankruptcy," *Washington Post,* April 17, 1985,
https://www.washingtonpost.com/archive/business/1985/04/17/steel
-firm-to-file-for-bankruptcy/43cbc58c-94de-4942-80da-b5467722de7b/.
Robert Kearns, "Wheeling-Pittsburgh Files Chapter 11 Bankruptcy,"
*Chicago Tribune,* April 17, 1985, https://www.chicagotribune.com/news/ct
-xpm-1985-04-17-8501220534-story.html.

## CHAPTER 2

*Julia Lefever was looking for answers:* "Witnesses Take Stand at Rape Trial,"
*Weirton Daily Times,* March 14, 2013, https://www.weirtondailytimes.com
/news/local-news/2013/03/witnesses-take-stand-at-rape-trial/.

*"I don't remember":* "Witnesses Take Stand at Rape Trial," *Weirton Daily
Times,* March 14, 2013. https://www.weirtondailytimes.com/news/local
-news/2013/03/witnesses-take-stand-at-rape-trial/.

*Coach Reno:* Reno Saccoccia, Interview with Det. Rigaud, Police Interview,
Steubenville, Ohio, October 10, 2013.

*For Detective Rigaud:* J. P. Rigaud, Interview with Nancy Schwartzman, Personal Interview, Steubenville, Ohio, October 4, 2016.

## CHAPTER 3

*Bought from Cox Enterprises by conservative conglomerate:* Paul J. Gough,
"Sinclair Acquires Steubenville, Johnstown stations," *Pittsburgh Business
Times,* May 3, 2013, https://www.bizjournals.com/pittsburgh/blog/morning
-edition/2013/05/sinclair-acquires-steubenville.html.

*"I'm working on a story out of Steubenville":* David "Bloomdaddy" Blomquist,
Legendary News Radio, Wheeling, West Virginia: 1170 WWVA, August
2012–April 2013.

*"2 juveniles arrested in connection":* Kelly Camarote, "2 Juveniles Arrested
in Connection with Alleged Sex Assault in Jefferson Co.," *Dayton Daily
News,* August 22, 2012, https://www.daytondailynews.com/news/juveniles

-arrested-connection-with-alleged-sex-assault-jefferson/gIbbwy85x DuilVm5hx7dRM/.

*…who notoriously received multiple DUIs:* "Domenick Mucci Jr.," Wikipedia, last modified December 12, 2020, https://en.wikipedia.org/wiki/Domenick_Mucci_Jr.

*Paul Volcker, who testified before Congress:* Steven Rattner, "Volcker Asserts U.S. Must Trim Living Standard," *New York Times*, October 18, 1979, https://www.nytimes.com/1979/10/18/archives/volcker-asserts-us-must-trim-living-standard-warns-of-inflation.html.

*In 1989, a Steubenville Steelworkers Memorial:* Steubenville, Atlas Obscura, "Steubenville Steelworkers Memorial," accessed December 15, 2021, https://www.atlasobscura.com/places/steubenville-steelworkers-memorial.

*In Winant's book:* Gabriel Winant, *The Next Shift: The Fall of Industry and the Rise of Healthcare in Rust Belt America* (Cambridge, Harvard University Press, 2021).

*Winant referenced* Striking Steel: Jack Metzgar, *Striking Steel* (Philadelphia: Temple University Press, 2000).

## CHAPTER 4

*In a later* New Yorker *article, she was quoted as saying*: Ariel Levy, "Trial by Twitter," *New Yorker*, July 29, 2013, https://www.newyorker.com/magazine/2013/08/05/trial-by-twitter.

*fifty-two accounts of rape by members:* Mike Coppinger, "Baylor Lawsuit Alleges Football Players Committed 52 Rapes in Four Years," *USA Today*, January 27, 2017, https://www.usatoday.com/story/sports/ncaaf/2017/01/27/baylor-lawsuits-52-rapes-football-players/97157276/.

*these allegations:* Jessica Luther and Dan Solomon, "Changes at Baylor," *Texas Monthly*, May 26, 2016, https://www.texasmonthly.com/the-daily-post/end-art-briles-era/.

*Art Briles:* Jason Kirk, "We Finally Know More about Why Baylor Fired Art Briles," *SBNation*, October 28, 2016, https://www.sbnation.com/college-football/2016/10/28/13460830/art-briles-fired-baylor-coach-report.

*"I see the same story play out time and again," wrote Amanda Rodriguez:* Amanda Rodriguez, "The Myth of the 'Perfect Victim' of Sexual Assault," *Baltimore Sun*, May 4, 2021, https://www.baltimoresun.com/opinion/op-ed/bs-ed-op-0505-assault-victim-myth-20210504-yflhw5jh3zffddxbuwjqm664me-story.html.

*A study conducted at one major northeastern university:* David Lisak, Lori Gardinier, Sarah C. Nicksa, and Ashley M. Cote, "False Allegations of Sexual Assault: An Analysis of Ten Years of Reported Cases," *Violence Against Women* 16, no. 12 (December 16, 2010): 1318–1334, https://pubmed.ncbi .nlm.nih.gov/21164210.

*DJ Bloomdaddy:* David "Bloomdaddy" Blomquist, Legendary News Radio, Wheeling, West Virginia: 1170 WWVA, August 2012–April 2013.

*August 23, she posted her first story:* Alexandria Goddard, "Big Red Players Accused of Rape & Kidnapping," Prinniefied, August 23, 2012, https://prinniefied .com/wp/2012/08/23/steubenville-high-school-gang-rape-case-firs/.

*She wrote that she was "utterly disgusted":* Alexandria Goddard, "Steubenville Big Red Rape Accusations: The Other Perpetrators," Prinniefied, August 26, 2012, http://prinniefied.com/wp/2012/08/26/steubenville-big-red-rape -accusations-the-other-perpetrators.

*two days later on August 28:* Alexandria Goddard, "Some People Deserve to Be Peed on #whoareyou," Prinniefied, August 28, 2012, https://prinniefied .com/wp/2012/08/28/some-people-deserve-to-be-peed-on-whoareyou-2/.

*weighed in on her involvement:* David "Bloomdaddy" Blomquist, Legendary News Radio, Wheeling, West Virginia: 1170 WWVA, August 2012–April 2013.

*"Rape charges against high school players divide football town of Steubenville, Ohio":* Rachel Dissell, "Rape Charges against High School Players Divide Football Town of Steubenville, Ohio," *Plain Dealer*, September 2, 2012, https://www.cleveland.com/metro/2012/09/rape_charges_divide_football _t.html.

*The expression "witch hunt" has origins:* "Witch-hunt," Brian P. Levack, *The Witch-Hunt in Early Modern Europe* (Oxfordshire: Routledge: 2015).

*according to* The Nation: Alice Markham-Cantor, "What Trump Really Means When He Cries 'Witch Hunt'," *Nation*, October 28, 2019, https://www .thenation.com/article/archive/trump-witch-hunt/.

*Mark Nelson had spent time in prison:* Christian P.L.A.N., *ProLife News*, Special Issue: Vol 1, No. 3, accessed December 10, 2021, https://christian.net/pub /resources/text/ProLife.News/1991/pln-0103s.txt. Sarah Eekhoff Zylstra, "Why There Are Way More Pro-Life Protesters Than You Think," *The Gospel Coalition*, January 15, 2020, https://www.thegospelcoalition.org/article /way-pro-life-protesters-think/.

*"[Reno] is talking X's and O's":* Rachel Dissell, "Rape Charges against High School Players Divide Football Town of Steubenville, Ohio," *Plain Dealer*, September 2, 2012, https://www.cleveland.com/metro/2012/09/rape_charges_divide _football_t.html.

CHAPTER 5

*The Steelers were led by "Big Ben" Roethlisberger:* Big Ben 7, The official web site of Super Bowl Champion Ben Roethlisberger: "Biography," accessed December 16, 2021, http://bigben7.com/biography/.

*Shortly thereafter, the unsavory details:* "Big Ben Settles Suit Alleging '08 Rape," Fox Sports, January 20, 2012, https://www.foxsports.com/stories/nfl/big -ben-settles-suit-alleging-08-rape.

*In early 2010:* Todd Venezia, "Big Ben 'Rape' Tape," *New York Post*, June 10, 2010, https://nypost.com/2010/06/10/big-ben-rape-tape/.

*where he cornered and raped her:* Jacob Klinger, "Steelers Deny Knowledge of Sexual Assault, Rape Accusations against Antonio Brown," *PennLive Patriot-News*, September 11, 2019, https://www.pennlive.com/steelers/2019 /09/steelers-deny-knowledge-of-sexual-assault-rape-accusations-against -antonio-brown.html.

*"We have a problem":* Jonathan D. Silver and Dan Majors, "Roethlisberger Documents Give Details," *Pittsburgh Post-Gazette*, April 16, 2010, https:// www.post-gazette.com/sports/steelers/2010/04/16/Roethlisberger -documents-give-details/stories/201004160149.

*Their controversial one-time wide receiver:* Jacob Klinger, "Steelers Deny Knowledge of Sexual Assault, Rape Accusations against Antonio Brown," *Penn Live*, September 11, 2019, https://www.pennlive.com/steelers/2019/09 /steelers-deny-knowledge-of-sexual-assault-rape-accusations-against -antonio-brown.html.

*Jerry Sandusky was arrested and charged with fifty-two counts:* NPR, "Sandusky Presentment," accessed December 15, 2021, https://legacy.npr.org/assets /news/2011/11/sandusky_presentment.pdf. CNN, "Penn State Scandal Fast Facts," May 2, 2021, https://www.cnn.com/2013/10/28/us/penn-state -scandal-fast-facts/index.html.

*Joe Paterno, a revered, iconic father figure for the state:* Will Hobson, "What Did Joe Paterno Really Know about the Sandusky Scandal at Penn State?" *Washington Post*, April 7, 2018, https://www.washingtonpost.com/news

/sports/wp/2018/04/07/what-did-joe-paterno-really-know-about-the-sandusky-scandal-at-penn-state/.

*Reno Saccoccia was born:* Roll Red Roll, "2020 Big Red Coaching Staff," accessed December 16, 2021, https://www.rollredroll.com/2012coaches.htm.

*In 1984, the school won their first state championship:* Roll Red Roll, "1984," accessed November 3, 2021, https://www.rollredroll.com/playoffs1984.htm.

*The two men empowered Coach to investigate the crime: Roll Red Roll,* directed by Nancy Schwartzman, New York: Artemis Rising Foundation, 2018.

*for her* Plain Dealer *story:* "Rape Charges against High School Players Divide Football Town of Steubenville, Ohio," *Plain Dealer,* September 2, 2012, https://www.cleveland.com/metro/2012/09/rape_charges_divide_football_t.html.

*Dissell's article quoted:* "Rape Charges against High School Players Divide Football Town of Steubenville, Ohio," *Plain Dealer,* September 2, 2012, https://www.cleveland.com/metro/2012/09/rape_charges_divide_football_t.html.

*Way back since the days of old:* Roll Red Roll, "A Brief History of Big Red Football," accessed December 15, 2021, https://www.rollredroll.com/history.htm.

*including one three-day prison sentence for drunk driving in 2011:* "Domenick Mucci Jr.," Wikipedia, last modified December 12, 2020, https://en.wikipedia.org/wiki/Domenick_Mucci_Jr.

*see increased instances of assaults on women on football game days:* Bianca Padró Ocasio, "Is the Super Bowl the Most Dangerous Day for Domestic Abuse Victims? No, Experts Say," *Miami Herald,* February 9, 2021, https://www.miamiherald.com/article239584138.html#storylink=cpy.

*A study by the National Bureau of Economic Research:* Scott Jaschik, "College Football, Parties and Rape," *Inside Higher Ed,* January 4, 2016, https://www.insidehighered.com/news/2016/01/04/study-finds-increased-rapes-campus-areas-days-big-time-college-football-games.

Inside Amy Schumer: Comedy Central, 2015, *Inside Amy Schumer,* "Football Town Nights (ft. Josh Charles)," Uploaded April 22, 2015, YouTube video, 5:23, https://www.youtube.com/watch?v=TM2RUVnTlvs.

*Department of Education under Trump:* Laura Meckler, "Betsy DeVos Announces New Rules on Campus Sexual Assault, Offering More Rights to the Accused,"

*Washington Post*, May 6, 2020, https://www.washingtonpost.com/local
/education/betsy-devos-announces-new-rules-on-campus-sexual
-assault-offering-more-rights-to-the-accused/2020/05/06/4d950c7c-8fa0
-11ea-a9c0-73b93422d691_story.html.

*A state profile of Ohio's sex ed policies in 2007:* SIECUS, "State Profile: Ohio
Sexuality Education Law and Policy," New York, NY, 2007.


CHAPTER 6

*1964 based on the Kitty Genovese:* Farnam Street Media, "The Murder of Kitty
Genovese and the Bystander Effect," (blog), accessed December 16, 2021,
https://fs.blog/video-the-bystander-effect-the-murder-of-kitty-genovese/.
Nicholas Goldberg, "Column: The Urban Legend of Kitty Genovese and
the 38 Witnesses Who Ignored Her Blood-Curdling Screams," *Los Angeles
Times*, September 10, 2020, https://www.latimes.com/opinion/story/2020
-09-10/urban-legend-kitty-genovese-38-people.

*A 1968 study by American social psychologists John M. Darley:* John M. Darley,
Bibb Latané, "Bystander Intervention in Emergencies: Diffusion of Responsibility," *Journal of Personality and Social Psychology* 8, no. 4, pt. 1: 377–383,
1968, https://psycnet.apa.org/record/1968-08862-001.

*"That night [of the incident]:* Rachel Dissell, "Rape Charges against High School
Players Divide Football Town of Steubenville, Ohio," *Plain Dealer*, September
2, 2012, https://www.cleveland.com/metro/2012/09/rape_charges_divide
_football_t.html.

*"The thing I found most disturbing about":* Juliet Macur and Nate Schweber,
"Rape Case Unfolds on Web and Splits City," *New York Times*, December
16, 2012, https://www.nytimes.com/2012/12/17/sports/high-school-football
-rape-case-unfolds-online-and-divides-steubenville-ohio.html.

*But perhaps there were less obvious problems at home:* @FreethinkerKW, post
to "Steubenville, OH: The Rape Case Which Won't Die." The Motley Fool
Forum, January 7, 2013. https://boards.fool.com/this-makes-me-seethe
-evidence-shows-these-thugs-30472322.aspx.

*"There are all those studies:* Andra Teten Tharp, Sarah DeGue, Linda Anne Valle,
Kathryn A. Brookmeyer, Greta M. Massetti, and Jennifer L. Matjasko, "A Sys-
tematic Qualitative Review of Risk and Protective Factors for Sexual Violence
Perpetration," *Trauma Violence Abuse* 14 no. 2: 133–167, National Center for
Injury Prevention and Control, Centers for Disease Control and Prevention,

https://www.pubfacts.com/detail/23275472/A-systematic-qualitative -review-of-risk-and-protective-factors-for-sexual-violence-perpetration.

*Burned by a recent breakup:* Reno Saccoccia, Interview with Det. Rigaud, Personal Interview, Steubenville, Ohio, October 10, 2013.

*the Saltsman family had filed charges: Saltsman v. Goddard,* October 25, 2012, Complaint in Defamation and Injunctive Relief and for Monetary Judgment, Digital Media Law Project, January 17, 2013, https://www.dmlp.org /threats/saltsman-v-goddard#node-legal-threat-full-group-description; https://www.dmlp.org/sites/citmedialaw.org/files/2012-10-25-Saltsman %20v.%20Goddard%20Complaint.pdf; https://www.dmlp.org/sites /citmedialaw.org/files/2012-11-29-Saltsman%20v.%20Goddard%20Order %20Authorizing%20Discovery.pdf.

*"We believe the real goal of this lawsuit":* ACLU of Ohio, "ACLU of Ohio Offers to Represent Anonymous Defendants in Jefferson County Defamation Case," December 14, 2012, https://www.acluohio.org/en/press-releases /aclu-ohio-offers-represent-anonymous-defendants-jefferson-county -defamation-case.

*the* New York Times *took the Steubenville:* Juliet Macur and Nate Schweber, "Rape Case Unfolds on Web and Splits City," *New York Times*, December 16, 2012, https://www.nytimes.com/2012/12/17/sports/high-school-football -rape-case-unfolds-online-and-divides-steubenville-ohio.html.

*murder of a young medical intern in Delhi:* Niharika Mandhana and Anjani Trivedi, "Indians Outraged over Rape on Moving Bus in New Delhi," *New York Times*, December 18, 2012, https://india.blogs.nytimes.com/2012/12 /18/outrage-in-delhi-after-latest-gang-rape-case/.

CHAPTER 7

*"Anonymous vs. Steubenville":* David Kushner, "Anonymous vs. Steubenville," *Rolling Stone*, November 27, 2013, https://www.rollingstone.com/culture -news/anonymous-vs-steubenville-57875/.

*According to Kushner's article:* David Kushner, "Anonymous vs. Steubenville," *Rolling Stone*, November 27, 2013, https://www.rollingstone.com/culture -news/anonymous-vs-steubenville-57875/.

*Noah McHugh from Virginia Beach:* Michael D. McElwain, "Roll Red Roll Hacker Sentenced to Two Years," *Weirton Daily Times*, March 9, 2017, https://www.weirtondailytimes.com/news/local-news/2017/03/roll-red-roll-hacker-sentenced-to-two-years/.

*"NBC, CBS, CNN, Fox, ABC":* David "Bloomdaddy" Blomquist, Legendary News Radio, Wheeling, West Virginia: 1170 WWVA, August 2012–April 2013.

*"remember that," said DJ:* David "Bloomdaddy" Blomquist, Legendary News Radio, Wheeling, West Virginia: 1170 WWVA, August 2012–April 2013.

*Daisy Coleman and Paige Parkhurst:* Peggy Lowe and Monica Sandreczki, "Why Was the Maryville Rape Case Dropped?," Kansas City Public Radio, July 11, 2013, https://www.kcur.org/community/2013-07-11/why-was-the-maryville-rape-case-dropped.

*In July 2014:* Michelle Denise Jackson, "In Defense of Jada: The Danger of Being a Black Girl in a Rape Culture," *For Harriet*, July 12, 2014, http://www.forharriet.com/2014/07/in-defense-of-jada-danger-of-being.html.

*In all this, Deric Lostutter, aka KYAnonymous:* David Kushner, "Anonymous vs. Steubenville," *Rolling Stone*, November 27, 2013, https://www.rollingstone.com/culture-news/anonymous-vs-steubenville-57875/.

*"#OccupySteubenville had another great rally today":* Alexandria Goddard, "Solidarity for Jane Doe," Prinniefied, February 3, 2013, https://prinniefied.com/wp/2013/02/03/occupy_steubenville_rally_feb2/.

CHAPTER 8

*George Stephanopoulos teased an upcoming 20/20 segment:* George Stephanopoulos, "High School Football Sex Scandal: Player Set for Trial Speaks Out," *Good Morning America*, March 12, 2013, https://abcnews.go.com/2020/steubenville-rape-case-script-awry-accused-teen/story?id=18712245.

*On January eighth, he appeared on the* Today *show:* Matt Lauer, Ron Allen, "Former Guardians Defend Ohio Teen Rape Suspect," *Today*, January 7, 2013, https://www.today.com/video/former-guardians-defend-ohio-teen-rape-suspect-13942851871.

*Back in the studio, George Stephanopoulos:* Matt Lombardi, Lisa Soloway, and Sean Dooley, "The Steubenville Rape Case: The Story You Haven't Heard," *ABC News*, March 11, 2013, https://abcnews.go.com/2020/steubenville-rape-case-story-heard/story?id=18705357.

*Trent and Ma'lik in January:* "Request for separate trials in rape case denied," *Weirton Daily Times*, January 23, 2013, https://www.weirtondailytimes

.com/news/local-news/2013/01/request-for-separate-trials-in-rape
-case-denied/.

*Gun violence in Steubenville:* The Intelligencer, "City Plagued by Gun Violence,"
*Wheeling News-Register,* July 21, 2013, https://www.theintelligencer.net
/news/top-headlines/2013/07/city-plagued-by-gun-violence/.

*Inside, the wood-paneled courtroom:* "Rape Trial: Complete Day One Coverage," *Weirton Daily Times,* March 13, 2013, https://www.weirtondailytimes
.com/news/local-news/2013/03/rape-trial-complete-day-one-coverage/.

*Hemmeter stood to begin her opening statement:* "Steubenville Rape Trial:
Prosecution Says Defendants Knew Girl Was Impaired," *Plain Dealer,* March
13, 2013, https://www.cleveland.com/steubenville-rape-case/2013/03
/steubenville_rape_trial_prosec.html.

*Ohio rape law was clear:* Ohio Revised Code: Crimes-Procedures, U.S.C. §
2907.02 (2021).

*Thursday at nine a.m.:* "Rape Trial: Complete Day Two Coverage," *Weirton
Daily Times,* March 14, 2013, https://www.weirtondailytimes.com/news
/local-news/2013/03/rape-trial-complete-day-two-coverage/.

*Traci Lords appeared on* Piers Morgan Live: Philip Caulfield, "Ex-Porn Star
Traci Lords talks of Childhood Rape in Steubenville When She Was
10-Years-Old," *New York Daily News,* March 15, 2013, https://www.nydai
lynews.com/news/national/ex-porn-star-lords-raped-steubenville-arti
cle-1.1289435. "Traci Lords–Piers Morgan Live interview on CNN (March
14, 2013)," YouTube, 3:40, March 15, 2013, https://www.youtube.com
/watch?v=uY9EvFEoPBc.

*On Friday, March 15 the early morning buzz in the court room had an elevated
tenor:* Chris Togneri and Bobby Kerlik, "Friend Says He Saw Steubenville
Rape Suspects Sexually Assaulting the Victim," *TRIB Live,* March 15,
2013, https://archive.triblive.com/news/friend-says-he-saw-steubenville
-rape-suspects-sexually-assaulting-the-victim/. Drew Singer, "Witnesses
Describe Sex Acts in Ohio Football Rape Trial," Reuters, March 15, 2013,
https://www.reuters.com/article/us-usa-crime-ohio/witnesses-describe
-sex-acts-in-ohio-football-rape-trial-idUSBRE92E0ZS20130315. "Steubenville Rape Case: Friend Testifies about Accuser's Behavior the Night of the
Alleged Attack," Associated Press, March 16, 2013, https://www.nydailynews
.com/news/national/girl-tells-accuser-behavior-ohio-rape-case-article
-1.1290613. "Witness Gets Immunity," *Weirton Daily Times,* March 15, 2013,

https://www.weirtondailytimes.com/news/local-news/2013/03/witness
-gets-immunity/. "7 p.m. Testimony Centers on DNA Samples," *Weirton
Daily Times,* March 15, 2013, https://www.weirtondailytimes.com/news
/local-news/2013/03/7-p-m-testimony-centers-on-dna-samples/.

*Evan claimed to be "stunned" by what he saw at Mark's house:* Evan Westlake,
Police Interview, Steubenville, Ohio, August 17, 2012.

*As Jane Doe settled into the witness stand:* Connor Simpson, "The Steubenville
Victim Tells Her Story," *Atlantic,* March 16, 2013, https://www.theatlantic
.com/national/archive/2013/03/steubenville-victim-testimony/317302/.

*According to an article in the* Atlantic: Connor Simpson, "The Steubenville
Victim Tells Her Story," *Atlantic,* March 16, 2013, https://www.theatlantic
.com/national/archive/2013/03/steubenville-victim-testimony/317302/.

*"the people who did that to her are held responsible":* "Steubenville Rape Trial
Ends with Victim's Testimony; Ruling Today," *Columbus Dispatch,* March 17,
2013, https://www.dispatch.com/story/news/crime/2013/03/17/steubenville
-rape-trial-ends-with/24223742007/.

*"Many of the things that we learned":* "Steubenville Rape Trial Verdict," WRAL
News, March 17, 2013, https://www.wral.com/news/video/12233419/.

*Both defendants:* "Hear from Steubenville Defendants," CNN, March 17, 2013,
https://www.cnn.com/videos/crime/2013/03/17/sotu-harlow-steubenville
-rape-trial-verdict.cnn.

*Attorney General Mike DeWine announced he would be convening a grand jury:*
Richard A. Oppel Jr., "Ohio Teenagers Guilty in Rape That Social Media
Brought to Light," *New York Times,* March 17, 2013, https://www.nytimes
.com/2013/03/18/us/teenagers-found-guilty-in-rape-in-steubenville-ohio
.html.

*Traci Lords appeared on* Piers Morgan *again:* "Actress Traci Lords on 'Piers
Morgan Live': The Steubenville Rape Trial Verdict 3/18/13," CNN, YouTube,
March 18, 2013, https://www.youtube.com/watch?v=Ljl_3P7btkw&ab
_channel=IntegratedPRChannel.

*two local fifteen- and sixteen-year-old girls were arrested:* Amanda Marcotte,
"Why Did Two Girls Threaten the Steubenville Rape Victim?" *Slate,*
March 19, 2013, https://slate.com/human-interest/2013/03/two-girls-from
-steubenville-are-arrested-for-threatening-the-victim-why-do-women
-blame-rape-victims.html.

*Elizabeth Vargas's* 20/20 *segment aired:* Elizabeth Vargas, "20/20: Exclusive

Interview with Defendant Ma'lik Richmond," ABC News, March 22, 2013, https://abcnews.go.com/2020/steubenville-rape-case-script-awry-accused -teen/story?id=187122.

*Even DJ Bloomdaddy seemed to have new insight:* DJ Bloomdaddy: David "Bloomdaddy" Blomquist, Legendary News Radio, Wheeling, West Virginia: 1170 WWVA, August 2012–April 2013.

## CHAPTER 9

*February 14, 1861:* Jefferson County Historical Association: "Abraham Lincoln Visits Steubenville," May 26, 2015, https://www.jeffcountyhistorical .org/abraham-lincoln-visits-steubenville/#:~:text=In%201860%2C%20 the%20Democratic%20Party%20had%20split%20into%20two%20 factions.

*one resident stood and proclaimed without apparent context:* "Fri., 1:05 pm: NAACP Official Says Steubenville Rape Defendant Didn't Get Fair Trial," *Tribune Chronicle,* March 29, 2013, https://www.tribtoday.com/news/latest -news/2013/03/fri-1-05pm-naacp-official-says-steubenville-rape-defendant -didn-t-get-fair-trial/.

*DeWine, a born-and-bred Ohioan:* "Governor Mike DeWine," accessed December 16, 2021. https://governor.ohio.gov/wps/portal/gov/governor/administration /governor.

*March 17 press conference:* "Ohio Attorney General: 16 More People Face Charges in Steubenville Rape Case," YouTube, 11:32, March 17, 2013, https://www.youtube.com/watch?v=53rc5iiQuQ0&t=87s&ab_channel =LeakSourceNews.

*On Prinnified, weeks later:* Alexandria Goddard, "Onward and Upward," Prinniefied, April 8, 2013, https://prinniefied.com/wp/2013/04/08/onward-and -upward-2/.

*It received 136,405 signatures:* Elizabeth Beier, "Steubenville Schools: Fire Coach Reno Saccoccia," *Change.org* (petition), March 29, 2013, https:// www.change.org/p/steubenville-schools-fire-coach-reno-saccoccia.

*"What the Hell?":* Dave Zirin, "'What the Hell!': Steubenville High School Football Coach Gets a Two-Year Contract Extension," *Nation,* April 22, 2013, https://www.thenation.com/article/archive/what-hell-steubenville-high -school-football-coach-gets-two-year-contract-extension/.

*She called out adults in Steubenville:* Alexandria Goddard, "Steubenville: Roll

Red Role Models," Prinniefied, April 8, 2013, https://prinniefied.com/wp/2013/08/24/steubenville-roll-red-role-models/.

*The* New Yorker *published a piece by staff writer Ariel Levy:* Ariel Levy, "Trial by Twitter," *New Yorker,* July 29, 2013, https://www.newyorker.com/magazine/2013/08/05/trial-by-twitter.

*"You're going to get yours":* Kat Stoeffel, "Times Reporter Threatened When Reporting on Ohio High-School Rape," The Cut, *New York,* December 17, 2012, https://www.thecut.com/2012/12/times-reporter-threatened-when-reporting-on-rape.html.

*crisis pregnancy center:* Amy G. Bryant, MD, MSCR, and Jonas J. Swartz, MD, MPH, "Why Crisis Pregnancy Centers Are Legal but Unethical," *AMA Journal of Ethics,* 20(3): 269–277, 2018, https://journalofethics.ama-assn.org/article/why-crisis-pregnancy-centers-are-legal-unethical/2018-03. Joanne D. Rosen, "The Public Health Risks of Crisis Pregnancy Centers," *Perspectives on Sexual and Reproductive Health,* 44(3): 201–205, 2012, https://www.guttmacher.org/journals/psrh/2012/09/public-health-risks-crisis-pregnancy-centers. Women's Justice Now, "Get the Facts, Crisis Pregnancy Center," accessed January 25, 2022. https://nownyc.org/womens-justice-now/issues/get-the-facts-crisis-pregnancy-centers/.

## CHAPTER 10

*"This is the first indictment in an* ongoing *grand jury investigation":* Ohio Attorney General, "First Indictment Issued by Steubenville Special Grand Jury," October 7, 2013, https://www.ohioattorneygeneral.gov/Media/News-Releases/October-2013/First-Indictment-Issued-by-Steubenville-Special-Gr.

*a former adjunct professor:* "Bill Rhinaman LinkedIn Profile," LinkedIn, accessed April 16, 2021, https://www.linkedin.com/in/bill-rhinaman-5b937262/.

*Alex Goddard reposted a leaked group email chain:* Alexandria Goddard, "Steubenville: Email supporting SHS IT Director After Arrest," Prinniefied, October 24, 2013, https://prinniefied.com/wp/2013/10/24/steubenville-email-supporting-alleged-it-director-indicted-for-covering-up-rape/.

*Townspeople began posting and debating on online forums:* @Roxine, 2013, "Action Diary—Steubenville: Email Supporting Alleged IT Director Indicted for Covering Up Rape," Daily Kos (Forum), October 24, 2013, https://www.dailykos.com/stories/2013/10/24/1250200/-Action-Diary-Steubenville-Email-supporting-alleged-IT-Director-indicted-for-covering-up-rape.

*That thread also included a comment:* Laura Collins, "Steubenville High School Employee's Daughter Becomes Second to Be Indicted by Grand Jury Investigating Ohio Rape Case," *Daily Mail,* October 23, 2013, https://www.dailymail.co.uk/news/article-2474151/Hannah-Rhinaman-indicted-Daughter-Steubenville-High-School-employee-indicted-Ohio-rape.html.

*She faced up to three years in prison:* Alastair Jamieson, "Steubenville Teen Rape Case; Ohio Grand Jury Indicts Daughter of School Employee," NBC News, October 23, 2013, https://www.nbcnews.com/news/us-news/steubenville-teen-rape-case-ohio-grand-jury-indicts-daughter-school-flna8c11448096.

*the younger Rhinaman, who had been arrested the month before:* Katie J. M. Baker, "Steubenville Rape Case Update: Daughter of School's IT Director Indicted," *Newsweek,* October 23, 2013, https://www.newsweek.com/steubenville-rape-case-update-daughter-schools-it-director-indicted-785.

*Newsweek:* Katie J. M. Baker, "Steubenville Rape Case Update: Daughter of School's IT Director Indicted," *Newsweek,* October 23, 2013, https://www.newsweek.com/steubenville-rape-case-update-daughter-schools-it-director-indicted-785.

*four more indictments were handed down:* Ohio Attorney General Dave Yost, "Statement As Prepared Ohio Attorney General Mike DeWine Steubenville Special Grand Jury Steubenville, OH November 25, 2013," November 25, 2013, https://www.ohioattorneygeneral.gov/Files/Briefing-Room/News-Releases/Special-Prosecutions/Mike-DeWine-Statement-As-Prepared-Steubenville.aspx.

*According to* Campus Safety Magazine*:* "Sexual Assaults on College Campuses Involving Alcohol," Alcohol.org, May 8, 2020, https://www.alcohol.org/effects/sexual-assault-college-campus/#:~:text=Approximately%2090%20percent%20of%20rapes,assaults%2C%20the%20aggressor%20is%20intoxicated.

*Big Red's assistant wrestling coach:* Rachel Dissell, "Former Coach in Steubenville Gets 10 Days in Jail," *Plain Dealer,* April 23, 2014, https://infoweb-newsbank-com.ezproxy2.cpl.org/apps/news/document-view?p=AMNEWS&docref=news14D6004724CB9228.

*"maintain appropriate boundaries":* Ohio Department of Education, "Licensure Code of Professional Conduct for Ohio Educators," Columbus, Ohio, September 17, 2019, https://education.ohio.gov/getattachment/Topics/Teaching

/Educator-Conduct/Licensure-Code-of-Professional-Conduct-for-Ohio
-Ed/Licensure-Code-of-Professional-Conduct.pdf.aspx.

*Steubenville Superintendent Michael McVey faced the most serious charges:* Rachel Dissell, "Steubenville Schools Chief Indicted with Three Others, Charges Involve Obstructing Justice in Rape Investigation," *Plain Dealer*, November 26, 2013, https://infoweb-newsbank-com.ezproxy2.cpl.org/apps/news /document-view?p=AMNEWS&docref=news/14A51B1421278C80.

*"While this started out being about the kids":* Ohio Attorney General Dave Yost, "Statement As Prepared Ohio Attorney General Mike DeWine Steubenville Special Grand Jury Steubenville, OH November 25, 2013," https://www .ohioattorneygeneral.gov/Files/Briefing-Room/News-Releases/Special -Prosecutions/Mike-DeWine-Statement-As-Prepared-Steubenville.aspx.

*The fourth and final person indicted was Lynnette Gorman:* Rachel Dissell, "Steubenville Schools Chief Indicted with Three Others, Charges Involve Obstructing Justice in Rape Investigation," *Plain Dealer*, November 26, 2013, https://infoweb-newsbank-com.ezproxy2.cpl.org/apps/news/document -view?p=AMNEWS&docref=news/14A51B1421278C80.

*According to police reports, just days after:* Police Reports, Steubenville, Ohio, April 2012.

*According to the* Washington Post: Cari Simon, "On Top of Everything Else, Sexual Assault Hurts the Survivors' Grades," *Washington Post*, August 6, 2014, https://www.washingtonpost.com/posteverything/wp/2014/08/06 /after-a-sexual-assault-survivors-gpas-plummet-this-is-a-bigger-problem -than-you-think/.

*innocent until proven guilty:* The Intelligencer, "Indicted School Officials Reinstated," *Wheeling News Register*, December 4, 2013, "https://www .theintelligencer.net/news/top-headlines/2013/12/indicted-school -officials-reinstated/.

*Ma'lik Richmond:* Jessica Testa, "Convicted Steubenville Rapist Returns to School Football Team," BuzzFeed News, August 11, 2014, https://www .buzzfeednews.com/article/jtes/convicted-steubenville-rapist-returns -to-school-football-tea.

*"Lynnette Gorman believes she committed no crime":* Elizabeth Daley, "Charge Dropped against Principal in Ohio Rape Case Investigation," Reuters, January 8, 2014, https://www.reuters.com/article/us-usa-crime-ohio/charge

-dropped-against-principal-in-ohio-rape-case-investigation-idUKBRE
A071GG20140108.

*"This is about the long-term healing of the community":* Cleveland 19 Digital
Team, "Steubenville Rape: AG Mike DeWine issues statement in Lynnett
Gorman Case," Cleveland 19 News, January 8, 2014, https://www.cleveland
19.com/story/24397116/ag-mike-dewine-issues-statement-in-lynnett
-gorman-case/.

*"I have read tweets disputing rape vs. digital penetration":* Alexandria Goddard,
"Why Steubenville Matters," Prinniefied, January 25, 2014, https://prinniefied
.com/wp/2014/01/25/why-steubenville-matters/.

*Hannah Rhinaman pled guilty:* "Steubenville Rape Defendant Guilty of Unrelated Theft," WKYC February, 26, 2014, https://www.wkyc.com/article
/news/crime/steubenville-rape-defendant-guilty-of-unrelated-theft
/95-241891490.

*Seth Fluharty was also granted a deal:* "Deal Reached with Indicted Steubenville Wrestling Coach," Cleveland 19 News, April 11, 2014, https://
www.cleveland19.com/story/25225089/deal-reached-with-indicted
-steubenville-wrestling-coach/.

*"There was a reason that locals were worried about a cover-up":* Alexandria Goddard, "Steubenville: Time to Take Out the Trash," Prinniefied, June 3, 2014,
https://prinniefied.com/wp/2014/06/03/steubenville-time-to-take-out
-the-trash/.

*"We must treat rape and sexual assault":* Ohio Attorney General Dave Yost,
"Statement as Prepared Ohio Attorney General Mike DeWine Steubenville
Special Grand Jury Steubenville, OH November 25, 2013," November 25,
2013, https://www.ohioattorneygeneral.gov/Files/Briefing-Room/News
-Releases/Special-Prosecutions/Mike-DeWine-Statement-As-Prepared
-Steubenville.aspx.

## CHAPTER 11

*News interview with local affiliate WTOV-9:* "Steubenville Rapist Ma'lik Richmond Back on School Football Team," NBC News, August 13, 2014, https://
www.nbcnews.com/news/crime-courts/steubenville-rapist-malik-richmond
-back-school-football-team-n179331.

*It's Time to Stop Shaming the Steubenville Rapists:* Amanda Hess, "It's Time to
Stop Shaming the Steubenville Rapists," *Slate,* August 11, 2014, https://

slate.com/human-interest/2014/08/ma-lik-richmond-returns-to-football
-in-steubenville-let-s-let-him-get-on-with-his-life.html.

*based on another article that ran on* Slate *the same day:* Matt Mellema,
Chanakya Sethi, and Jane Shim, "Sex Offender Laws Have Gone Too Far,"
*Slate*, August 11, 2014, https://slate.com/news-and-politics/2014/08/sex
-offender-registry-laws-have-our-policies-gone-too-far.html.

*In her book:* Mariame Kaba, *We Do This 'Til We Free Us: Abolitionist Organizing
and Transforming Justice* (Chicago: Haymarket Books, 2021).

*In an email interview with BuzzFeed:* Jessica Testa, "Convicted Steubenville
Rapist Returns to School Football Team," BuzzFeed News, August 11,
2014, https://www.buzzfeednews.com/article/jtes/convicted-steubenville
-rapist-returns-to-school-football-tea.

*allowing a Tier II registered sex offender on the team:* Jessica Testa, "Convicted
Steubenville Rapist Returns to School Football Team," BuzzFeed News,
August 11, 2014, https://www.buzzfeednews.com/article/jtes/convicted
-steubenville-rapist-returns-to-school-football-tea.

*That November 2014,* Salon *ran an article:* Emma Goldberg, "Steubenville Hasn't
Changed at All: 'You Trying to Write about That Whole Rape Thing?'"
*Salon*, November 30, 2014, https://www.salon.com/2014/11/30/steubenville
_hasnt_changed_at_all_%E2%80%9Cyou_trying_to_write_about_that
_whole_rape_thing%E2%80%9D/.

*In December, assistant coach Matthew Belardine:* "Belardine on Probation
Arrested for Violation," *Weirton Daily Times*, December 12, 2014, https://
www.weirtondailytimes.com/news/local-news/2014/12/belardine
-on-probation-arrested-for-violation/.

*On Prinnified, she reposted:* Alexandria Goddard, "State of Ohio Says Belardine
Violated Probation," Prinniefied, December 12, 2014, https://prinniefied
.com/wp/2014/12/12/state-of-ohio-says-belardine-violated-probation/.

*"By no means do I take this lightly":* Elizabeth Daley, "Former Coach in Ohio Rape
Case Sentenced for Probation Violation," Reuters, December 22, 2014, https://
www.reuters.com/article/us-usa-ohio-coach/former-coach-in-ohio-rape
-case-sentenced-for-probation-violation-idUSKBN0K01T720141222.

*"We hope the guilty parties hold a higher standard":* Ray Jablonski, "Steubenville
Rape Convict Trent Mays Released from Juvenile Detention," Cleveland.com,
January 8, 2015, https://www.cleveland.com/metro/2015/01/steubenville
_rape_convict_tren.html.

*"The Mays family is elated to be reunited with their son after this trying ordeal":* Nemann Law Offices, "Trent Mays Released from Ohio Juvenile Detention Facility," accessed December 16, 2021, https://www.nemannlawoffices .com/blog/trent-mays-released-from-ohio-juvenile-detention-facility .cfm.

*"She's been around the block more than 5 times…was it rape?":* "Steubenville Rapist Ma'lik Richmond Back on School Football Team," NBC News, August 13, 2014, https://www.nbcnews.com/news/crime-courts/steubenville -rapist-malik-richmond-back-school-football-team-n179331.

*"THIS is what is wrong with the lunatic fringe of Steubenville":* Alexandria Goddard, "Trent Mays & the Lunatics of Steubenville," Prinniefied, January 7, 2015, https://prinniefied.com/wp/2015/01/07/trent-mays-the-lunatics-of -steubenville/.

*Mike McVey was finally scheduled to begin:* Ray Jablonski, "Steubenville Superintendent Mike McVey Resigns after Charges against Him Dismissed," Cleveland.com, January 12, 2015, https://www.cleveland.com/metro/2015 /01/steubenville_superintendent_mi.html.

*"I think a lot of people are just glad to see this case finally put to rest":* Alexandria Goddard, "Charges Dropped Against McVey, Former Steubenville Superintendent," Prinniefied, January 12, 2015, https://prinniefied.com/wp/2015/01/12 /charges-dropped-against-mcvey-former-steubenville-superintendent/.

*"I am satisfied that he has been held accountable for his actions with this agreement and consider this a just result":* Mark Law, "McVey Resigns, Charges Dropped," *Weirton Daily Times*, January 13, 2015, https://www .weirtondailytimes.com/news/local-news/2015/01/mcvey-resigns-charges -dropped/.

*William Rhinaman, the IT director accused of wiping:* "Former Steubenville School Official Pleads Guilty to Erasing Files Sought in Rape Investigation," Cleveland.com, February 27, 2015, https://www.cleveland.com/open /2015/02/former_steubenville_school_off.html.

*Steubenville made the state semifinals:* Roll Red Roll, "State Champs," accessed June 14, 2021, https://www.rollredroll.com/football.htm.

*"What has changed?" she wrote:* Alexandria Goddard, "When Steubenville Rapists Go Free," Prinniefied, January 31, 2015, https://prinniefied.com /wp/2015/01/31/when-steubenville-rapists-go-free/.

CHAPTER 12

*Eleanor Bishop:* Eleanor Bishop, "Eleanor Bishop State Director," Personal Web Page, accessed August 20, 2021, http://www.eleanorbishop.org/steubenville-1.

Good Kids *by Naomi Iizuka:* Department of Theatre, Film, and Media Arts, "Good Kids," The Ohio State University College of Arts and Sciences, October 2015, https://theatreandfilm.osu.edu/events/good-kids.

*Brock Turner, was arrested for assaulting:* "Court Documents: Stanford Rape Case," *Los Angeles Times*, accessed December 16, 2021, https://documents .latimes.com/stanford-brock-turner/.

*case led to the judge being recalled:* Richard Gonzales and Camila Domonoske, "Voters Recall Aaron Persky, Judge Who Sentenced Brock Turner," NPR, June 5, 2018, https://www.npr.org/sections/thetwo-way/2018/06/05/617071359 /voters-are-deciding-whether-to-recall-aaron-persky-judge-who-sentenced -brock-tur.

*Huffington Post:* Emma Gray, "This Letter from the Stanford Sex Offender's Dad Epitomizes Rape Culture," *Huff Post*, June 6, 2016, https://www.huffpost .com/entry/brock-turner-dad-letter-is-rape-culture-in-a-nutshell_n _57555bace4b0ed593f14cb30.

*Brock Turner's victim:* Phil Helsel, "Judge Recalled over Brock Turner Sentence Fired as Girls' High School Tennis Coach," NBC News, September 12, 2019, https://www.nbcnews.com/news/us-news/judge-recalled-over-brock -turner-sentence-fired-girls-high-school-n1052916.

Know My Name: Chanel Miller, *Know My Name: A Memoir* (New York: Penguin Books, 2019). Emily Doe, "Victim Statement to Brock Turner," BuzzFeed News reported by Katie J. M. Baker, June 2, 2016, https://www .buzzfeednews.com/article/katiejmbaker/heres-the-powerful-letter -the-stanford-victim-read-to-her-ra.

*Supreme Court ruling against the NCAA: National Collegiate Athletic Assn. v. Alston*, 20-512 U.S. (2021).

*Ohio's Hocking College:* Tom Archdeacon, "Steubenville Offender Gets Second Chance at Central State," *Dayton Daily News*, April 27, 2017, https:// www.daytondailynews.com/sports/tom-archdeacon-polarizing-player -gets-second-chance-central-state/FdHHkpFheNnTIFHvfMMTLP/.

*According to an Associated Press story:* Associated Press, "QB's Role in Steubenville Rape Hangs over College's New Team," ESPN, September 16, 2015, http://www.espn.com/espn/wire/_/section/ncf/id/13667779.

*"I think it's our history"*: Kendall Forward, "Finishing Touches Are Going onto Steubenville's Newest Mural Restoration," WTOV-9, October 9, 2015, https://wtov9.com/news/local/finishing-touches-are-going-onto-steubenvilles-newest-mural-restoration.

*"This historic fort originally was built in 1786–1787"*: Steubenville Visitor Center, "Historic Fort Steuben," accessed November 7, 2021, https://www.visitsteubenville.com/what-to-do/historic-sites-museums/historic-fort-steuben/.

*"The Steubenville Nutcracker Village"*: The Steubenville Nutcracker Village, "The Steubenville Nutcracker Village," accessed December 16, 2021, https://www.steubenvillenutcrackervillage.com/.

*"It seems like a real strategic misstep for him"*: Amy Chozick and Ashley Parker, "Donald Trump's Gender-Based Attacks on Hillary Clinton Have Calculated Risk," *New York Times*, April 28, 2016, https://www.nytimes.com/2016/04/29/us/politics/hillary-clinton-donald-trump-women.html.

*"You've called women you don't like fat pigs"*: Kayla Epstein, "Trump Responds to Megyn Kelly's Questions on Misogyny—with More Misogyny," *Guardian*, August 6, 2015, https://www.theguardian.com/us-news/2015/aug/06/donald-trump-misogyny-republican-debate-megyn-kelly.

*As an "October surprise" just before the election*: David A. Fahrenthold, "Trump Recorded Having Extremely Lewd Conversation about Women in 2005," *Washington Post*, October 8, 2016, https://www.washingtonpost.com/politics/trump-recorded-having-extremely-lewd-conversation-about-women-in-2005/2016/10/07/3b9ce776-8cb4-11e6-bf8a-3d26847eeed4_story.html.

*65.9 percent for Trump*: Associated Press, "2016 Ohio Presidential Election Results," Politico, December 13, 2016, https://www.politico.com/2016-election/results/map/president/ohio/.

*They took steps*: Laura Meckler, "Betsy DeVos Set to Bolster Rights of Accused in Rewrite of Sexual Assault Rules," *Washington Post*, November 14, 2018, https://www.washingtonpost.com/local/education/betsy-devos-set-to-bolster-rights-of-accused-in-rewrite-of-sexual-assault-rules/2018/11/14/828ebd9c-e7d1-11e8-a939-9469f1166f9d_story.html.

*63 percent of cases that go unreported*: National Sexual Violence Resource Center, "False Reporting," accessed August 20, 2021, https://www.nsvrc.org/sites/default/files/Publications_NSVRC_Overview_False-Reporting.pdf.

*The inaugural Women's March:* John P. Rafferty, "Women's March," *Encyclopedia Britannica*, January 14, 2021, https://www.britannica.com/event/Womens-March-2017.

*"university president Jim Tressel":* Mark Schlabach, "Scandal Tarnishes Tressel, Ohio State," ESPN, March 8, 2011, https://www.espn.com/college-football/columns/story?columnist=schlabach_mark&id=6195223. Associated Press, "Tressel Quits Ohio State amid Embarrassing Tattoo Scandal," *New York Post*, May 31, 2011, https://nypost.com/2011/05/31/tressel-quits-ohio-state-amid-embarrassing-tattoo-scandal/.

*August 21, his biological father:* Associated Press, "Father of Football Player Convicted in Steubenville Rape Case Shoots Judge," *Sports Illustrated*, August 21, 2017, https://www.si.com/more-sports/2017/08/21/stuebenville-rape-case-nate-malik-richmond-judge-shooting.

*A petition was immediately launched:* K Davis, 2017, "Remove Steubenville Rapist, Ma'lik Richmond, from YSU's Football Team," Change.org (petition), accessed June 13, 2021, https://www.change.org/p/bo-pelini-remove-steubenville-rapist-ma-lik-richmond-from-ysu-s-football-team.

*"post-Trump world":* https://www.record-courier.com/story/news/2017/06/26/dewine-makes-governor-bid in/19994085007/.

*"This is a very humble and emotional moment for me":* Dave Gossett, "Jerry Barilla Will Take Over as Mayor in Steubenville," The Intelligencer: *Wheeling News-Register*, November 8, 2017, https://www.theintelligencer.net/news/top-headlines/2017/11/jerry-barilla-will-take-over-as-mayor-in-steubenville/.

*"Sexual Misconduct Claims Trail a Hollywood Mogul":* Jodi Kantor and Megan Twohey, "Harvey Weinstein Paid Off Sexual Harassment Accusers for Decades," *New York Times*, October 5, 2017, https://www.nytimes.com/2017/10/05/us/harvey-weinstein-harassment-allegations.html.

*"If all the women who have been sexually harassed":* Nadja Sayej, "Alyssa Milano on the #MeToo Movement: 'We're Not Going to Stand for It Any More,'" *Guardian*, December 1, 2017, https://www.theguardian.com/culture/2017/dec/01/alyssa-milano-mee-too-sexual-harassment-abuse.

*Soon after,* Today *anchor Matt Lauer:* Aurelie Corinthios, "Everything We Know About the Allegations Against Matt Lauer," *People*, December 2, 2020, https://people.com/tv/matt-lauer-sexual-harassment-assault-allegation-breakdown/.

*Blasey Ford said in her opening statement:* "READ: Christine Blasey Ford's Opening Statement For Senate Hearing," NPR, September 26, 2018, https://www.npr.org/2018/09/26/651941113/read-christine-blasey-fords-opening-statement-for-senate-hearing.

*"When Boys Become Men Like Brett Kavanaugh":* Nancy Schwartzman, "When Boys Become Men Like Brett Kavanaugh," *Ms.,* September 27, 2019, https://msmagazine.com/2019/09/27/when-boys-become-men-like-brett-kavanaugh/.

*Betsy DeVos filed her new Title IX rule:* Valerie Strauss, "Betsy DeVos's Controversial New Rule on Campus Sexual Assault Goes into Effect," *Washington Post,* August 14, 2020, https://www.washingtonpost.com/education/2020/08/14/betsy-devoss-controversial-new-rule-campus-sexual-assault-goes-into-effect/.

*"Dear Colleague Letter":* U.S. Department of Education, "Dear Colleague Letter," April 4, 2011, https://www2.ed.gov/print/about/offices/list/ocr/letters/colleague-201104.html.

*By the end of 2018:* "2018," Wikipedia, 2018, last modified December 15, 2021, https://en.wikipedia.org/wiki/2018.

*more than half the world's population, at 51.2 percent:* "More than Half of Global Population Now Online: UN," Yahoo News, December 7, 2018, https://sg.news.yahoo.com/more-half-global-population-now-115946999.html.

*song that he covered with Kelly Clarkson:* Olivia B. Waxman, "'Baby, It's Cold Outside' Was Controversial from the Beginning. Here's What to Know About Consent in the 1940s," *Time,* December 5, 2019, https://time.com/5739183/baby-its-cold-outside-consent/.

## CHAPTER 13

*home page of Reddit:* "*Roll Red Roll* (2018) - An underage girl is raped at a party in Steubenville, Ohio by two football players. The town tries to protect the boys and the team, but the evidence exposes a culture ingrained with a 'boys will be boys' mentality. [1h20m]," u/moviemakr, Reddit, 2020, https://www.reddit.com/r/Documentaries/comments/cp68wu/roll_red_roll_2018_an_underage_girl_is_raped_at_a/.

*"That was certainly a bill that I wanted to sign":* Karen Kasler, "DeWine: Proud to Sign 'Heartbeat Bill' but Total Abortion Ban Can Wait," Statehouse News Bureau, December 13, 2019, https://www.statenews.org/government-politics/2019-12-13/dewine-proud-to-sign-heartbeat-bill-but-total-abortion-ban-can-wait.

*"I don't believe we can talk":* "Our Story," Set the Expectation, accessed December 16, 2021, https://www.settheexpectation.org/about-ste/our-story.

*"The Tracy Rule":* "The Tracy Rule," Set the Expectation, accessed November 22, 2021, https://www.settheexpectation.org/our-impact/tracy-rule.

*"What is Dignity?":* Rosalind Wiseman, "What is Dignity? Rosalind Wiseman from Cultures of Dignity & Cognitive Media," Uploaded January 23, 2020, YouTube, 1:58 min., https://www.youtube.com/watch?v=OcSg 66kudFQ.

*85 percent of today's sexual assaults:* Lucy Adams, "Sex Attack Victims Usually Know Attacker, Says New Study," BBC News, March 1, 2018, https://www .bbc.com/news/uk-scotland-43128350.

*In fact, from 2007 to 2017:* "Why Are Young Adults Having Less Casual Sex?" Rutgers Today, March 22, 2021, https://www.rutgers.edu/news/why-are -young-adults-having-less-casual-sex.

*Paul Voltz was found guilty on seven counts:* "Voltz Found Guilty on All Counts," WTOV-9, June 8, 2021, https://wtov9.com/news/local/breaking-voltz-found -guilty-on-all-counts.

*Recent findings from a multi-campus study:* Jeremy Bauer-Wolf, "Repeat Rapists on Campus," *Inside HigherEd,* April 12, 2019, https://www.inside highered.com/news/2019/04/12/study-repeat-rapists-committing-vast -majority-sexual-crimes.

*Larry Nasser, a doctor who swore a Hippocratic oath:* Eric Levenson, "Larry Nassar Sentenced to Up to 175 Years in Prison for Decades of Sexual Abuse," CNN, January 24, 2018, https://www.cnn.com/2018/01/24/us/larry-nassar -sentencing/index.html.

*R. Kelly, after thirty years of abusing girls:* "R. Kelly Is Found Guilty of All Counts and Faces Life in Prison," *New York Times,* last modified October 20, 2021, https://www.nytimes.com/live/2021/09/27/nyregion/r-kelly-trial-news.

*"college athletes can lose their NCAA eligibility":* Kenny Jacoby, "NCAA Looks the Other Way as College Athletes Punished for Sex Offenses Play On," *USA Today,* December 12, 2019, https://www.usatoday.com/in-depth /news/investigations/2019/12/12/ncaa-looks-other-way-athletes-punished -sex-offenses-play/4360460002/.

*quarterback Deshaun Watson:* Amy Dash, "Exclusive: Prosecutors Likely Presenting Deshaun Watson Case to a Grand Jury in January, Attorney Says," League of Justice, December 6, 2021, https://leagueofjustice.com

/exclusive-prosecutors-likely-presenting-deshaun-watson-case-to-a
-grand-jury-in-january-attorney-says/.

*known abusers such as Dr. Robert Anderson:* "37 Years of Sexual Abuse: This Is the Dr. Robert Anderson Story," *Michigan Daily*, November 4, 2021, https://www.michigandaily.com/news/robertanderson/.

*Courtney Smith:* Diana Moskovitz, "Courtney's Story," Defector, September 13, 2021, https://defector.com/courtneys-story/.

*"Trent Mays Accused of Sexual Assault…AGAIN":* Alexandria Goddard, "Trent Mays Accused of Sexual Assault…AGAIN," Prinnified, March 25, 2019, https://prinniefied.com/wp/2019/03/25/trent-mays-accused-of-sexual
-assault-again/.

*"necessary for Juvenile Sex Offender Registrants":* "Judge Removes Ma'lik Richmond from Sex Offender List," ESPN News, May 11, 2018, https://www.espn
.com/college-football/story/_/id/23473841/malik-richmond-youngstown
-state-penguins-removed-sex-offender-list.

*Their lives in somewhat predictable ways:* Alexandria Goddard, "Steubenville Case: Where Are They Now?" Prinniefied, June 18, 2019, https://prinniefied
.com/wp/2019/06/18/steubenville-case-where-are-they-now/.

*we can look at the deadly example:* María Luisa Paúl, "Police Mishandled 'Red Flag' of Domestic Violence in Gabby Petito Confrontation, Experts Say," *Washington Post*, October 2, 2021, https://www.washingtonpost.com
/nation/2021/10/02/gabby-petito-new-video/.

*These officers had little to no effective training in the dynamics of violence against women:* María Luisa Paúl, "Police Mishandled 'Red Flag' of Domestic Violence in Gabby Petito Confrontation, Experts Say," *Washington Post*, October 2, 2021, https://www.washingtonpost.com/nation/2021/10/02
/gabby-petito-new-video/.

*justice for George Floyd:* Tara Jabour, "Protesters Gather in Steubenville Calling for Justice for George Floyd," WTOV-9, May 30, 2020, https://
wtov9.com/news/local/protesters-gather-in-steubenville-calling-for
-justice-for-george-floyd.

*to the US:* Jeffrey Kluger, "Domestic Violence Is a Pandemic Within the COVID-19 Pandemic," *Time*, February 3, 2021, https://time.com/5928539
/domestic-violence-covid-19/.

*Daisy Coleman:* Diane Barth, "Daisy and Melinda Coleman's Suicides Lay Bare How Public Attention Can Mask Ongoing Trauma," NBC News, December

10, 2020, https://www.nbcnews.com/think/opinion/daisy-melinda-coleman -s-suicides-lay-bare-how-public-attention-ncna1250627.

*also committed suicide:* Doha Madani, "Melinda Coleman, Mother of Daisy Coleman, Dies by Suicide 4 Months after Daughter," NBC News, December 7, 2020, https://www.nbcnews.com/news/obituaries/melinda-coleman -mother-daisy-coleman-dies-suicide-4-months-after-n1250287.

*Donald Trump's campaign:* Andrew Grimm, "Trump Jr. Draws a Crowd at Bully Tools in Steubenville," *Herald Star,* October 23, 2020, https:// www.heraldstaronline.com/news/local-news/2020/10/trump-jr-draws -a-crowd-at-bully-tools-in-steubenville/. Gage Goulding, "EXCLUSIVE: Donald Trump Jr. One-on-One, Speaks about Issues in Ohio Valley," WTOV9, October 22, 2020, https://wtov9.com/news/local/donald-trump -jr-steubenville-ohio-campaign-rally-bully-tools.

*The state and Jefferson County went for Trump by a slightly larger margin:* Céilí Doyle and Sheridan Hendrix, "Trump Promised to Bring Back Coal in Appalachia. Here's Why That Didn't Happen," *Columbus Dispatch,* October 20, 2020, https://www.dispatch.com/story/news/environment/2020/10/20 /trump-promised-bring-back-coal-appalachia-has-he/5866420002/.

*Mike DeWine:* Howard Wilkinson, "Commentary: DeWine, Portman and the Wrath of Trump," WVXU, November 20, 2020, https://www.wvxu.org/politics /2020-11-20/commentary-dewine-portman-and-the-wrath-of-trump.

*Kirsten Hill, was not only in attendance:* WKYC Staff, Jake Zuckerman (*Ohio Capital Journal*), " 'Kirsten Hill Goes to Washington': Ohio Board of Education Member from Amherst Who Organized Bus Trip to D.C. Responds to Criticism," WKYC Studios, January 13, 2021, https://www.wkyc.com /article/news/local/ohio/kirsten-hill-elyria-ohio-board-of-education -bus-trip-washington-capitol-riot/95-40dc7f22-d24e-430e-a67e-3c9d3dd 039a5.

*to the "Stop the Steal" rally:* Jake Zuckerman, "Ohio Board of Ed Member Organized Bus Trip to D.C. for "Stop the Steal" Rally," *Ohio Capital Journal,* January 12, 2021, https://ohiocapitaljournal.com/2021/01/12/ohio -board-of-ed-member-organized-bus-trip-to-d-c-for-stop-the-steal-rally/.

*"The president's continued refusal to accept":* Andrew Welsh-Huggins, "Ohio Governor: Trump Started Fire that Threatens Democracy," AP News, January 7, 2021, https://apnews.com/article/election-2020-donald-trump-mike -dewine-democracy-elections-82a8e55300e19aba64927f2bfab59580.

*According to NPR:* Tom Gjelten, "Amy Coney Barrett's Catholicism Is Controversial but May Not Be Confirmation Issue," NPR, September 29, 2020, https://www.npr.org/2020/09/29/917943045/amy-coney-barretts-catholicism-is-controversial-but-may-not-be-confirmation-issu.

*Municipal abortion bans doubled in 2021:* Jacob Fulton, "As Supreme Court Considers Abortion Cases, Local Governments Impose Bans," NBC News, November 6, 2021, https://www.nbcnews.com/politics/politics-news/supreme-court-considers-abortion-cases-local-governments-impose-bans-n1281999.

*the school made a public statement:* Jenn Morson, "Franciscan University Vows to Stop Sexual Assault, but Victims Need Convincing," *National Catholic Reporter*, October 9, 2018, https://www.ncronline.org/news/accountability/steubenville-vows-stop-sexual-assault-victims-need-convincing. Jenn Morson, "Franciscan University of Steubenville, Ohio, Takes Steps to Address Sexual Assault, Title IX issues," *National Catholic Reporter*, September 4, 2018, https://www.ncronline.org/news/accountability/franciscan-university-steubenville-ohio-takes-steps-address-sexual-assault-title.

*raping a girl as she slept:* Cliff Pinckard, "Ohio High School Football Star Accused of Raping Sleeping Girl," Cleveland.com, July 20, 2021, https://www.cleveland.com/nation/2021/07/ohio-high-school-football-star-accused-of-raping-sleeping-girl.html.

*As Mariame Kaba wrote:* Mariame Kaba, *We Do This 'Til We Free Us: Abolitionist Organizing and Transforming Justice* (Chicago: Haymarket Books, 2021).

# RESOURCES

*ROLL RED ROLL* FILM WEBSITE  *http://rollredrollfilm.com*
The official website for *Roll Red Roll*, where you will find information on upcoming screenings, how to host screenings in your own community, opportunities to take action, and more.

## FOUNDATIONAL INFORMATION ABOUT SEXUALITY AND HEALTH

**Scarleteen**  *http://www.scarleteen.com*
Scarleteen is an independent, grassroots sexuality and relationships education and support organization and website, founded in 1998. Visit for information on understanding abuse and assault, help getting out of danger, understanding consent, learning how to advocate for yourself, and self-care tips.

## FOR MEN LOOKING TO GET MORE INVOLVED IN VIOLENCE PREVENTION

**A Call To Men**  *http://www.acalltomen.org*
A Call To Men works to promote a healthy and respectful manhood and shift attitudes and behaviors that devalue women, girls, and other marginalized groups. It is a great resource for violence prevention education and training and promotion of healthy manhood.

**He For She**  *https://www.heforshe.org/en*
HeForShe is a United Nations global solidarity movement for gender equality and provides models of ways to take action in your community.

**It's On Us**  *https://www.itsonus.org*
It's On Us is a national movement to end sexual assault that was launched following recommendations from the White House task force to prevent sexual assault. The campaign combines innovative creative content and grassroots organizing techniques to spark conversation on a national and local level.

**Men Can Stop Rape**  *http://www.mencanstoprape.org*
Men Can Stop Rape is an international organization that mobilizes men to use their strength for creating cultures free from violence, especially men's violence against women. Find a local Men of Strength (MOST) club, for mobilizing young men to prevent sexual and dating violence.

**MenChallenging**  *http://www.menchallenging.org*
MenChallenging offers resources for taking action and making that action as effective as possible.

**Men Stopping Violence**  *https://www.menstoppingviolence.org*
Men Stopping Violence organizes men to end male violence against women and girls through innovative training, programs, and advocacy. Visit for resources, internships, trainings, and other opportunities to learn strategies to create safer communities for women and girls.

**Promundo**  *https://promundoglobal.org*
Promundo is a global leader in promoting gender justice and preventing violence by engaging men and boys in partnership with women and girls. Check out the group's "The Man Box" report (https://promundoglobal.org /resources/man-box-study-young-man-us-uk-mexico/) for data on young men's attitudes, behaviors, and understandings of manhood.

## INITIATIVES GEARED TO COLLEGE AND HIGH SCHOOL STUDENTS

**InSideOut Initiative**  *https://insideoutinitiative.org*
This organization provides a blueprint for change to the current win-at-all-costs sports culture and promotes the use of sports to foster human growth.

**Know Your IX**  *https://www.knowyourix.org*
A project of Advocates for Youth, Know Your IX is a survivor- and youth-led initiative that empowers students to end sexual and dating violence in their schools.

## GET INVOLVED WITH *ROLL RED ROLL*'S NATIONAL PARTNERS

**Breakthrough**  *https://us.breakthrough.tv*
Breakthrough is a global human rights organization working to drive the cultural change we need to build a world in which all people live with dignity, equality, and respect. It works to change the attitudes and assumptions around gender that lead to violence and discrimination.

**Calcasa** *http://www.calcasa.org*
The California Coalition Against Sexual Assault (CALCASA) provides leadership, vision, and resources to rape crisis centers, individuals, and other entities committed to ending sexual violence. CALCASA works through a multifaceted approach of prevention, intervention, education, research, advocacy, and public policy.

**End Rape On Campus** *http://endrapeoncampus.org*
For survivors in higher-ed seeking support: End Rape On Campus works to end campus sexual violence through direct support for survivors and their communities; prevention through education; and policy reform at the campus, local, state, and federal levels.

**I Have the Right To** *https://www.ihavetherightto.org*
For parents and survivors: This organization started as a social media campaign using the hashtag #IHaveTheRightTo to bring safety and respect to all cultures. As an organization, it promises to be a safe place where survivors and families of survivors can come to find support, belief, advocacy, and community.

**Raliance** *http://www.raliance.org*
A collaborative initiative dedicated to ending sexual violence in one generation, Raliance strongly believes that sport is a critical partner in preventing sexual and domestic violence, both on and off the field. Learn more about strategies and programs to support your sport community to prevent sexual and domestic violence at the Sport and Prevention Center: http://www.raliance.org/sport-prevention-center.

**Relationship Abuse Prevention Program (RAPP)**
*https://www.dayoneny.org/rapp*
RAPP partners with high schools across New York City to provide critical teen dating violence prevention and intervention. The program provides trauma-informed individual and group counseling, classroom workshops to educate school populations on relationship abuse, professional development for teachers and school staff, and community outreach.

**SafeBAE** *https://www.safebae.org*
SafeBAE is a survivor-founded, teen-led organization that educates middle- and high-school students about healthy relationships, dating violence, and sexual assault prevention, affirmative consent, safe bystander intervention, survivor self-care, and survivor rights under Title IX.

**Set the Expectation** *https://www.settheexpectation.com*
For safer athletic communities: This organization (which uses the hashtag #SetTheExpectation) is dedicated to combating sexual and physical violence through education and direct engagement with coaches, young men, and boys in high school and college athletic programs.

**Steps to End Family Violence** *https://www.egscf.org/programs/steps*
This program of Edwin Gould Services for Children and Families offers services for victims of gender-based violence and focuses on prevention, intervention, and policy advocacy.

**Vital Voices** *https://www.vitalvoices.org*
Vital Voices was created to make space for women to be heard through investment in community leaders worldwide.

## GET SAVVY ON YOUR MOBILE DEVICE

**Circle of 6** *https://www.circleof6app.com*
Circle of 6 is a White House award–winning mobile safety app designed to reduce sexual violence. It is currently used by over 350,000 people in thirty-six countries.

## ADDITIONAL RESOURCES FOR SURVIVORS

**National Sexual Assault Telephone Hotline: 1-800-656-HOPE (4673)**
*https://www.rainn.org/about-national-sexual-assault- telephone-hotline*
National hotline providing a wide range of support.

**National Sexual Assault Online Hotline** *https://hotline.rainn.org/online*
Private and secure online hotline.

**National Sexual Assault Resource Center** *https://www.nsvrc.org*

**RAINN** *https://www.rainn.org*

**Anti-Violence Project (AVP)** *https://avp.org*
Support specifically for LGBTQ folk.

**Black Women's Blueprint** *https://blackwomensblueprint.org*
Community support for black women.

**1IN6** *https://1in6.org*
The mission of 1in6 is to help men who have had unwanted or abusive sexual experiences live healthier, happier lives. It was founded in 2007 in response to

a lack of resources addressing the impact of negative childhood sexual experiences on the lives of adult men.

**The Mount Sinai Sexual Assault and Violence Prevention Program (SAVI)** *https://www.mountsinai.org/patient-care/service- areas/community -medicine/sexual-assault-and- violence-intervention-program-savi*
Free and confidential counseling, and community education.

# ACKNOWLEDGMENTS

This book wouldn't be possible without the interviews and insights of Jeno Atkins, Jerry Barilla, Rachel Dissell, Alexandria Goddard, J. P. Rigaud, Michele Robinson, and Sandra. Thank you for your time and trust.

I want to thank my family for their love and support, especially my father, who enjoyed reminding me that he has three books to my one. Thanks to my brilliant friends and fellow artists who cheered me on: Deborah Kampmeier, Maxyne Franklin, Yael Luttwak, Natalie Difford, Steven Lake, Jed Mellick, Jennifer MacArthur, Craig DeLeon, Jeremy Tamanini, Nick Syrett, Margot Spindelman, Shira Tarrant, Angela Tucker, and Nicola Kraus. Thanks to Lily Donnell and Vivien Jastrzebski for your incredible support.

Thank you to Nora Zelevansky, for your intelligence, skill, and above all, kindness.

Thanks to Mollie Weisenfeld at Hachette Books, and Lucinda Blumenfeld, for taking a chance on a filmmaker who knew there was more to the story.